THE
NOUVEAU ROMAN READER

edited by

JOHN FLETCHER AND JOHN CALDER

JOHN CALDER · LONDON
RIVERRUN PRESS · NEW YORK

First published in Great Britain in 1986 by
John Calder (Publishers) Limited
18 Brewer Street, London W1R 4AS

and in the United States of America in 1986 by
Riverrun Press Inc
1170 Broadway, New York, NY 10001

British Library Cataloguing in Publication Data
The Nouveau roman reader.
    1. French fiction——20th century——History and criticism
    I. Fletcher, John, *1937–* II. Calder, John *1927–*
843'.912'09   PQ671

ISBN 0–7145–3720–9

Library of Congress Cataloging in Publication Data
The Nouveau roman reader.
    Bibliography: p. 246
    1. French fiction—20th century—History and criticism.
    I. Fletcher, John, 1937– . II. Calder, John.
    PQ629.N67 1985   843'.914'09   85–18353
    ISBN 0–7145–3720–9

Typeset in 10 on 11 pt Times Roman by Photobooks (Bristol) Ltd.
Printed in Great Britain by Photobooks (Bristol) Ltd.

CONTENTS

EDITORS' NOTE

The translations used in this 'Reader' are sometimes British and sometimes American, so that there is a marked contrast in spelling and phraseology. It would not have been possible to impose a single style as the translations used are those currently approved, often with the collaboration of the author.

INTRODUCTION

The Post-Modern situation

> *Oh! Blessed rage for order, pale Ramon,*
> *Thé maker's rage to order words of the sea*
> Wallace Stevens

'Do we have a "rage for order"?' asks Frank Kermode rhetorically in his essay 'Modernisms', published in Bernard Bergonzi's important symposium *Innovations* (Macmillan, 1968), consciously echoing the serene lines quoted above which close Wallace Stevens's poem 'The Idea of Order at Key West'; and, like Stevens, Kermode considers that we do. For although he distinguishes two phases of modernism—which he designates respectively as palaeo-modernism, whose 'peak period . . . must be placed somewhere around 1910–1925', and neo-modernism, which postdates the Second World War—he believes in their fundamental, if diverse, continuity. 'There has been,' he writes, 'only one Modernist Revolution, and it happened a long time ago. . . . There has been little radical change in modernist thinking since then.' He reinforces this point a little further on:

> Neo-modernists have examined. . . . various implications in traditional modernism. As a consequence we have, not unusually, some good things, many trivial things, many jokes, much nonsense. Among other things they enable us to see more clearly that certain aspects of earlier modernism really were so revolutionary that we ought not to·expect—even with everything speeded up—to have the pains and pleasures of another comparable movement quite so soon.

In consequence Frank Kermode rejects the two other possible views of modernism—Cyril Connolly's, as expressed in his survey *The Modern Movement* (1965) that 'it is virtually all over', and Leslie Fiedler's proposition in a famous essay (also in *Innovations*) that the new art is so radical, both aesthetically and socially, that its proponents should be called 'the New Mutants', Kermode's sense of continuities is in its turn qualified by another chronicler of the fortunes of modernism, Ihab Hassan, who writes in a 'paracritical bibliography' published in *New Literary History* (Autumn, 1971) that 'we will not grasp the cultural experiences of our moment if we insist that the new arts are "marginal developments of older modernism;" or that distinctions between "art" and "joke" are crucial to any future aesthetic'. To Kermode's categories palaeo- and neo- (which presuppose variations upon an on-going theme rather than any radical discontinuity), Hassan prefers as his formulae the more definite and final terms 'modernism' and '*post*-modernism'. Like Fiedler, he takes more seriously than Kermode does the 'apocalyptic' quality of much recent art, especially the works of John Cage, William Burroughs and Robert Rauschenberg; and unlike Kermode, he is not inclined to consider that such manifestations merely reveal 'that the Last Days are good for a giggle'. In other words, where Kermode views neo-modernism as a 'marginal development' on palaeo-modernism, Hassan sees his post-modernism—for it is quite clear they are both talking about the same movement—as being much more radically and disturbingly distinct. The scenario, as Hassan would sketch it, goes something like this:

We have all in recent years been preoccupied with the special quality of the art of our own century, and have come to look upon what has happened since the early 1900s as constituting a divide or rift which separates us irrevocably from such crises of the past as the Renaissance, or the Romantic agony. This recent cataclysm can be situated, with some degree of assurance, in the years before and immediately after the First World War, and its tremors were provoked by artists like Proust, Joyce and Kafka in the novel, Strindberg, O'Neill and Pirandello on the stage, Yeats, Rilke and Eliot in poetry, Debussy, Schoenberg and Bartok in music, and Cézanne, Picasso and Klee in painting. Then, as if the shock administered to our sensibilities by this unheaval were too great to bear, there seemed to occur a lull, even a reaction. During the 1930s and 1940s the rise of political ideology led people to belittle, even to reject violently, the absolute dedication to art of these practitioners. Committed writers like George Orwell and Louis-Ferdinand Céline, Gottfried Benn and Alberto Moravia, set a new tone of asperity, of austerity, of ironic casualness, which—as was intended—contrasted with what was seen as the Apollonian dignity and majestic decorum of the previous generation. In France, for example, Gide's elegant, measured periods quite suddenly looked old-fashioned beside the harsher cadences of Malraux and Sartre writing under the influence of the recently translated laconic and ungenteel prose of a Dos Passos or a Hemingway; and Valéry, of all people, sounded effete beside the colloquial brashness of Aragon. This is of course not by any means the whole story; others carried on as if nothing had altered, but they attracted less attention at the time and tend not to provoke much discussion now.

Then gradually, and apparently quite unpredictably, a new tendency began to assert itself vociferously in the late 1930s (two key works, Sartre's *Nausea* and Beckett's *Murphy*, were both published in 1938), and we still live in its shadow. In the often violent reaction to the social and political concerns of the previous generation, of the movement which received its testament, as it later turned out, in Sartre's *What is Literature?* of 1947, this new force was ostentatious in its preoccupation with forms and structure, taking up again, after an interval, the aesthetic obsession of earlier modernist writers, but with a difference: the new 'post-modernism' was more irresistibly drawn to anarchism, iconoclasm and anti-formalism than its precursor, as well as feeling itself more self-consciously an heir to dada and surrealism, and much more interested in both nihilism and play, in subverting structures rather than in exploiting their full potential. The 'crucial text' of post-modernism, in Hassan's view, is not *Ulysses*, for all its 'contemptuousness of its own formal and stylistic elaborateness', because it derives from and makes studied reference to a whole tradition of epic and mock-epic, but *Finnegans Wake*, in which destruction is a mode of creation, and iconoclasm and remake go hand in hand. We still have not, Hassan believes, adjusted to all the consequences of that radical gesture of Joyce's mature years. So it is not surprising that his successor Samuel Beckett should be the acknowledged high priest of this new apostolate, and that its idiosyncratic votaries are called William Burroughs, John Barth and Michel Butor in the novel (Hassan is alert to the coincidence of the frequent occurrence in post-modernism of the initial B), Edward Albee, Harold Pinter, Peter Weiss and Fernando Arrabal in the theatre, Allen Ginsberg in poetry, John Cage in music, and the followers of Marcel Duchamp in the visual arts. Hassan is quite clear about who is the remote progenitor of these lusty and rebellious infants: it is our old friend the Marquis de Sade. The line Ihab Hassan traces from Sade to Beckett in his book *The Dismemberment of Orpheus: Toward a Postmodern Literature* (New York: Oxford University Press, 1971), deftly hopping over 'the age of Novalis and Rimbaud in order to reach the present swiftly', is, he admits, 'hypothetical'. The theme he pursues through his major figures Sade, Hemingway, Kafka, Genet and Beckett is silence, the 'sovereignty of the void': a silence that may be either nihilist or plenary, or both ('contrapuntally') at once. His controlling image, the dismemberment of Orpheus at the hands of the Maenads for having 'offended life in some hidden and original manner', symbolizes for him the true meaning of the post-modern avant-garde; Orpheus now consents to being dismembered, and Hassan sees this attitude on the part of the artist as the culmination of a long evolutionary process.

Whether it is itself a stable attitude is another question. There are signs of a new outlook developing without post-modernism itself, and in particular a return to political involvement. A quarter of a century after the publication of *What Is Literature?* the French avant-garde, or at least that section of it grouped around the review *Tel Quel* and its editor Philippe Sollers, is once again heavily influenced by marxist conceptions of the role of literature in a capitalist consumer society. How *Tel Quel* will manage to reconcile the extreme formalism of its literary theory with its militant anti-bourgeois stance in political and social philosophy is as yet difficult to predict. But John Cage's scores, William Burroughs's cut-up fold-in novels, other artists' ready-mades and photo-realism are by no means the last word of the avant-garde; if anything, such *dernier cri* is beginning to sound a trifle dated.

Indeed, the danger with the Hassan/Fiedler version of the new modernism is that it tends to overemphasize the flashier and more strident avant-gardes, the sort egregiously characterized by the products of the Warhol factory. On the other hand, because we are in the middle of the phenomenon it is not easy to reconcile such odd bedfellows as the beat poet Allen Ginsberg and the Roman Catholic novelist Muriel Spark, and yet both writers exemplify important, if rather different, aspects of neo-modernism. Nevertheless, we do seem to be able to discern a pattern, at least through the contrast with what has gone immediately before; and it is natural we should look for some term which will adequately describe it. The 'new literature' is obviously unsatisfactory, for the same reason that desert mirages are always one jump ahead of the parched traveller. Claude Mauriac's neologism 'aliterature' (after 'atonal' in music), for which Hassan has considerable liking, is as inaccurate in its way as Martin Esslin's phrase 'the theatre of the absurd': not all post-modern writing can be desribed as 'aliterature', any more than all contemporary experimental drama is preoccupied with the absurd.

Frank Kermode, as we have seen, has coined the rather unpretty term 'neo-modernism', which has however the virtue of being precise. But the difficulty with Kermode's version of the contemporary situation is that it does not account very adequately for the big slump in modernist values brought about by the renewed interest in political commitment at a time of world crisis in the twenty-year period between about 1930 and 1950. On the whole I share Kermode's view that palaeo- and neo-modernism are essentially continuous in spite of the hiatus and that the development of the new forms can be seen 'as following from palaeo-modernist premises without any violent revolutionary stage'; that neo-modernists are 'stealthy classicists' and that both phases share the conviction that 'research into form is the true means of discovery, even when'—as with Beckett—'form is denied existence'. I share, too, his belief that neo-modernism has thrown up 'some good things' (as far as I am concerned they have been produced by, amongst others, the writers who are featured in this book), just as I feel the same distaste as he does for the excesses and muddle often associated with neo-modernism's more eccentric manifestations. My own version of the new modernism, while it derives from his attempts to account for the impression of hiatus we experience as we look back over the Second World War decade, goes something like this:

Neo-modernism emerged in France about 1950 and spread fairly rapidly to most countries of predominantly European civilization—though not without strong local opposition in several places, which led to their undergoing its influence later than others did. Moreover, it has had, for obvious reasons, no perceptible impact in the Soviet Union, though there has been some echo in such member-countries of the Communist bloc as have been able at certain times to achieve a degree of freedom for artists, mainly Poland and Czechoslovakia; Martin Esslin rightly includes playwrights from these nations in *The Theatre of the Absurd*. And—with the exception of Latin America— the Third World has proved largely indifferent to neo-modernism: indeed the reaction there has occasionally been hostile, as was shown at the 1964 Formentor conference when delegates from developing countries expressed their disgust at the award of the International Publishers' Prize to *The Golden Fruits* by Nathalie Sarraute, an author whose concerns seemed utterly remote from those exercising readers in their home countries: 'are we to be national writers,' one of them pointly asked, 'or Parisians?' In fact, just as modernism sprang from and remained largely centred upon Europe and places mainly colonized by Europeans, so its reincarnated form has tended to spread little beyond the same confines. But wherever it has spread, it has been a cosmopolitan rather than a regional phenomenon. Its characteristic figures are writers like Vladimir Nabokov, Samuel Beckett, Eugene Ionesco and Fernando Arrabal, who may have their roots in a national tradition, but no longer contribute to it. Their works are like fruit-grafts: the trunk is of one variety, the graft (a different language and milieu) another, and the result a hybrid. Nabokov is that extraordinary phenomenon, an 'American-Russian' novelist; Beckett has, in his post-war works, gone far beyond Anglo-Irish literature; and Ionesco keeps no links with Rumanian writing, and Arrabal few with Spanish. Even a writer like Jorge Luis Borges, who writes in his mother tongue and resides in the same country (Argentina) in which he was born, is a cosmopolitan figure, a man of universal culture whose work transcends the confines of his own nation and is addressed to those whose reading is as eclectic as Borges's own.

As an aesthetic movement, literary neo-modernism is primarily rooted in three media: the novel, drama and the film. It shows little interest in lyric poetry, at least of the more traditional, i.e. the non-concrete variety, or in dance, or in music (at least of a non-electronic kind). In this it differs from a movement which originated earlier in France, symbolism, and which was rooted in poetry, music and dance; and unlike another French-led movement, surrealism, it maintains only a fairly episodic interest in the visual arts. So it will principally be with the so-called *nouveau roman* or new novel, the new wave in the cinema, and the not necessarily absurdist 'theatre of the absurd' that I shall be concerned in pressing my own version of neo-modernism. All three of these artistic manifestations arose in France in the early nineteen-fifties.

Why this was so is a complicated problem of the sociology of art which it is impossible to answer satisfactorily in the present state of our knowledge. But one can give some idea of the political and social climate in which it arose, and which goes some way towards suggesting an explanation. To do so we need to go back to the period before the Second World War. The rise, diffusion and triumph of fascism in a number of European countries, and the consolidation of Stalinism in the Soviet Union, cast a pall of political dread not only over countries directly affected but over most others in the civilized world. These developments in the political sphere were of course often triggered off by crises in the economic domain, such as runaway inflation in Germany and the reverberations later of the 1929 Wall Street crash. New, aggressive, totalitarian regimes raised once again the threat of war which the generation that survived 1914–18 had hoped to have seen exorcized for ever. And in this general climate of unsettlement and tension it was natural that palaeo-modernism should fall into abeyance, plunge beneath the surface like a river in limestone country, and re-emerge only when conditions altered. It took some time for the shock administered by the horrors of the First World War to affect what was most dynamic in creative endeavour, but this it did, and by the mid-1920s palaeo-modernism was losing its impetus. It never disappeared entirely, of course; the magazine *transition* was published during the 1930s, Beckett began his literary career in that decade, and Joyce published *Finnegans Wake* at the end of it, but nothing of this created anything like the impact provoked by the appearance of *Journey to the End of the Night* in 1932 and *Man's Estate* in 1933 by Céline and Malraux respectively—two voices profoundly characteristic of the thirties—or, in a more popular vein, by the publication of Erich Maria Remarque's *All Quiet on the Western Front* a year or so previously.

Once the Second World War had broken out, France suffered

further severe shocks: the collapse of her army and occupation by the enemy realized in concrete terms the imprecise fears of the uneasy peace. After 1940 intellectuals had the opportunity to engage in clandestine activities of resistance to the invader, and at last the issues became as simple as the life hard and dangerous. The majority opted for resistance, active or passive according to their situation and opportunities. Nearly every name of importance in modern French literature is associated with the resistance under one guise or another. Some, like Malraux, took to the maquis and narrowly escaped torture and death. Others, like Samuel Beckett, acted in a humbler but still dangerous capacity as collectors and transmitters of information. Others again, like Sartre, Eluard, Mauriac, Jouve, Aragon and so on, militated in literature, overt or clandestine, and Camus helped produce the underground newspaper *Combat*. It was naturally in the area of journalism and propaganda that the intellectual was most effective, as German efforts to trace secret presses showed. The size of printings and extent of distribution of clandestine publications reached impressive levels, and Camus's famous article of May 1944—'For Five Hours They Shot French People'—exposed in the best traditions of journalism the mass execution at Ascq. Of course, a handful of writers adopted the opposite ideological stand and collaborated actively with the occupying forces; their journalism in the tolerated, pro-German press aroused the strongest feelings of resentment. Robert Brasillach, one of the best of them, was executed at the Liberation; another, Drieu la Rochelle, committed suicide; and Céline went to ground, disgraced, in Denmark. The rest were small fry, like Lucien Rebatet, and survived.

But even if finer points of humanity were sacrificed both during and after the war, the main issue was clear-cut and admitted of few doubts: one was either for or against the Vichy regime. But the euphoria resulting from the success of the liberation of France did not long survive the complexities of the post-war world and particularly the development of the cold war. By 1950 the spirit of Resistance, of comradely brotherhood in the face of a common enemy, was dead. The Communist Party had retreated into its Stalinist bastion; the Fourth Republic had settled down to its wrangles; Madagascar, Morocco, Indochina and Algeria were so many episodes of which the liberal intellectual could feel only ashamed, or inwardly torn apart and impotent, as Camus was over Algeria. Memories of guilt over Dresden and Hiroshima returned to haunt minds formerly accustomed to suppose that one side had held the monopoly of evil. By 1950 the atmosphere was therefore ripe for a reaction against commitment in literature, or *littérature engagée*, the concept of which had grown out of the experience of writing under the occupation and been provided, in Sartre's essay *What is Literature?* of 1947, with an elaborate theoretical basis. But whereas during the Resistance literary commitment posed few difficulties for the writer, after the war the issues became so complex that they admitted of no clear-cut stand that was not fraught with insonsistencies: the history of Sartre's bewildering love-hate relationship with the French Communist Party is a case in point. Quite suddenly, around 1950, it began to be felt that *littérature engagée*, with its rash claim to be able to alter life rather than simply to reflect it, was too simple and naive.

This, then, was the atmosphere of disenchantment in which, in May 1950, the first of the 'absurdist' plays, Ionesco's *Bald Prima Donna*, was performed in Paris, and in which, a mere ten months later, Samuel Beckett's novel *Molloy* appeared. The impact of the two events was immediate, and their significance far-reaching; it is now quite clear that in so far as any single occurrence can mark the beginning of a new era, the arrival of Beckett and Ionesco at the forefront of the literary arena was just such a turning-point. And yet neither Beckett, nor Ionesco, nor Arthur Adamov, who achieved notoriety at the same time only to fade away later, were young Turks. In 1950 Beckett was forty-four years old, Adamov forty-two and Ionesco thirty-eight; all had been around literary Paris for several years, writing and working in relative obscurity. They were, therefore, mature men, who certainly owed little or nothing to such contemporary fads as Saint-Germain-des-Prés existentialism, to which they tended at first to be assimilated by commentators who were slow to perceive how radical was their originality. In any case, their literary allegiances lay further back, indeed were formed before the Second World War. Beckett had in his youth been influenced by the aesthetics of the circle of writers grouped around the magazine *transition* (published between 1927 and 1938), in particular of course by the experiments of Joyce in *Work in Progress*. Surrealism, too, had been a minor influence on him, but it had had a major formative impact on Ionesco and Adamov's development, deriving in particular from Raymond Roussel, Vitrac and Artaud. In other words, the movement was launched by men who had been young in the inter-war years, and who also—and this was quite new in the history of French literature—were all of alien origin. Adamov was of Armenian extraction, Ionesco Rumanian, and Beckett Irish. Ionesco was always the most naturalized of the three—and is now a member of the French Academy—but throughout his life Adamov continued to speak French with a noticeable accent, and Beckett has never renounced his Eire citizenship. This foreign background goes some way towards explaining why, although they wrote in perfectly fluent French, their tone sounded so radically different from that of the reigning native intellectuals.

They were, however, soon followed by Frenchmen of the next generation, who had been children when surrealism was in its heyday, and teenagers when the war broke out. Alain Robbe-Grillet (born in 1922) submitted his second novel *The Erasers* to Beckett's publishers (Editions de Minuit) and it appeared in 1953; Michel Butor, four years his junior, followed suit in 1954 with *Passage de Milan*. Older writers were sufficiently impressed to modify and develop their style or at least to associate themselves with the same current: Nathalie Sarraute, born in 1902, who had published her first book as early as 1938, when it had passed virtually unremarked; Claude Simon, born the same year as Camus (1913), who had already published four books with other firms before he joined the Editions de Minuit in 1957; and Robert Pinget, born 1920, who had launched himself unnoticed in 1951 with *Entre Fantoine et Agapa*, the source of much of his later writing and especially of his masterpiece *The Inquisitory* (1962). Such disparate individuals have never constituted a 'school' or even a close band of friends as the surrealists did, and they are not all even published by the same firm, though Minuit issue the bulk of their work.

It follows that there was no one source of this literary re-volution—or, more accurately, resurgence of an earlier revolution —though it is possible to trace a lineage which most writers I have just mentioned would not repudiate, and which for all practical purposes goes back to Flaubert. He was probably the first writer to take the novel completely seriously as an art form with rigorous principles of its own. In doing so, he envisaged a 'book about nothing', a book without 'external attachments' which would, as he put it, 'stand by itself through the internal forces of its style as the earth stands without being supported, a book with hardly any subject, or at least with an almost invisible subject'. Flaubert himself never wrote any such book, but his ideal of the novel as a perfect formal structure, owing little to the world outside it, was taken up after 1950 as a battle-cry in the attack on 'committed literature', which was seen as owing too much to external considerations; as Robbe-Grillet put it, the artist can only be committed to literature. One might think that this was nothing more than the old business resurrected of 'art for art's sake', and no doubt there was an element of that in it. But with a difference: these writers did not retreat to ivory towers, but continued—as intellectuals—to take an active interest in national and international affairs. Most of them were, for instance, signatories to the famous 'Declaration of the 121' on the necessity of military insubordination in Algeria, and were prosecuted in consequence. But they no longer felt able to weave allusions to, and attitudes against, current or past injustices into their creative works, except in quite incidental ways. Claude Simon, for instance, set *The Palace* in Barcelona during the Spanish civil war, but his novel is an elegy, quite unlike Malraux's *Days of Hope* which was written in the thick of the struggle. And if Marguerite Duras focuses her screenplay *Hiroshima mon amour* on the occupied French town of Nevers, and the devastated Japanese city, her chief concern is with the grief over a first love which a successful actress and fairly happily-married woman has buried in her psyche, until the day when a chance encounter in present-day Hiroshima permits her to exorcize it in a hysterical but memorably liberating cry, 'but it was my first love!' It is of note, too, that both *The Palace* and *Hiroshima mon amour* flout deep-rooted French political taboos: Simon in demythifying the struggle against Franco's fascism. Duras in giving her heroine a German soldier as a lover; and yet both writers have identified themselves with left-wing causes, Marguerite Duras even militantly so.

Flaubert—to return to him—is usually portrayed as a detached, even cold author, but his detachment was more apparent than real: there is no such thing as complete detachment on the part of the writer in his fictions, any more than there is such a thing as total realism. It is all a matter of degree. The narrator in *Madame Bovary* certainly seems detached if you compare him with the narrator in a book by Balzac or by Dickens, where the narrative voice is much more insistently in evidence. Both *Hard Times* and *Madame Bovary* open with a scene set in a schoolroom, for instance; but the manner is very difficult. Flaubert's narrator identifies himself at once as one of Charles Bovary's school-fellows; but after the initial paragraphs he only reappears two or three times more throughout the whole novel. He might be supposed to serve as the silent objective reporter of the events related, adding nothing of his own; but he is, in fact, a mere front for Flaubert himself, who intervenes surreptitiously at intervals to make comments of a general nature about people, society, or existence, like this one provoked by Leon the clerk, Emma's second lover:

> For every bourgeois, in the heat of his youth, be it only for one day, one minute, has believed himself capable of huge passions and high adventures. The most mediocre libertine dreams of the harem; every clerk bears in his heart the remains of a poet.
>
> (*Madame Bovary*, Part III, ch. 6)

Flaubert is able in this way to comment on the general implications of the particular happenings his narrator is describing: because he holds the reporter's impassive mask over his face he beguiles us into assuming that he too is detached. Which he certainly is not: he gave the game away when he confessed privately, 'Madame Bovary, c'est moi.' Dickens, on the other hand, has no need for such subterfuges. Although his narrator does not introduce himself, he is very much in evidence from the outset, manipulating our vision and appraisal of the opening scene by his choice of angle and imagery:

> The scene was a plain, bare, monotonous vault of a schoolroom, and the speaker's square forefinger emphasized his observations by underscoring every sentence with a line on the schoolmaster's sleeve. The emphasis was helped by the speaker's square wall of a forehead, which had his eyebrows for its base, while his eyes found commodious cellarage in two dark caves, overshadowed by the wall. The emphasis was helped by the speaker's mouth, which was wide, thin, and hard set. The emphasis was helped by the speaker's voice, which was inflexible, dry, and dictatorial. The emphasis was helped by the speaker's hair, which bristled on the skirts of his bald head, a plantation of firs to keep the wind from its shining surface, all covered with knobs, like the crust of a plum pie, as if the head had scarcely warehouse-room for the hard facts stored inside. The speaker's obstinate carriage, square coat, square legs, square shoulders—nay, his very neckcloth, trained to take him by the throat with an unaccommodating grasp, like a stubborn fact, as it was—all helped the emphasis.
>
> (*Hard Times*, Book I, ch. 1)

In passages like this Dickens's language is overt in its direction of his reader's feelings and attitudes, and most of the time it works superbly well (think of the atmospherics of *Bleak House*, for instance, generated by the opening litany on fog, both literal and metaphorical); but sometimes it is too blatant, and the reader refuses to co-operate. Flaubert offers us very little of such flamboyant drama, but his subdued and subtle devices are sometimes more effective, as in the famous sequence of short and long sentences which bridge sixteen years of historical time in the existence of his 'superfluous hero', Frédéric Moreau:

> He travelled.
> He came to know the melancholy of the steamboat, the cold

> awakening in the tent, the tedium of landscapes and ruins,
> the bitterness of interrupted friendships.
> He returned.
> He went into society, and he had other loves. . . .
>
> (*Sentimental Education*, Part III, ch. 6)

By similarly discreet rhetorical devices, Flaubert leads us, in his earlier novel, to sympathize with his foolish, romantic, thoroughly misguided but fundamentally rather decent and sympathetic heroine Emma Bovary. And another of his most remarkable creations—a real *défi de maître*, this, since the material is so negative—can be found in the late short story 'A Simple Soul', the principal character of which is the illiterate, idolatrous servant woman Félicité. He holds us fascinated with the changing personality and narrowing vision of this person as fifty years and about as many pages pass over her in order, as he put it, 'to make sensitive people weep, being one of them myself.'

Flaubert's modernity, like Baudelaire's, clearly announces new attitudes which half a century later were to come to dominate the literary world. It has been said of modernists that they are romantics, albeit stealthy ones, with a sense of, and feeling for, the ironic. It has also been said that modernism seems to have something to do with 'the intersection of apocalyptic or modern time and the timeless symbol, with the ironic relationship between contingent history and the formal wholeness of art'. The origins of such attitudes can clearly be discerned in Flaubert. After him, the great writers of modernism—late Henry James, Conrad, Joyce, Proust, Kafka, Faulkner and Virginia Woolf—are of course also rightly looked upon as important precursors in the field of experimental fiction: precursors, indeed, whose achievement is not likely soon to be surpassed, and whose formal innovations are still being absorbed. The palaeo-modernist novel, with its high degree of technical sophistication, particularly its tendency towards interiorization or turning structurally in upon itself, and also what Malcolm Bradbury has called its 'air of exhausting itself formally in each new work', sets the standard against which neo-modernist fiction must be judged.

The transition between these novels of early modernism, and the works of the *nouveaux romanciers* which began to appear after 1950, was provided by books whose authors probably had quite different intentions in mind. The apparent neutrality of the opening lines of Ernest Hemingway's *A Farewell to Arms* (1929) offered French writers who were young in the inter-war years an example of what they saw as 'constat literature', although the flat, even subdued tone of the prose conceals the impassioned and rather naive quality of the novel's denunciation of war and exaltation of the thirties' version of the drop-out syndrome. The sentimentality of the story, the hip remarks about life being a 'dirty trick', the tedious harping on a 'good time' (until the hero is redeemed from boozing and wenching by true love) do not detract from the beauty of the novel's opening paragraphs. The famous Hemingway rhythms in these sentences are based on one of the most ancient of prosodic measures, the hexameter. This occurs in the phrases italicized in the following extract.

> In the late summer of that year we lived in a house in a village that looked across the river and the *plain to the mountains*. In the bed of the river there were *pebbles and boulders*, dry and white in the sun, and the water was clear and swiftly moving and *blue in the channels*. Troops went by the house and down the road and the dust they raised powdered the leaves of the trees. The trunks of the trees too were dusty and the leaves fell early that year and we saw the troops marching along the road and the dust rising and leaves, stirred by the breeze, falling and the soldiers marching and afterwards the road bare and white except for the leaves.
>
> The plain was rich with crops; there were many *orchards of fruit trees* and beyond the plain the mountains were brown and bare. There was fighting in the mountains and at night we could see the flashes from the artillery. In the dark it was like summer lightning, but the nights were cool and there was not the feeling of a storm coming.
>
> (*A Farewell to Arms,* Book I, ch. 1)

Hemingway, like Erskine Caldwell and John Dos Passos, has exerted an immense influence on French writing, largely through the translations of Maurice Coindreau, who has done for this phase of American fiction what Baudelaire did for Edgar Allan Poe, that is incorporate it into the native tradition. Inter-war American writing presented an example of freshness, of direct, blunt, even brutal transcriptions of modern urban and industrial reality, of a world where man was shown as dehumanized and nature sterilized by the machine, by the conveyor belt in the factory and the combine harvester on the land; the cities' *lumpenproletariat*, the dispossessed share-cropper of the plains, found their spokesmen in novels which provoked widespread enthusiasm when they were translated into French.

The direct result of this kind of writing was the first part of Camus's novel *The Outsider*, which Robbe-Grillet admires, although he has reservations about what happens to it later in the novel because, he claims, the book isn't 'written in as *purified* a language as the first few pages might lead one to suppose' (nor, as we have noted, is *A Farewell to Arms*). And this comes about naturally enough, Robbe-Grillet points out, since Camus's 'intention is to reveal to us, as Pascal put it, "the natural misfortune of our condition".' What Robbe-Grillet seeks is the rigorous exclusion of such 'anthropomorphism'; he wants the neutrality of tone to be consistent and thorough-going, as it undoubtedly is in one of his own early texts, 'The Dressmaker's Dummy' (see p. 189).

Robbe-Grillet backed up the example of writing of this kind in a carefully argued theoretical attack against the indulgent humanism of the previous generation, and particularly Sartre's view of literature. In advocating a fresh approach to the purpose of writing he diverged radically from the tenets Sartre expounds in *What is Literature?* For Robbe-Grillet, the writer's first duty is to his art, which he alone is equipped to advance; his effectiveness in the political arena is no greater than any other citizen's, and may well be smaller. In line with this scepticism about the efficacy of ideological commitment is his advocacy of a new approach to characterization and psychology in fiction. Nathalie Sarraute, in her essay *The Age of Suspicion*, claims that the novelist no longer 'believes' in his characters (we have come a long way since Flaubert made himself ill by sharing so intensely in Emma Bovary's sufferings under arsenic); and even if the writer does still believe in his characters the reader no longer will. The history of the novel reveals increasingly elaborate and sophisticated devices being invented by authors to convince their increasingly sceptical readers of the 'reality' of their fictions. In this writers have managed to keep only a step or two ahead, and then not always; we have all experienced annoyance with stories in which we find the characters 'unconvincing'. The new novelists maintain that they no longer *can* be made convincing, so the writer might as well own up to his impotence and not seek to deceive anyone about the reality of his creations. Detailed psychological analyses of the feelings and motives of a character sound more and more 'phoney' to the reader. So, instead of doing a 'straight' study of a jealous man in the classical manner, Robbe-Grillet wrote a novel which itself *constitutes* a fit of jealousy, becoming gradually more and more irrational and fanciful as the obsession feeds upon itself. In this way Robbe-Grillet's novels are themselves, as much as his essays, an aesthetic. The same is true of Nathalie Sarraute. Her interest lies in the area of wordless, instinctive behaviour which, like a subterranean power, or like 'tropisms' in biology, governs our relations with other people. Since she cannot analyse the unsayable verbally, she indicates through dialogue, interior monologue and situation the antagonisms, resentments and sudden sympathies which activate her characters.

Moreover, time in the *nouveau roman* is never a straightforward matter of hour added to hour and day to day, since the human imagination is continually extending crucial but very brief moments (such as the seconds during which a road accident takes place), and drastically compressing much longer stretches of duration, like tedious periods of work. Nor is the order in which events actually occur often respected by the human memory: so the new novel is similarly disrespectful of it, rarely signalling its transitions (by tense or otherwise) from present to past time and back again. And sometimes the human consciousness harbours flagrant inconsistencies, even logical impossibilities of the sort which occur in Robbe-Grillet's novel *The House of Assignation*, where the mysterious circumstances surrounding Manneret's death make it imperative for Johnson to quit Hong Kong, so before he leaves he asks Manneret to lend him the money he needs, and so on. The new novelists believe that it is quite legitimate for the novel, like the mind, to stretch, abridge, shuffle and repeat, with or without variations, any particular occurrence or event.

They also are convinced (by developments in phenomenology in recent French philosophy) that the external world can only be taken at face value, and that there are no hidden depths, such as might harbour malevolent feelings towards man, in things like the notorious root of the chestnut tree which, in Sartre's novel *Nausea*, seems to claw like a vulture's talon at the hero Roquentin. On the contrary, writes Robbe-Grillet, 'man looks at the world, but the world doesn't look back at him,' though it may willy-nilly act as a focus for his emotions, and like the centipede in *Jealousy* (see p. 193) or like the piece of string in *The Voyeur*, release their pent-up force just as contact with an earth will discharge static electricity; but it always remains passive and irremediably external, totally unaffected by the touch of man who is 'no more, from his own point of view, than the only witness'. But if he can learn to live with the smooth, meaningless, mindless and amoral surface of things he will, says Robbe-Grillet, 'reject communion' with them, and in so doing reject the 'tragedy' which inevitably follows when he is made aware of their utter indifference. Robbe-Grillet thus flatly refuses to embrace the 'tragic' vision of an 'absurd' world which he finds in the work of Camus and Sartre; the world is not absurd, he argues, it is simply there. He likewise rejects the accusation that his own writings are 'inhuman'; by constantly maintaining that everything in the novel must be seen from a human, circumscribed and relativistic point of view, and that nothing pseudo-human should be posited about the external world, Robbe-Grillet claims that he is more genuinely a humanist than his predecessors, whose anthropomorphism tended to belittle man in relation to the surrounding hostile universe.

The reader of novels inspired by this new attitude is not treated to the hectorings of authorial rhetoric, but expected to co-operate with the writer of the joint elaboration of a world which is open to infinite development by the reader's imagination. His activity is therefore creative, prolonging that of the author, as is only to be expected in an era which 'is less sure of itself and more modest, perhaps because it has abandoned the idea of the omnipotence of the individual'. From this it follows that form must logically be prior to content: neither writer nor reader will know in advance what the novel is going to 'contain', what it is going to be about: they will both discover that in the process of creating it. The novelist can have no previously determined 'message' for which he merely requires a vehicle in order to put it across, or if he has, he can only expect to produce the most dreary *roman à thèse* written didactically, to a formula. The true artist, on the contrary, starts writing in order to find out what it is precisely he wishes to convey. Content can only be a function of form, and the determining factor in all literary creation must be the formal decisions (how long?, what tense?, from which point of view?, etc.) taken in the very process of the undertaking. To write according to a prior ideological commitment, as recommended by Sartre, is therefore a contradiction in terms as far as Robbe-Grillet is concerned.

Of course, as I have already indicated, the new approach threw up works before theory, which has tended always to be *post hoc* and indeed to leave largely out of account aspects of the works, such as humour or myth in Robbe-Grillet's case, which are if anything more significant than those on which the heaviest stress is laid in the essays. And in any case independent figures like Beckett and Genet had already been writing for some time oblivious of the theory, but within its general spirit and certainly affecting its elaboration by their example (Robbe-Grillet's *Towards a New Novel* contains a short study of Beckett, for instance). For there can be no doubt that Beckett's novels, because they call into question the validity of the expressive act itself, are new in a more radical way even than Robbe-Grillet's. But even though he and Genet stand outside all schools and coteries, rarely discuss their work in public and never theorize in a general fashion about it or its place in the contemporary movement, they are clearly two of the major figures in the neo-modernist revival. For, now that several years have elapsed since *Molloy* appeared, it is evident that this current, greeted at first with the derision that hails all avant-gardes, represents a profound renewal in literary aesthetics, one of which maintains rhetoric even in its anti-rhetoric, and holds to the highest ideals of art even when it appears at first sight to be anti-art. For of course neo-modernism is not anti-art; it is opposed only to a certain kind of art, which it considers outdated and thus irrelevant to the contemporary world. This includes conventional socialist realist art just as much as conventional bourgeois art. It is concerned to drive the money-changers out of the temple, not to tear down the icons: 'far from making a clean sweep of the past,' says Robbe-Grillet, 'it is on the names of our predecessors that we find it easiest to agree, and our only ambition is to continue where they left off' (*Towards a New Novel*, p. 137). And this they have certainly achieved. In a talk critical of Robbe-Grillet's theories Bernard Bergonzi argued that 'the novel cannot, in fact, escape from the limitations of lineality and chronology' (*The Listener*, 23 March 1967), but I believe that both in theory and in practice Robbe-Grillet and others have shown that it can indeed escape from these limitations, while still remaining recognizably a fictive structure enriching and extending our experience of the world we inhabit.

This, then, would be how I would describe and define neo- (or post-) modernism. I have laid most stress on the novel, since novelists are the subject of this book, but in the theatre and the cinema it is obvious that a similar exploration into formal possibilities is taking place. Narrational chronology, consistency of characterization, conventional dialogue, all are subverted in the search for fresher, more vivid, more natural and more genuine forms of the medium. Superficially unconventional, Harold Pinter's plays have a classical rigour about them; and even though nothing much may appear to 'happen' in them in the traditional sense of theatrical development, they generate considerable tension by timing and the judicious use of silence. They are certainly as dramatically expressive, if not as rich, as the great works of palaeo-modernism, Strindberg's *A Dream Play*, or Chekhov's *Three Sisters*. And in the cinema the directors of the 'new wave' acknowledge a clear debt to the classics of the film, to Lang, Ford, Hitchcock and Renoir, while developing a free, loose style which differs radically from the more rigid structures that were necessitated by less flexible and sophisticated technical equipment. And in this medium, too, neo-modernism has already produced its own masterpieces, films like *Zabriskie Point* directed by Antonioni and *Persona* directed by Bergman, which in terms of subtlety and range can compare with anything palaeo-modernism created in the silent film. In none of these areas, fortunately, do we appear to be near to seeing an end to what Kermode sees as modernism's distinguishing characteristic, its 'formal desperation': the restless play with structures continues to excite us. And in the forefront of this endeavour stand some of neo-modernism's greatest novelists, the *nouveaux romanciers* of France.

J.F.

2

The British have seldom admitted to any influence from France other than fashions in clothes, furniture and architecture, but there are moments in the arts when the French influence has been decisive, even when it has not been purely French, as for instance the influence of Lully (Italian born) on Purcell or the Parisian post-impressionists (often, like van Gogh, not French) on the Bloomsbury painters. Our music has closer links to Italy, Germany and even Holland than to France, and our painters have looked more to the Italian and Dutch Renaissance than to the French School. It is in literature that the closest influence can be felt, although few people in Britain are aware of it, because few French writers have ever been really popular here in the sense that Tolstoy, Chekhov and Dostoyevsky have been popular, or respected as Goethe, Schiller and the German poets and philosophers were respected in the early nineteeth century.

Any influence between the French and English (by now largely Scottish and Irish) literatures of the eighteenth century are not particularly significant, although they both reflected a preoccupation with man and his discoveries rather than with nature, until the romantics came into the limelight. But the parallels between Sir Walter Scott and Stendhal are striking. Stendhal, ultimately a much better writer, popularized Scott in France and frequently wrote for the *Edinburgh Review* (their mutual admiration is strangely never mentioned in Lockhart's biography of Scott) and both were interested in a contemporary form of 'outsider' for hero, anticipating the existentialist hero of our own time. Balzac, who started writing at about the same time as Stendhal and a little earlier than Dickens, is not likely to have been 'influenced' by him, but he must have been aware of the world of real people created by the French novelist and his way of creating character. Such an awareness can have an influence on what is attempted by a younger novelist of similar outlook in another country.

A generation later Flaubert dominates French literature. Interestingly his great parallel is Dostoyevsky, born the same year and dying a year after him. Dostoyevsky's popularity in Britain had always outstripped Flaubert's, but his translations came too late to be a significant influence except on twentieth-century writers. On the other hand Dostoyevsky was an avid follower of French literature, especially of the journals of the day, and *Madame Bovary*, serialized in the *Revue de Paris* in 1856-7, preceded by some years the great novels of the Russian master, and *Anna Karenina* by twenty, which it probably to some extent influenced. But there is no direct link to English literature here. Thackeray may have been aware of Stendhal, but hardly Flaubert.

Two things first brought French literature to the attention of English writers: the later stage of naturalism and the neo-romantic rise of interest in the gothic, the occult and the decadent. In fact there are so many points of contact between the naturalists and the decadents that it is easy to see them as one school and most of their critics and denigrators have preferred to do so. The taint of pornography is responsible both for this identification and their rapid translation into English at a time when the old Franco-British political animosities had died down and British artists of all kinds looked to Paris for ideas, freedom and stimulation. The titillating novels of Gauthier, the exploration into life on the streets and in the back rooms that characterizes Zola's Rougon-Macquart novels on the one hand, and the various exotic productions of the decadent aesthetes, from Gerard de Nerval (1808-1855) to Georges Charles Huysmans (1848-1907) became known in Britain through translation. The publisher Vizetelly, who spent many years in prison for publishing Zola and other French naturalist writers considered obscene here, championed Zola passionately in England and his influence can be felt in Hardy, Lawrence and much modern writing in both Britain and America. Oscar Wilde was fascinated by the fastidious gothic extravagances of Huysmans and Villiers de l'Isle Adam with their interest in occultism, secret orders, black magic and sex; their influence is evident in his own work, for instance *The Portrait of Dorian Gray*, but it spread through the influence of his circle. Baudelaire and the symbolists too influenced not only poetry in Britain—Swinburne and Yeats are only two examples—but introduced subjects that had been taboo, sexual psychology, black magic, the structure of the mind. Darwin, Havelock-Ellis, Freud, and the political writers and philosophers all combined by the end of the century to give the novelist and the poet a whole new range of ideas, mystiques and subjects to explore and a new morality to invent. André Gide is a good prototype, having absorbed all these influences and

Les Nourritures Terrestres, often described as a work of 'moral subversion', published in 1897, demonstrates the return of the polemical novel, intended to change the reader's outlook. The early novels of Aldous Huxley are a good example, and an anglicized form of the same thing, and later, the work of Genet can be seen both as an extension of Gide and a throw-back to nineteenth-century decadence, as well as a move forward into new forms of literary extravagance.

What is common in much French literature from Sade, through Baudelaire, the decadents, Rimbaud, Gide and Genet, and central to dadaism and surrealism, is a thread of gratuitousness, the *acte gratuit*. If order, law-keeping, stability is the French bourgeois ideal, then the action committed for its own sake or perhaps for no reason at all is dear to the French artist, indeed it is a possible definition of art. Sartre explains it away by his concept of 'the look' (that we are what we are seen to be). A person expected to be a criminal, because of his background, personality, behaviour, or purely prejudice on the part of another, will become a criminal. He may commit a crime for no reason at all. The *acte gratuit* is beautifully exemplified in Baudelaire's short story *Le Mauvais Vitrier*, in which the narrator deliberately smashes all the window panes of a glazier, after making him pointlessly climb the stairs to the top of the building and go down again, while shouting in glee, 'life is beautiful.' He finishes by pointing out that such evil can have its consequences, but 'what does an eternity of damnation matter to someone who has enjoyed a second of infinite joy.'

During the twentieth century the culture gap between nations has been rapidly reduced and most writers have been anxious to have some knowledge of what their contemporaries have done elsewhere, although this was not especially true of the thirties, the forties and the seventies in Britain, when there has usually been positive hostility to foreign ideas and techniques. Flaubert has long been recognized as a great novelist, but he is considered alien and unexciting, little read. But for the French novelist of today he is the father of modern literature, the man who gave the post-romantic novel its essential form. He has no comparable British contemporary like Balzac or the generation born in the 1840s. The decadents made their mark in Britain, even among such minor figures as Aleister Crowley the diabolist, and Gide had his followers among the post-1918 avant-garde in Britain, not only Aldous Huxley, but the Bloomsbury group as well, who looked much to Paris and were especially interested in the symbolists. T.S. Eliot and Ezra Pound, Americans in Europe, did much to bring French literature to the attention of British writers in spite of the opposition of the establishment that still considered Hardy a shocking novelist and Swinburne an 'advanced' poet.

Laforgue's influence on Eliot is well known, but he had been dead thirty years when 'Prufrock' was published. French poetry was not to have a decisive influence on British poetry again, although the techniques and ideas of the surrealists are only now beginning to be understood. Éluard is perhaps the last important French poet to have a fair number of British admirers.

The depression discouraged publishers from translation, bringing to an end the golden age of the twenties when Gide, Roger Martin du Gard and other French novelists were available in English, and the thirties was such an age of political rather than literary commitment that André Malraux, whose *Les Conquerants* appeared in 1928 in Paris and the following year in London, had to wait from 1933 until 1948 for his masterpiece *La Condition Humaine* to be translated. And yet here was a Hemingway-like political novel. But it was the high-brows who lost most and whose influence diminished. Even Joyce's *Ulysses*, banned from 1922 until 1936 in Britain, was little read until the 1950s. Later Sartre and Camus became well known in Britain, largely because the first was identified with the St Germain life-style popularized through films, and the latter satisfied the hunger for a more intellectual and allegorical style, otherwise only found in Graham Greene, by a culture-hungry post-war generation. Proust was known to an élite before the war through the influence of the Bloomsbury group, but it is difficult to see whom he has influenced, although mistaken claims are made for Anthony Powell.

But all this time, during the thirties and forties when experiment and new literary forms were totally out of fashion, new roots were growing underground and there was an astonishing outburst in France during the early fifties in the theatre and the novel. Beckett, Ionesco and Adamov, followed shortly after by Arrabal, Dubillard, Obaldia, Billetdoux and others, caught the imagination of a bored French intellectualate. In a short time they had come across the channel. Peter Hall put on *Waiting for Godot*, Laurence Olivier played in Ionesco's *Rhinoceros* and Alec Guinness in *Exit the King*. The *theatre of the absurd*, as Martin Esslin dubbed it, found its British exponents with Pinter, N.F. Simpson, Saunders, Rudkin and Bond. In the novel Beckett and that group of novelists who are the subject of this *Reader*, brought new techniques, some of them learned from the cinema, to the attention of the public. The group of British writers who made a mark in the late fifties and early sixties all consciously used some of the techniques of the *nouveaux romanciers* and the theatrical absurdists, although Canetti, Grass and Böll also had an influence. They had a brief vogue: Alan Burns, Ann Quin, Brian Johnstone, Paul Ritchie, Peter Everett, Eva Figes. But only Burns and Figes are still writing novels. Personal disaster, or discouragement as the established critics came back to the attack, stopped the others. Anthony Burgess, the last genuinely experimental writer in Britain, and John Berger who is more of a political polemicist, continue to exhibit some French influence. But the tides of recession have already reduced translation between English and French to a trickle and it may be some years before cross-fertilization is evident again. In the meantime, underground, something is always stirring for the future. The editors hope that this volume may contribute to it.

3

The Nouveau Roman

New literary movements are usually brought into being by the dissatisfaction of a generation of writers with the current literary mode. Usually too, a new literary approach is one aspect of an outlook that is taking hold in the intellectual and artistic thinking of the time, which one would expect to find in the other arts as well. In the early nineteenth century, both the English and the French novel felt a need to take a new path away from the unrealities of the romantic novel with its cardboard characters and 'idealized' view of human motivation, sacrificing real observation to poetic sentiment. The movement that started around 1830 with Balzac in France and Dickens in England resulted in a naturalistic novel that concentrated on the accurate observation and description of character and of real life as people lived it. A generation later Flaubert took naturalism a step further, enquiring more deeply into human behaviour and the workings of the mind, and his exact contemporary Dostoyevsky, did the same thing in Russia. Another generation on, Zola examined and described human activities that had previously been unmentionable, continuing, after Flaubert's problems with *Madame Bovary*, the great censorship debate that is still with us today, and he took naturalism to its limit as far as the human eye and the time of the clock was concerned. After that, man and his behaviour had to be seen through a microscope to get a more detailed picture.

Looking at the French novel in particular, one can say that every twenty years after 1830 a new school of the novel came into being, each one stretching the framework a little further in the search for truth and more accurate description. Zola in particular was interested in science and the development of scientific method in terms of objectivity and of experiment, and he tried to apply these techniques to literature. Each new generation came to think of itself as a lap in a race, relaying the torch of artistic progress on to the next generation. But every artistic doctrine helps to bring its opposite into existence and the growth of ever more detailed naturalism with its sceptical view of what cannot be seen and proved is accompanied by a parallel growth of speculative, metaphysical and decadent literature. These movements are observable in painting, music and philosophy as well. The shared outlook of intellectual and creative people gives common *style* to each discipline.

So parallel to Zola we find a mystical expressionistic literature represented by Villiers de l'Isle Adam and Huysmans in France, and Oscar Wilde in England; and a generation later, both traditions are continued in a more impressionistic manner, the naturalist tradition by Proust and the mystical by Gide.

But Proust not only carried naturalistic observation a stage further by stretching out clock time to memory time, he also turned naturalism into anti-naturalism, or more accurately, he transferred the techniques of painterly and musical impressionism into literature, so that it is not the measured pace of events observed and accurately described that takes on importance, but the significant moments in memory (all description in art—with certain exceptions like speculative fiction—must in any case be memory as a thing cannot be described until after it has happened). Memory is selective and it distorts, so that what is important at the time may be unimportant in retrospect, and vice-versa. Modernism in the novel begins with Proust, although he is also the end of the nineteenth-century naturalistic tradition. In British terms the same can be said of Joyce, who brought the novel even further into the 'reality' of the mind, rather than of the camera. Joyce also stretched time, using impressionistic technique, and went still farther into abstraction in *Finnegans Wake*, a work that will keep literary critics, philosophers and psychologists busy for the next century. One should mention two other names here: Kafka, Joyce's central European contemporary, who, closer to expressionism and the aura of Dostoyevsky than the naturalistic impressionism of Western Europe, first conveyed the overwhelming sense of morbid and doom-ridden unreality that is now in the psyche of all intelligent mortals; and Beckett, still writing at his peak as these words are written, must be thought of as a predecessor, but also as a contemporary of and a subliminal influence on the eight writers who are the subject of this *Reader*. And brief mention should perhaps also be made of Sartre and Camus, who revived the philosophical novel, a form, which as far as any influence on the history of literature is concerned, has been almost unknown since the eighteenth century and the dawn of the romantic revolution; mention must be made, because their existentialist novels constitute a hiatus between important pre-war literary art in the increasingly abstract writing of Proust, Joyce and Kafka (abstract in the sense that it examines man and his mind through an ever more microscopic lens), and the arrival of the *nouveau roman*. In terms of literary history, the novels of Sartre and Camus can be criticized for sharing many of the drawbacks of the romantic novel; they are an island in the river, not part of the current.

And perhaps one other fore-runner of the *nouveau roman* must be mentioned: surrealist literature which, like surrealist painting and film, has added to the contemporary unease and sense of unreality, emphasizing that what man wants to see is as important as what he does see, and refuting the determination and logic that characterized scientific, political and philosophical thinking until belief in progress and the perfectibility of human life foundered in the irrational carnage of the 1914–18 war. Surrealism was a reaffirmation of free will and of the creative power of the irrational and metaphysical, offering a short cut to discovery by giving the imagination precedence over logic.

It is difficult as yet to date accurately the arrival of the *nouveau roman*. It was a revolt against the 'committed' novels of Malraux, Sartre and Camus, and one might as well say of Koestler, Huxley, Orwell, etc, not that the *nouveaux romanciers* were necessarily aware of the non-French novel of the thirties and forties, although they knew what they were like. Very disparate writers, sharing a dissatisfaction with the accepted novel form, which seemed to them inadequate to express the state of the world and their own preoccupations, particularly in regard to truth and observation, each writing in isolation around 1950, became recognized and merged together as a group under a variety of epithets (their novels were referred to as the anti-novel, a-novel, *chosism*) largely because they were read, liked and offered to the public by one remarkable publisher, Jérôme Lindon of Editions de Minuit, who after the war had taken over a war-time clandestine publishing company founded by Vercors and used it to promote his own publishing vision.

The doyenne of the group, Nathalie Sarraute, does not belong to the *Minuit* stable, although her *Tropisms* (first published 1939) were reissued by them in 1957. These short texts are miniatures and models for her later work. They take their title from the response that a plant or sedentary animal shows to an external stimulus, such as light or heat. In the same way, Nathalie Sarraute argues, people respond to each other, often unconsciously recognizing what is going on in the mind of another person by recognizing a tic or mannerism or false inflection in the voice. All her novels and plays are based on fictionalization or dramatization of the interaction of people to each other, where the human 'tropisms' of the outer mask often reveal what people are really thinking and where their intentions belie their words. Popular psychology in such books as *Games People Play* make the same points on a non-literary and less subtle level. Nathalie Sarraute is therefore basically a social novelist, describing behaviour in a very special way, but like Proust making a number of very relevant points about love, affection, hypocrisy and such other failings of bourgeois society as avarice, greed and malice. She can sensitively describe the differing attitudes and the real, as opposed to the pretended, reason for antagonism between two generations of the same family and she has a sensitive and original way of making political points. In her essays *The Age of Suspicion*, first collected into a book in 1956, she states that the author has become 'suspicious' of his characters, no longer believes in their credibility, and even if the author does, the reader will not. She therefore, through dialogue, conversation, interior monologue and the description of mannerisms, manages to strip her characters down to their uncertain and dishonest real selves, very different from their public personas. She sees her roots particularly in Dostoyevsky and Kafka, but expresses admiration for many English novelists such as Virginia Woolf and Ivy Compton Burnett, and of course she owes much to Proust and to her French predecessors.

Alain Robbe-Grillet has done most to unify, promote and theorize the *nouveau roman* and many consider him the first pope of the movement. A brilliant speaker with the ability to explain ideas in lucid terms, he has been generous with his time in reading the work of younger writers who share his dissatisfaction with the 'old novel' and in helping them to publication and critical attention. Generosity in helping one's rivals is a rare quality in the *tous contre tous* battleground of literary Paris, but as for many years principal reader for Les Editions de Minuit, as an indefatigable debater and lecturer, a principal founder of the *Prix des Critiques* and the *Prix Médicis*, each a prize designed to help promote new literary talent, he has fused a variety of different writers, who were more in agreement as to what they were against than what they were for, into a viable school of literature, the first to do so since André Breton created the surrealist school. Even those who criticized his flamboyance and distrusted his motives were only too happy to take advantage of his activities to become better known themselves, once the *nouveau roman* had become a topic for fashionable discussion. One writer included in this volume, Marguerite Duras, insisted that whatever her contracts with her normal publisher stipulated, she had to have one book published by Minuit.

Robbe-Grillet was trained as an agricultural engineer and he brings an architect's technique to his work. He starts with the plans and then the blueprint for his structure: the theory comes first. Brilliant, determined and ambitious, he has never been willing to spend his life basking in the admiration of a small circle of intelligent friends in semi-poverty like Joyce, but has used his ingenuity and flair for publicity to combine critical acceptance with the best possible financial rewards. His work is therefore calculated to give him the maximum advantage from all quarters. He plans his basic structure, his plot, his technique, his puzzles and surprises, and only then writes the book. He has enough humour to admit that he sometimes teases and tricks his readers, often with buried and even outrageous puns. But above all, he has studied the linear descent of French literature with its accretions and influence from other languages and taken the logical next step forward, centreing his work on an extension of fictional time, on a rejection of objective reality and a refusal to play God. Ambiguity and doubt abound in his work. He will tell you what someone is saying or thinking, give you a description of what one of his characters sees, but you have no way of knowing whether the speech, the thought or the observation is true or false, whether the character is sane or demented or even if he exists at all. The effect on the reader is to disorientate him, so that he sees everything in relative terms, is forced to play God himself in deciding what is reality and what illusion, and is obliged in so doing to share the task of writing the novel with the author.

For both artistic and financial reasons Robbe-Grillet moved from the novel to the film, and has extended his theories and techniques to that medium. *Last year at Marienbad*, made with Alain Resnais as director, originally had a final word for the viewer, cut after the first showings: 'If you have not understood this film, ask yourself if you have really understood your life.' One reason for Robbe-Grillet's success and importance is that he has so accurately conveyed the doubt—about the world we inhabit, the society we live in, the meaning of our lives and actions, and what kind of person each one of us is—so accurately, that a thinking person cannot help but see the relevance to himself and make new discoveries about himself and his environment. And Robbe-Grillet is not an especially difficult writer to read, indeed his more recent work often contains so much erotic content that he has occasionally been criticized for commercializing and trivializing. But he is not a writer who would accept a curb on his imagination, and it is in imagination that he excels. Like Raymond Roussel who could build a novel of adventure from the chance meeting of two words to form a third as a starting point, he can take his point of departure from the gesture of opening the door to his Paris flat (in *Project for a Revolution in New York*), closing it, describing the back of the door and then the varnish of the woodwork around the window, in which thin lines suggest to him a young woman, naked, lying on her left side. At that moment he has a scene in his mind and he adds to it, bringing in another character, and a story starts to unfold that has nothing to do with a revolution in New York or anywhere outside the author's mind and imagination as he transfers it to the printed page.

The freedom from having to describe any reality known to the reader, the total rejection of any naturalism, and the continual dissolving of scene into scene according to the associations, observations, preoccupations and random interruptions that occur to the author, do however have the effect of creating a new kind of reality which the reader can recognize in himself, and which *he can create himself.* The novel invents itself, the novelist gives it birth, his mind is the womb, his typewriter the midwife, and it is the reader who must take the responsibility for bringing it up and for deciding what kind of novel it is going to be. And another reader may in fact see the book in a very different light without any objection from the author. Like Kafka, Robbe-Grillet is able to help the reader make order out of chaos by understanding and accepting the chaos, by inventing and imposing his own order on it, not according to any set of rules, but according to his will. Robbe-Grillet's basic philosophical message is that there is no objective reality, that reality is what we choose to make it and the will of man is more important and offers more hope and happiness to mankind than any attempt to deduce doubtful truths from nature with our discredited scientific and critical investigative methods. These words should not be read in an ecological sense: man can will himself back to a pre-industrial environment if he wishes.

Situated in age between Nathalie Sarraute and Alain Robbe-Grillet is Claude Simon (born 1913), whose work has a more baroque flavour, and often a kinship with the novels of Faulkner. Obsession is his hallmark and his characters confuse past, present and possible future, changing chronology and recounting events according to a logic which is peculiar to the novel in question, meticulously plotted and often very complex. And all this is done in a language that often resembles *The Wind*, title of his first novel, driving the reader on with great gusts of rich, ebullient language.

A year younger is Marguerite Duras (born 1914), who started her career as a writer committed to the Communist Party, but only found her voice after recovering her intellectual freedom. Nevertheless her work, and in particular her films, hint more at direct political issues than does the work of any other writer in this volume. The films *Hiroshima, Mon Amour* and *After Such a Long Absence* are love stories, each with a background of tragedy resulting from the last war, but concerned with later political issues, although obliquely. The death of a German soldier, the disgrace of his French girl friend, the bomb on Hiroshima, or the lost memory of a war victim, the Algerian war, these tragedies can only be brought home to the film viewer by empathy and identification with someone else's loss, not by polemic or direct propaganda. The oblique approach characterizes all Mme. Duras's novels and plays. In *The Square*, a chance conversation between a commercial traveller and a house-maid reveals their loneliness, poetically expressed through the associations that certain moods and longings have for each of them with places and things. In *Ten-Thirty on a Summer Night*, a young wife's awareness of her husband's infidelity and of the plight of an escaped murderer become fused in her mind, and to face the first situation she does something positive about the second. In *The Afternoon of M. Andesmas*, an old man who has been temporarily forgotten by the architect who is to build him a new house, realizes that he will soon die and be forgotten by everyone. In *Moderato Cantabile*, the novel that the author insisted go to Editions de Minuit, the bored wife of a rich man finds an outlet for her *ennui* and death-wish through her fascination with a *crime passionel* that she partly witnesses. Although a more 'popular' writer than those already mentioned, Marguerite Duras has the preoccupations, practices and techniques which have come to be associated with the *nouveau roman*. Her strong poetic and romantic bent, allied with formidable intellectual talent, have earned her a special place in modern literature. She writes especially perceptively about women and their emotional problems, while her horror of war, injustice and oppression have made her known to many who have not read her work.

Claude Mauriac was born the same year as Marguerite Duras and is the son of the great catholic writer, François Mauriac. He has had a distinguished career as a film critic, and his first novel *Toutes les femmes sont fatales* (1957) has a film critic as its hero, who appears again with less importance in the novels that followed it. This novel is reasonably conventional, a sequence of successful seductions and their aftermath, but with its successor *Dinner in Town*, he developed a technique that has much in common with Nathalie Sarraute, mingling the conversations and thoughts of the people around a table at a dinner party to give a multi-faceted picture of their relationship to each other, but leaving it to the reader to identify who is who. In his next novel, *The Marquise Went Out at Five*, the setting is a busy crossing of narrow streets in the Latin Quarter: the novelist, working on his book, looks down on it from his window, and the thoughts and conversations of shopkeepers, shoppers and pedestrians mingle with his own. There are three other novels in the sequence where many of the characters from earlier novels make appearances, older and often in different circumstances and liaisons, which still have to appear in English.

Robert Pinget (born 1920), belongs, like Marguerite Duras, to the more poetical wing of the *nouveau roman*, and like her makes his points through oblique associations. In his novel *No Answer* and its stage version *Dead Letter*, an elderly father living in a small village writes to his son who has gone to the city. The appeal to return is never stated directly, but is clear enough between the lines of local gossip and information which he relays in letters, that are never answered. His best-known book *The Inquisitory* is a technical masterpiece, filled with vague menace, in which the caretaker of a deserted house is questioned by a mysterious inquisitor about the past events and the previous inhabitants of the establishment, so recently deserted. It is a large novel consisting entirely of question and answer, and it becomes obvious that the caretaker is often lying. The reader must work out the truth and its meaning for himself.

Pinget has been prolific in the novel, and in the stage and radio play, and is one of the most respected of the Minuit authors, although to date he has attracted less academic interest than others of the same generation. He has often been associated with Samuel Beckett because of certain similarities in outlook and style, but he is very much of an individualist whose influences lie largely in the work of pre-war writers, like the poet and prose stylist Max Jacob. He does not indulge in theory, although he has occasionally written intro-ductory statements about his own work and had lectured on other writers.

Michel Butor (born 1926) has been one of the most successful of the *nouveaux romanciers*, although he has become more of a critic in recent years and his imaginative work has become experimental in a direction that is perhaps closer to the next generation than his own. His early work is still much admired and shows many similarities with the techniques of Robbe-Grillet at the same period. In *Second Thoughts* (1957) a man is on a train from Paris to Rome, leaving his wife for his mistress. On the long journey he comes to realize the associations that each woman has for him and the reasons he is making this break, and decides to return to Paris. In *Passing Time* (a mis-translation of *L'Emploi du Temps*—'The Time Table'), probably his best novel, a French lecturer spending a year in a British city (clearly identifiable as Manchester) works out his association with the city and its people and manages to remain aloof from both. *Degrees* describes a boy's school in great detail and infuses it with a strange human presence.

The present volume covers two generations of writers. Some, like Nathalie Sarraute and Claude Mauriac, have extended the scope of the social novel as well as developing new methods of presenting characters and situations. Others like Alain Robbe-Grillet and Michel Butor have been more interested in how the mind works, and in subjective description of places and objects that become human because human properties are read into them. Previously it was frequently said by literary critics that Robbe-Grillet and his school were only interested in describing *things* and in 'removing Man from the novel'. Better understanding has shown that the opposite is true. Marguerite Duras and Robert Pinget are poetic novelists primarily, impressionists whose work is rooted in the significant moment, the moment of awareness when things become clear, at least to the reader. Claude Simon stands alone, has certain similarities with Robbe-Grillet, particularly in the way he shows the mind's working and in his interest in obsession. He is a high stylist in the way that Joyce was a stylist, rejoicing in the myriad possibilities of words. Finally, Jean Ricardou, the pope of the second generation, like Robbe-Grillet is a theorist, an organizer and publicist, whose name and ideas are much better known than his books, giving the reader much greater difficulty than his predecessors.

The *nouveau roman* has become a prime subject for academic study in Britain and America, both in French departments and comparative literature courses, and the present volume is partly designed to make that study easier. But above all, the new novel, like all novels, is written not just to show off the cleverness and virtuosity of the author, but also to entertain, divert, provoke and interest the mind, to enlarge the reader by increasing his awareness of his times and the world in which he lives, above all to increase his awareness of himself. The eight writers included in this reader all in their different ways do this, and they complement each other. The volume is intended to give the essence and the flavour of each, together with such information about the authors themselves and their works as can be contained in a book of this size.

Size has made it impossible to include many others who might claim some space here and mention is made of them and their books in the bibliography. But the reader has a fair survey, never attempted in Britain before, of one of the really significant literary movements of the twentieth century, and it would have little value if it were to leave out any of the key figures included here, all of whom have some work available in good English translations, while some of them are completely translated, or eventually will be.

J.C.

NATHALIE SARRAUTE

Nathalie Sarraute was born in Ivanova in Russia in 1902, travelled widely when a young girl and spent a time as a student at Oxford, which explains her command of many languages. Since before the war she has been married to a distinguished French jurist and the worldly Parisian circles in which she moves have undoubtedly provided the background for much of her work. She is nevertheless very much in the forefront of French intellectual life and her public appearances always attract a large following of admirers.

The subtlety with which she reveals the thoughts and motivations that lie under our formal behaviour and the front we present to the world is difficult to describe, but fascinating to read. From a method of revealing personality, her novels and plays have taken on a deeper significance and in her important novel *Fools Say!* (1976) she has advanced a theory of human value developing directly out of her observation. She makes it clear that each one of us considers him- or herself to be the centre of the world, which means that all external value of other people or things must develop out of their relationship to ourselves. But at the same time we must live in a world of others' values and come to terms with them. Each of us lives inside an image accepted by others and by oneself. The images of a group or a family are interdependent and if one image is shattered, by, for instance, one member stepping outside his role, the certainties of the whole group disintegrate.

When writing about artists, she poses difficult questions about the problems of aesthetics, the attitudes of generations and what is acceptable by current fashion. Ultimately Sarraute has much to teach the philosopher and the psychologist, because her unusual methods of investigating behaviour evoke a shocked recognition in the reader as he perceives an unexpected truth. Reality cannot be directly described, indeed she says that the writer must 'seem incapable of describing anything but appearances', but she delineates appearances so accurately that a deeper meaning emerges. At the same time different social milieus, that of the ambitious bourgeoisie in *Portrait of a Man Unknown*, her first novel, that of the minor aristocracy in *The Planetarium* or of Parisian literary circles in *The Golden Fruits*, come vividly to life because she is also writing a social novel where conversations and interchanges are close to their real-life models. Initial penetration of Nathalie Sarraute's style requires a certain intellectual effort, but once the reader has made it, he will find himself fascinated for life.

The first five texts that follow are complete and taken from *Tropisms*, first published in 1939. They demonstrate in essence the technique and subject matter of her novels, descriptions of people and events that give away the underlying ennui or sub-conversation in the minds of the participants. The other extracts are taken from *The Planetarium*, the novel that achieved the greatest commercial success on publication, and from *Between Life and Death*, her fifth novel. This is followed by a complete play, written as if for radio like all Nathalie Sarraute's plays, but it has been successfully staged by the Renaud-Barrault Company in Paris, in a production devised by Claude Régy. The play emphasizes a difference in generational attitudes and the defensiveness that covers up the basis insecurities of that section of French society that must have opinions about culture, but does not hold them very deeply.

(J.C.)

Tropisms (1939)

XIX

He was smooth and flat, two level surfaces—his cheeks which he presented first to one then to the other, and upon which, with their pursed lips, they pressed a kiss.

They took him and they crunched him, turned him over and over, stamped on him, rolled, wallowed on him. They made him go round and round, there, and there, and there, they showed him disquieting painted scenery with blind doors and windows, towards which he walked credulously, and against which he bumped and hurt himself.

They had always known how to possess him entirely, without leaving him a fresh spot, without a moment's respite, how to devour him to the last crumb. They surveyed him, cut him up into dreadful building lots, into squares, traversed him in every direction; sometimes they let him run, turned him loose, but they brought him back as soon as he went too far, they took possession of him again. He had developed a taste for this devouring in childhood—he tendered himself, relished their bitter-sweet odour, offered himself.

The world in which they had enclosed him, in which they surrounded him on every side, was without issue. Everywhere their frightful clarity, their blinding light that levelled everything, did away with all shadows and asperities.

They were aware of his liking for their attacks, his weakness, so they had no scruples.

They had emptied him entirely and restuffed him and they showed him everywhere other dolls, other puppets. He could not escape them. He could only turn politely towards them the two smooth surfaces of his cheeks, one after the other, for them to kiss.

XX

When he was little, he used to sit up straight in bed at night, call out. They would come running, light the light, they would take the white linens, the towels, the clothes, in their hands, and show them to him. There was nothing. In their hands the white linens became harmless, shrank, they became set and dead in the light.

Now that he was grown, he still made them come and look everywhere, hunt inside him, observe well and take in their hands, the fears cowering in the nooks and corners inside him, and examine them in the light.

They were accustomed to coming in and looking, and he prepared the way for them, he himself lighted all the lights so as not to sense their hands groping about in the dark. They looked—he remained motionless, without daring to breathe—but there was nothing anywhere, nothing that could cause fear, everything seemed in good order, in place, they recognised everywhere familiar, well-known objects, and they showed them to him. There was nothing. What was he afraid of? At times, here or there, in a corner, something seemed to tremble vaguely, to waver slightly, but with a pat they set it straight again, it was nothing, one of his usual fears—they took it and showed it to him: his friend's daughter was already married? Was that it? Or else, so-and-so, who although he was a former classmate of his, had been promoted, was to be decorated? They repaired, they righted that, it was nothing. For a moment, he believed he felt stronger, propped up, patched up, but already he sensed his legs and arms grow heavy, lifeless, become numb with this solidified waiting, he had, as one has before losing consciousness, a tingling sensation in his nostrils: they saw him withdraw into himself all of a sudden, assume his strangely preoccupied, absent look: then, with little pats on his cheeks—the Windsors' travels, Lebrun, the quintuplets—they revised him.

But while he was coming to himself and when they left him finally mended, cleaned, repaired, all nicely seasoned and ready, fear formed in him again, at the bottom of the little compartments, of the little drawers they had just opened, in which they had seen nothing, and which they had closed.

XXI

In her black alpaca apron, with her cross pinned every week on her chest, she was an extremely 'easy' little girl, a very docile, very good child: 'Is this for children, Madame?' she would ask the stationery woman, if she was not sure, when buying a comic paper or a book.

She never could have, oh no, for nothing on earth, already at that age, she could not have gone out of the shop with those eyes, the stationery woman's eyes, glued to her back, as she went to open the door to leave.

Now she was grown, little fish grow big, yes, indeed!, time passes fast, oh! it's once you're past twenty that the years begin to fly by, faster and faster, isn't that so? They think that too? And she stood there before them in her black ensemble, which goes with everything, and besides, black always looks well, doesn't it? . . . she remained seated, her hands folded over her matching handbag, smiling, nodding her head sympathetically, of course she had heard, she knew that their grandmother's death had been a lingering one, it was because she had been so strong, they weren't like us, at her age, imagine, she still had all her teeth . . . And Madeleine? Her husband . . . Ah! men, if they could give birth to children, they would only have one, that's sure, they would never go through it a second time, her mother, poor woman, had always said so—oh! oh! fathers, sons, mothers!—the eldest was a girl, and they had wanted to have a son first, no, no, it was too soon, she must not stand up already, not leave, she was not going to separate from them, she was going to stay there, near them, quite near, as near as possible, of course she understood, it's so nice to have an older brother, she shook her head, smiled, oh, not her, first, oh! no, they could be quite assured, she would not move, oh, no, not her, she would never break that up all of a sudden. Remain silent, look at them; and right in the middle of the grandmother's illness, rise and, making an enormous hole, escape, knocking against the lacerated walls, and run shouting amidst the crouched houses standing watch all along the grey streets, flee, stepping over the feet of the concierges seated in front of their doors taking the air, run with her mouth contorted shouting incoherencies, while the concierges looked up from their knitting and their husbands lowered their newspapers to their knees, to press their gaze the length of her back, until she had turned the corner.

XXII

Sometimes, when they were not looking at him, to try and find something that was warm and living around him, he would run his hand very gently along one of the columns of the sideboard . . . they would not see him, or perhaps they would think that he was merely 'touching wood' for luck, a very wide-spread custom and, after all, a harmless one.

When he sensed that they were watching him from behind, like the villain in the movies who, feeling the eyes of the policeman on his back, concludes his gesture nonchalantly, gives it the appearance of being off-handed and naïve, to calm their apprehension he would drum with three fingers of his right hand, three times three, which is the really effectual lucky gesture. For they were watching him more closely since he had been caught in his room, reading the Bible.

Objects, too, were very wary of him and had been for a long time, ever since, as a little child, he had begged their favour, had tried to attach himself to them, to cling to them, to warm himself, they had refused to 'play', to become what he had wanted to make of them, 'poetic memories of childhood'. They had been brought to heel, these objects had, being well trained, they had the unobtrusive, anonymous look of well-schooled servants; they knew their place and they refused to answer him, out of fear, no doubt, of being dismissed.

But with the exception, very rarely, of this timid little gesture, he really took no liberties of any kind. He had succeeded, little by little, in gaining control over all his stupid little manias, in fact, he had fewer of them now than were normally tolerated; he didn't even collect postage-stamps—which normal people did, for all to see. He never stopped in the middle of the street to look—the way he had once done, on his walks, when the nursemaid, come along, will you! come along! had had to drag him—he crossed quickly and never held up street traffic; he walked by objects, even the most hospitable, even the most alive of them, without casting a single look of complicity in their direction.

In short, the very ones among his friends and relations who were keen about psychiatry had nothing to reproach him with, unless, perhaps, in view of his lack of inoffensive, relaxing whims, in view of his too obedient conformity, it were a slight tendency towards asthenia.

But they tolerated that; all things considered, it was less dangerous, less indecorous.

From time to time only, when he felt too weary, on their advice, he took the liberty of going away alone on a little trip. And there, when he went walking at nightfall, in the quiet little snowy streets that were filled with a gentle indulgence, he would run his hands lightly over the red and white bricks of the houses and, clinging to the wall, sidewise, through fear of being indiscreet, he would look through the clear panes into downstairs rooms in which green plants on china saucers had been set in the window, and from where, warm, full, heavy with a mysterious denseness, objects tossed him a small part—to him too, although he was unknown and a stranger—of their radiance; where the corners of a table, the door of a sideboard, the straw seat of a chair emerged from the half-light and consented to become for him, mercifully for him, too, since he was standing there waiting, a little bit of his childhood.

XXIII

They were ugly, they were dull, commonplace, without personality, they were really too out-of-date, clichés, she thought, which she had already seen described everywhere, so many times, in the works of Balzac, of Maupassant, in Madame Bovary, clichés, copies, copies of copies, she decided.

She would have so liked to repulse them, seize them and hurl them away. But they stood quietly about her, they smiled at her, pleasantly, but dignifiedly, very decorously, they had been working all week, all their lives they had counted on nobody but themselves, they asked for nothing, except to see her from time to time; to rearrange a little the tie between them and her, feel that it was there, still in place, the tie that bound them to her. They wanted nothing more than to ask her—as was natural, as everybody did, when they went to call on friends, or on relatives—to ask her what she had been doing that was nice, if she had been reading a lot lately, if she had gone out often, if she had seen that, didn't she think those films were good . . . They, themselves, had so enjoyed Michel Simon, Jouvet, they had laughed so hard, had had such a delightful evening.

And as for all that, clichés, copies, Balzac, Flaubert, Madame Bovary, oh! they knew very well, they were acquainted with it all, but they were not afraid—they looked at her kindly, they smiled, they seemed to feel that they were safe with her, they seemed to know that they had been observed, depicted, described so often, been so sucked on, that they had become as smooth as pebbles, all shiny, without a nick, without a single hold. She could not get at them. They were safe.

They surrounded her, held out their hands to her: 'Michel Simon . . . Jouvet . . . Ah! she had been obliged to book seats well ahead of time, had she not . . . Later, there would have been no tickets to be had, except at exorbitant prices, nothing but boxes, or in the stalls . . .' They tightened the tie a little more, very gently, unobtrusively, without hurting her, they rearranged the slender tie, pulled . . .

And little by little a certain weakness, a certain slackness, a need to approach them, to have them approach her, made her join in the game with them. She sensed how docilely (Oh! yes . . . Michel Simon . . . Jouvet . . .) very docilely, like a good, amenable little girl, she gave them her hand and walked in a ring with them.

Ah! here we are at last all together, good as gold, doing what our parents would have approved of, here we all are then, well-behaved, singing together like good little children that an invisible adult is looking after, while they walk gently around in a circle giving one another their sad, moist little hands.

(Translated by Maria Jolas)

The Planetarium (1959)

Something inside her comes loose and falls . . . in the emptiness inside her something is quivering . . . Dizziness . . . Her head reels slightly, her legs weaken . . . But she must brace herself, she must hold on, just one second more, present a calm face for the light kisses on her cheek, offer a kiss in return, smile, talk . . . 'Well, goodbye, Maman, we'll see you soon . . . Why no, I'm not depressed, no, I'm not annoyed, what an idea . . . Why, of course, Maman, I understand, I know . . . And you, don't you worry, either . . . They're nothing serious, you know, in reality, those fads of Alain's . . . You'll see, we're not as bad as you think. Yes, yes, I'll speak to him. You're right, it will straighten out . . .'

As soon as the door is closed, as soon as she is alone on the silent staircase, the dikes break . . . Something boils up in her, runs over . . . She knows what it is, it's the old sensation she used to have, her own peculiar fear, still the same, the terror that had never left her, she recognizes it . . .

She is skipping along the walk in the Petit Luxembourg gardens, holding her mother's hand. The big pink blossoms on the horse-chestnut trees stand erect amidst the soft foliage, the damp grass sparkles in the sun, the air trembles slightly, but it's happiness, it's Spring that trembles above the lawns, between the trees . . . she inhales delightedly on her bare arm her own odour, the odour that will always recall that Spring, that happiness, the cool, bland odour of her child's skin, of the sleeve of her new cotton dress . . . And suddenly a shriek, an inhuman, strident shriek . . . Her mother shrieked, her mother is pulling back savagely, her head turned away, holding her nose . . .

The light has grown dim, the sun is shining with a dull lustre, everything is wavering with terror, and a strange vehicle, a high, slender, nightmarish cart, filled with a livid powder that exhales a frightful smell, comes bumping along towards them on the walk . . .

She feels now, as she did then, like hiding her head so as not to see, like holding her nose, she's going to be sick, she would like to sit down just anywhere, there, on one of the steps . . . or preferably, over there, out of doors, on a bench . . . Everything is wavering . . . Everything is going to collapse.

Smiles, knowing looks, murmurs . . . later, later, you'll see . . . Images proposed on every side, songs, films, novels . . .Promised, heralded, awaited, finally manifested, handsomer than she could possibly have imagined . . . a little shy, perhaps, but high-bred, smart, subtle smile of his grey eyes, everyone had agreed: a real Prince Charming. A little too young? Her father had patted her cheek as he gazed at her in his tender way . . . 'Don't complain, my daughter . . . You'll see, youth is a very brief illness, one gets quickly over it, believe me . . .' And his studies not completed? his doctor's thesis not yet finished? But it's so hard, the Doctor of Letters thesis especially, it's the hardest of all . . . the blotchy-cheeked woman looked at her with shining, slightly bulging eyes . . . 'Ah, my dear child, my husband was studying for his internship when we were married, and now, you see . . .'

No, nobody had had anything to say against it. If there had been something . . . the slightest crack . . . her mother, who saw everything, her mother who looked out for everything—nothing escaped her . . . No, there was nothing. It really was what you call happiness that people had looked at with tender smiles, moist eyes. You couldn't mistake it. It certainly was that. Everybody had been delighted with the very amusing fancies, the innocent teasing that happiness indulges in when its strength is overflowing, when it feels lighthearted, at ease, and sure of itself: the bridal train that an awkward little page had caught on a bench, as they started up the aisle . . . The 'yes' that she had answered a little too soon during the civil ceremony . . . the right hand she had stretched out instead of the left to receive the ring . . . It was all so funny, so charming . . . and they had all been delighted, laughing there under the refreshing caress of this joyful outburst, of this overflow of happiness . . .

And yet, even that day—now that she looks with all her might at the beautiful structure, which is wavering, which is listing—even that day, there had already been something, a crack, a defect . . . What was it? She feels, as she hunts about, a sort of excitement, almost a satisfaction, which mingles with her suffering . . . yes, already at that time, the edifice had not been so handsome, so perfect . . . There had been that tiny cranny through which an evil-smelling vapour,

exhalations, had leaked . . . That half-laughter, as she went from one
to the other in the drawing-room, all excitement, people calling her
from every side, congratulating her, that whisper, like a wheeze, of
the two baleful old women, the wicked fairies, leaning towards each
other . . . 'How much did you say?' How much? Eighty thousand
francs a month? Really? no more than that?'

She turned away, she fled, she ran to take refuge with her husband,
she laid her hand on his arm, they looked into each other's eyes, then
and there, in front of everybody . . . And she felt very strongly, for the
first time, she knew that the two of them . . . the pain comes back all
of a sudden, throbbing harder than before . . . that they formed
together something indestructible, unassailable . . . Not a flaw in the
hard, smooth wall. No way for others to see what was on the other
side.

On the other side, only they two knew it, everything was fluid, vast,
without outlines. Everything was in a state of constant movement,
changing. Impossible to find your way about, to give a name to
things, to classify them. Impossible to judge.

Who would dare? Indeed, nobody dared. Silence. The baleful
fairies themselves stopped talking, while they stood there like that,
facing the others, leaning towards each other, looking into each
other's eyes. Everybody kept a respectful distance and looked, with
emotion, at the handsome, congenial young couple, joined together,
the very image of happiness.

They two alone, he and she—they alone were able to enter at will into
the intimacy of others, to penetrate without effort on the other side of
the thin wall that others tried to oppose to them, behind which others
sought to hide . . . It was so amusing, so thrilling, it sufficed to make a
slight effort, everything was so well circumscribed with other people,
each thing in its place, immediately recognizable, they pointed it out
to each other . . . 'Uncle Albert, don't you think he has a very
hypocritical side? And Auntie, really she's stinginess itself. Frank,
though, that she is, her heart on her sleeve.' In the evening, after their
friends were gone, taking one last drink, just between themselves—it
was fun, this diversion, after all the effort, all the edginess, it was
delightful, this little surplus excitement mingled with a sensation of
relaxation—they amused themselves trying to find a set formula for
each guest, pigeonholing . . . At times, the tiniest thing suffices to
guide you . . . A word, a gesture, a mannerism, a silence . . . 'Did you
see that? Did you hear that? What do you think of it?' It's very
curious, occasionally astonishing, these discoveries, these glimpses,
these demolitions, they proceeded hand in hand, she let herself be

guided by him . . . He was so witty when he took hold of people, held them in the palm of his hand, showed them to her, when he drew them with such accurate, vivid strokes, he knew how to get such a good likeness, he imitated them so well, she laughed till she cried . . .

No one escaped. Not even their parents. She had been afraid—it was this same fear, the same sensation, as now, of wrenching, of falling into space—when, huddled up to him, she had seen her mother, who, thus far, like herself, had been unsurroundable, boundless, abruptly projected in the distance, suddenly grow petrified in an unfamiliar form with very precise contours . . . she would have liked to close her eyes, she had drawn close to him . . . 'Oh, no, Alain, this time it's not that, this time, I'm not so sure . . .' But he had forced her to look, he had laughed: 'What a child you are . . . why, it's obvious, see here, think it over . . . It's so simple, I don't understand what you are so surprised about, for it's clear. Your mother is, above all else, bossy. She loves you, that goes without saying, I don't say she doesn't, she always has your welfare in mind. But you must walk the straight and narrow path that she has laid down for you. She has probably been frustrated herself, not had in her own life what she would have liked. She wants to make up for it through you. I, as her son-in-law, actually suit her very well. She would have her hands full with anybody else but me, somebody older, more independent . . . I put up no resistance; at least, so she thinks. Just a few snubs here and there, to frighten her, to amuse myself . . . But I'm what she needs, with me, she can imagine that she can do as she does with you, that is, that she can continue to teach me how to behave . . .' She had drawn back. Sacrilege . . . Yet no, they had the right: thou shalt leave thy father and thy mother. What strength that had given her; what relief she had felt at finally seeing things clearly, at being able to look calmly at what, for so long, she had felt moving in the darkness, confused, disturbing, what she had tried in vain to flee, what she had struggled against with the awkwardness, the angry weakness, of a child . . .

In front of her, all about her, he was clearing the ground, cleaning out the underbrush, laying out roads, she had only to let herself be led, to remain supple, flexible, as one does with a good dancer. It was curious, this sensation she often had, that, without him, before, the world had been a bit inert, grey, formless, indifferent, that she herself had been nothing but expectation, suspense . . .

As soon as he was there, everything fell back into place. Things assumed form, moulded by him, reflected in his glance . . . 'Come and look . . .' He took her by the hand, lifted her up from the bench on to which she had dropped to rest her swollen feet, looking, without seeing them, at the tedious rows of frozen-faced Madonnas, of large, nude women. 'Do look at that. Not bad, eh? What do you think of it? He certainly knew how to draw, the old rip. Take a look at that draughtsmanship, those masses, that balance . . . Not to mention the colour . . .' From out of uniformity, chaos, ugliness, something unique emerged, something strong, alive (the rest now, all about her, the people, the view out of the windows overlooking gardens, seemed dead) something vibrant, traversed by a mysterious current, organized everything round about, lifted, sustained the world . . .

It was delightful to delegate him to do the sorting, to remain confident, in abeyance, acquiescent, to wait for him to give her her beakful, to watch him looking for their feed in old churches, in the book-stalls along the Seine, in old engraving shops. It was good, it was cheering.

Little by little, a sense of relaxation, of recovered security, overspread her suffering, her fear. He is so eager, so alive, he throws himself into things with such enthusiasm . . . That is what permits him to make discoveries, to invent, it's that fervour, the intensity of his sensations, his unbridled desires. She feels quite well now. The tottering, unstable edifice has little by little found its poise . . . It's what she lacks, this enthusiasm, this freedom, this boldness, she's always afraid, she doesn't know . . . 'You think so? In our place? Somehow I don't see it . . .' He laughed, held her arm tightly . . . 'Over there, silly, no, not that one, that's a Voltaire arm-chair, no, there, upholstered in pale pink silk, that *bergère* . . .' She had suddenly felt excited, she had joined in right away, it had touched one of her sensitive spots, hers too, the building of their nest; she was a little frightened . . . 'It must cost a fortune . . . Not that in our flat, Alain! That *bergère*?' Like her mother, she would have been more inclined to put comfort, economy before everything else, but he had reassured her: 'Do look at it anyway, it's a beauty, a magnificent piece of furniture . . . You know, it would change everything in our place . . .' Only marriage permits such moments as these, of fusion, of happiness, during which, leaning on him, she had gazed at the old silk with its ash-rose, its delicate gray tones, the large, nobly spreading seat, the broad back, the free, firm curve of the elbow-rests . . . A caress, a consolation emanated from its calm, ample lines . . . at their fireside . . . just what was needed . . . 'There would be room, you're sure?—Of course, between the window and the fireplace . . .' Tutelary, diffusing serenity, security about it—this was beauty, harmony itself, captured, subjugated, familiar, become part and parcel of their life, a joy constantly within their reach.

A passion had seized upon them, avidity . . . The door of the shop was closed, it was the lunch hour . . . they had to know right away, no obstacle could stop them . . . in those moments, he is seized with a sort of frenzy, and she too had felt within herself, a kind of emptiness that must immediately be filled, a sort of hunger, almost suffering, that must be appeased at all costs . . . they had turned the door-handle, the shop door was closed but the handle had not been removed, this augured well, the dealer could not be far . . . they had pressed their noses against the pane, they had knocked, they had gone into the courtyard to see if there was not a back room, behind the shop, where he might be having lunch . . . but he was not there . . . they had questioned the concierge . . . doubtless he wouldn't be long . . . 'We'll have to wait a bit, it's worth it, it's perhaps a unique bargain, you know, come on, let's go and look at it again . . .'

That's where it comes from, this sensation of weakness in the legs, this fear which she feels again now—our bodies are never wrong: before consciousness, they record, enlarge, assemble and reveal with relentless brutality to the outside world, tiny, intangible, scattered impressions—that sensation of flabbiness in her entire body, the shiver running up her spine . . . Hadn't she already experienced them at the moment when they went back to look, while they waited, leaning against each other, soaking up what emanated from the sheen of the faded silk, from the soft lustre of the mellowed wood, from the free, powerful curve of the arm-rests . . . Already at that moment, she had suddenly felt a sort of weakness, a pang in her heart, anguish . . . something like what the characters in a play she had once seen must have experienced. The scene was the bar of an ocean liner. The passengers gathered there were drinking and chatting, at first everything seemed commonplace, harmless enough. And then, little by little, something disquieting, slightly sinister, began to make itself felt, it was hard to say from where it came, perhaps from the strange manner of the pallid bartender standing behind his counter . . . Suddenly the hand of one of the passengers began to tremble, the glass it was holding fell and rolled along the floor . . . He had just realized that this liner on which they were drinking and chatting was the boat that transported the dead, they thought they were alive and they were dead . . . somewhere out there living persons had looked at them, touched them, examined them, turned them over, carried them

. . . and they themselves didn't know they were dead . . . she too had suddenly understood at the moment when they were standing there waiting in front of the shop window . . . she had seen herself, she had seen themselves, the two of them, as others, her mother, the living, saw them . . . They were dead. They are both dead, embarked they don't know how, swept along, carried away without their knowing it towards God knows what country of the dead . . . a dream, all that, Louis XVth *bergères*, antique-shop windows, visions that cross the minds of persons in a swoon, of drowning, frozen persons . . . She must ask for help, call out, she must pull herself together, break away from all that, from these drowsy shops filled with things that are long since dead, she had drawn aside abruptly, she had felt like running away . . . 'Oh, listen Alain, it doesn't matter, why insist, let's drop it, let's go home, shall we, don't you think we'd better go home?'

Complete fusion exists with no one, those are tales we read in novels—we all know that the greatest intimacy is constantly being traversed by silent flashes of cold clearsightedness, of loneliness . . . what her mother had seen, she too had seen, during the brief second when she had come to herself again, when she had come to her senses, the two figures coincide, no mistake is possible . . . it suffices to step away from ourselves and see ourselves as others see us, and immediately it knocks your eyes out . . . her mother has just tried to resuscitate them both, come to your senses, I beg of you, pats on the cheek . . . Life is flowing by all round them while they are numb with sleep, clinging weakly in their dreams . . . to what? I ask you . . . what is all this morbid excitement, this sudden necessity? why?

Quick, she must go home, throw herself on her bed, examine it all closely . . . she almost runs . . . the little empty street is sad, dreary, like this whole neighbourhood, she hates it. The entrance to the house, the neat, overheated stairway, remind one of a nursing home, a mental hospital . . . and the little nest, well, it's even smaller than she had remembered it . . . that enormous *bergère* in here would look absurd, ludicrous, it was ridiculous to think it could change the meagre, cramped look, it would even bring out all the more the diminutive size of the room: a real little tenement. She runs to her room and drops face down on her bed . . . Lets herself sink, farther, still farther down . . . voluptuousness of going down . . . down to the very bottom . . . It's all a fraud . . . she sits up in bed: she and Alain are a fraud. Imitation, sham, pictures supposed to represent happiness, and there's something on the back . . . the old witches' laughter . . . And her father's shrug, the way he hissed the day they showed him that they didn't much like the glass-doored book case he had bought himself . . . 'Oh, that aestheticism of yours . . .' It was like the over-flow of an acrid vapour that had filtered between his clenched teeth . . . Frivolous, weak, spoilt child . . . His contempt for all serious ambition, his amateurishness . . . already disenchanted, bored, at twenty-seven . . . and she clinging to him, she being swept along towards death . . .

That contemptuous smile of his, that sneer when she had said to him as they passed in front of the *Collège de France* . . . 'Who knows? perhaps one day you will go in through that door to give your lectures . . .' He had drawn away from her, the better to see her, his lip had curled in that contemptuous expression he can have . . . 'What do little girls dream of? So that's what you have in mind . . . What a joyful prospect to see me one day, bald and rotund, go and mumble a lecture before a lot of idiotic society women, tramps . . . No, really, you disappoint me . . . that makes me think of that poem of Rimbaud's, you remember? She, replying to all his invitations to go voyaging: and my office?' And she had felt herself blushing . . . How mature he was already, how clear-sighted, pure, strong . . . he sat enthroned, solitary, disillusioned, bitter, on the heights . . . all the others, dashing about somewhere down below, running stupidly hither and thither, with a busy air, comically lifting enormous burdens . . . She had snuggled up against him, they were alone, the two of them, very high up, she was a bit dizzy, she was a bit afraid, the air was hard to breathe, raw, rarefied. An icy wind blew against the bare peaks. She would have preferred—but she hardly dared to admit it—she would have loved to go down in the valley with the others, in that tiny miniature world that she saw in the distance, where everything was made for her, to her measure . . . peaceful villages, calm evenings, dreams of the future . . . He would have energy, ambition: you'll see, I'll be somebody . . . They would talk about their children's education, choose names for them . . . Everybody longed for that happiness, it was normal, it was wholesome . . . that was what she had expected, what had always been promised her . . . But her mother knew, her mother had understood a long time ago. It's unbearable, she can't face it . . .

What's done cannot be undone. Her mother finally decided to open her eyes, to show her things the way they are. They had been mistaken, it was not that, that was not happiness. She's not happy. Every one has noticed it. People remark about it, she has changed, grown thin, her eyes, her hair have lost their lustre . . .

She hears the little click of a key in the lock . . .

The wrench, the frightful separation will soon be finished. Like the dead passengers on the boat, he knows nothing as yet. As in their movements, there is in each of his gestures, when he quietly hangs his overcoat on the hall rack, when he smooths his hair in front of the mirror and moves towards the bedroom . . . 'Is that you, Gisèle? You're back . . .' there is something in his voice, in his natural, carefree tone, which is off key, strange. The gestures, the sayings of lunatics give normal persons observing them this impression of being disconnected, emptied of their substance. She hides her head in the pillows. It's impossible, she can't remain so far from him, watch him from a distance and then try coldly, prudently, with skill, the way a psychiatrist would do it, to slip the words into him that, without his being aware of it, are going to mould him, transform him, cure him . . . No, she hasn't the courage . . .

She feels the caress of his hand on her hair, he has that anxious, tender, protective tone that he takes when she has one of her moments of depression, one of her crying spells . . . And she lets him do what he wants with her. She lets him fondle her, pet her like a child . . . 'Gisèle, darling, what's the matter? What's wrong, Gisèle, tell me . . .' She feels her eyes fill with tears right away, she lifts her head, puckers her lips like a little girl: 'I don't know, I feel blue. It's idiotic. About nothing at all . . .' That nice look he can have, a very attentive, intelligent look, which penetrates her, searches . . . Impossible . . . she can't . . . let him see for himself, she can hide nothing from him, there's nothing that doesn't concern them both . . . it's there inside her, sunk down deep, buried, it hurts her, he must help her remove it, he alone can do it . . . 'You know, it's a sudden feeling of anguish . . . it's idiotic, we've often said so . . .' She's a little afraid . . . she hesitates . . . 'It starts from almost nothing . . . The slightest pretext will do . . . It's about that *bergère* . . .' She has the impression that he draws back a little, is on his guard: 'The *bergère?*—Yes, you know, the one we want to buy . . .' Something inside him closes; a glaze, a hard varnish veils his eyes: 'Well, what about it?' It can't be helped, she must risk everything . . . He must be made to see. It can't be helped if she appears hideous, second-rate, narrow-minded, she wants him to see her as she is . . . conceal nothing, she couldn't stand it . . . It's there inside her, let him look, it must be extracted right away, that must not be allowed to grow inside her, to embitter everything, he should not force her to withdraw within herself, to turn away from him and scrutinize herself all alone, he must not allow her to suffer far from him . . . 'Listen, Alain, I'm going to tell you. I have the impression, at certain moments, but you're not going to be angry? You know I can't hide anything from you . . . I am talking to you as I should to myself . . . It seems to me that we care a little too much for all that, for those *bergères*, those handsome things . . . we attach too much importance to them . . . You would think it was a matter of life and death, whether to take that or something else . . . Sometimes it seems to me . . . how shall I say it to you? . . . that we are a bit on the edge of life, that we are wasting our strength . . .' If only he would wake up, if only he would come to his senses . . . His face is inscrutable, frozen, he'll have to be given a shaking . . . Other people are there, all round us, other healthy, calm, clear-sighted, normal people, they see us . . . They pass judgment on us . . . They are right . . . 'Alain, listen to me, my mother spoke to me about it . . . I felt that it really hurt her when I refused her leather chairs . . . Not for herself . . . I assure you . . . for us . . . She is anxious . . .' He laughs with a laughter that rings false . . . 'Ha, ha, and if we accepted the leather chairs, would that reassure her?—No, but what would reassure her would be for us to attach less importance to all that . . . The leather chairs are sturdier, more comfortable, less expensive, and that's that. And for her, it would give her such pleasure . . .' He should come, he should join them, they're all there about him, they are calling him, they are stretching out their arms to him, he should understand, he should finally see things as they are, he should see himself as he is: weak, childish, a rebellious child; she will take him in her arms, she will press him close to her . . . He can let himself go, there, in her arms, she'll protect him, she'll help him to grow up, to change . . . he can change, if he wants to . . . 'Alain, I assure you, at our age we should have other fish to fry . . .' he laughs derisively, gives her a quick glance which skims lightly over everything with disdain, with loathing, a glance that judges things coldly, that classifies them rapidly: 'What fish?' No matter, it's too late to turn back, the only thing left to do is to seize him round the waist, bind him hand and foot, throw cold water on his head, to get the best of him: 'What fish? Well, work, imagine that. Some real work. Not just little amateur jobs that you do to earn a little money, but your thesis, for instance, you don't seem to care a rap about it . . . Something that really leads somewhere . . . there's our future, just the same, you should think about that, our children's future . . .' He draws back a little to examine her more closely and bursts into hate-filled laughter: 'Ha! that's a good one, a fine one . . . That's what *bergères* lead to . . . they lead a far way . . . That's what comes of so-called good upbringing. You never depart for long from the right principles. The slightest call to order suffices to make you walk straight again. But if you think you can get me that easily . . . A man is supposed to maim himself to fit into your picture, which is the dream of every little stenographer, the nursemaid's ideal . . . a good, reliable husband, a family, a career . . . And all of that represented by sturdy leather armchairs. What a magnificent symbol! From Maple's. Long-lasting. Economical. In the evening, to satisfy you both, you and your mother, I'll put on my embroidered house-slippers and sit in the chair opposite you to rest from my labours. We'll talk of my future, of my promotion. But how scared you look, you are indignant, aren't you, at what I just said . . . It wasn't exactly that . . . Whom did I take you for? . . . No . . . I forgot . . . Leather chairs, that's something else: it's the lighthearted-ness, the negligence of the artist, of the scholar, which should make me accept them . . . I should not even notice them, absorbed as I am by my research, by my work . . . An over-rich inner universe keeps me from being interested in these trivial details . . . It's all right for my mother-in-law, for my wife, to think about such things, it's their task to build me a comfortable little nest in which I can blossom forth . . . That's their role . . . Oh, you know, my husband . . . he simpers . . . he's a demon for work, a real seeker, the only thing that matters is his work . . . But the *bergère*, horrors . . . what a frightful revelation. Your mother was ashamed, the other day, in front of her friends, of those dubious tendencies of mine . . . Imagine, I seemed to understand only too well . . . what am I saying? I seemed to approve of my old lunatic of an aunt . . . Your mother was ashamed of me before her guests, she disavowed me . . . Fie upon me! Think of it . . . But my word, young man, if you don't speak as though you were a connoisseur . . . You come by it honestly . . . I answered her pretty sharply . . . It took her breath away . . . I know them, I know all of you only too well, do you understand, it's too easy, it's not even funny any longer. But she'll regret not having urged me to take it, that *bergère* . . . She'll be the one who will have to insist to get me to accept it, you'll see . . . It's the only means she has to keep her hold on us, these little treats, these little presents . . . In that way, she can own us . . . She would fall ill if the umbilical cord were cut . . . But I've had enough. I've had enough for a long time, if you want to know . . . I didn't want any of that, you know that quite well. I don't give a hang about the apartment, the furniture and all the rest . . . I can live on a park bench, I prefer to live just anywhere to putting up with all your preaching, your teaching, your martyred looks . . . Oh, I beg of you, you make me laugh with your tearful airs . . . There's only one victim here, and that's myself. My life is ruined . . . All I want . . . a little calm, freedom . . . And I have to listen to all these stupid things . . . these insinuations . . . 'Your tastes . . . You came by them honestly . . . Your career, my darling, you make maman anxious . . .' I've had enough. She'll see . . . I've had enough . . . he's hammering each word: Enough, you understand . . . I'm fed up with all that . . . Well, I'm leaving . . . I'm going out . . . I don't know when I'll be back. Good-night, don't wait up for me.'

They're upon him. They've encircled him. No way out. He's caught, locked in; at the slightest movement, at the faintest stray impulse on his part they spring up. Always on the watch, spying. They know where to find him now. He himself has submitted to their law, given himself up to them . . . so weak, confident . . . he's theirs, always within their reach . . . And she, supple, malleable—a tool fashioned by them, which they use to bring him to heel. Stupid faces, eyes shining with curiosity. Moist glances . . . It's such a touching sight . . . these turtledoves . . . so young . . . their little nest . . . Brief incursions, furtive leaps, prudent withdrawals, shy touchings, little surprises, presents . . . the old lady wiggling the mobile end of her nose, her skittish eyes under their worn lids . . . coy smile . . . holding out a lump of sugar . . . And right away he too, wretched dog, trained by them, wriggling, begging on his hind legs, eyes shining covetously, stretching out an avid neck . . . 'Really, auntie, you would do that for us? . . . You mean it, you're not joking?' They grow bolder every day. They're going beyond all limits, they're not afraid of anything any more. No shame in them, no reserve. They stick their noses into everything, attack openly. No more precautions, even before other people. No need to mind him, is there? With him, you can do as you like. Guileless fool, so sensitive . . . Pearls before swine . . . But they'll see. Of what stuff . . . he is skipping . . . Who laughs last . . . he almost runs, knocking into the passers-by.

Indignation and rage have aroused him, all his strength comes surging, he must take advantage of it, maintain his momentum, it will be right away or never . . . But he must not lose his head, above all, not act too hastily, he would have to start everything over again, prolong this apprehension, this suspense . . . Go easy . . . with the forefinger thrust well in the little metal circle, push the dial frame entirely to the right, let it come back to its starting point . . . one letter, then the next . . . now the figures . . . It's the first move he has made towards deliverance; it's a challenge which he's hurling at them, at all of them out there, from this narrow booth in the basement of the little bistro, by dialling this number: a simple telephone number like any other in appearance, and this commonplace appearance has something thrilling about it, it heightens its magic character: it is the talisman that he carries with him always—his safeguard when he feels that he is threatened. It's the password divulged to the privileged few: permission to make use of it is conferred as the highest of distinctions. And he has been given it, he has been deemed worthy, he, quite so . . . But don't rejoice, don't boast too soon, all can yet be lost, in an instant he can be ignominiously hurled back to them, humiliated, vanquished, immediately taken possession of by them—this time, their prey for ever . . . He feels like a hunted man on foreign soil, who is ringing the bell of the embassy of a civilized country, his own, to ask for asylum . . . The bell echoes in empty space. Each regular, prolonged buzz holds his life in suspense . . . A click . . . Someone has taken down the receiver . . .

It's astonishing to hear his own voice, as though detached from him, who is nothing now but disorder, confusion, palpitating shreds, answer of its own accord, very calmly: 'Is Mme. Germaine Lemaire in? This is Alain Guimiez speaking . . .' That name, Germaine Lemaire, which he has just spoken so calmly, constitutes a scandal. It's an explosion. That name alone would make them retreat. It would make those very perspicacious glances they're continually turning on him, those knowing smiles, disappear from their faces, the mobile end of his aunt's nose would stop wiggling, it would become set, tense, puzzled . . . But a few words can still make them rush upon him, hem him in . . . Those dreaded words, he might as well prepare himself, make a hollow to receive them, to deaden the shock . . . there they are, he feels them forming somewhere out there, he braces himself . . . Mme. Germaine Lemaire is out . . . when a deep, drawling voice, the voice he knows, replies: 'Why of course. It's me. No, I shall be in for some time yet. You won't disturb me, do come. I'll expect you.' The universe, calmed, subdued, charmed, stretches itself voluptuously and lies down at his feet. And he, standing there, very erect, he strong, master of all his movements, deploying all his faculties, clear-sightedness, cunning, dignity, replies with perfect ease, in a voice that is so warm, so pleasant, so engaging, that he himself is charmed by it: 'Very well, that's splendid. I'll come, then . . . In about half an hour, if I may . . .'

Thank God, he held his own, he didn't spoil things . . . What progress . . . In the old days, he would have lost his head, through some stupid weakness sacrificed these moments—one half-hour of happiness. Twenty-five minutes, to be exact. Seated on the banquette in the back of the little café, he can now relish this moment, when nothing has yet started, when nothing can yet be jeopardized, spoiled, when he still holds hugged to him, his unimparied treasure, absolutely intact.

Time stands almost still. The instants, closed in on themselves, smooth, heavy, full to the cracking point, advance very slowly, almost imperceptibly, move with precaution, as though to preserve their charge of dream, of hope.

In a little while, all will be haste, excitement, blinding light, scalding heat, the instants, like a fine gray dust blown by a burning hot wind, will bear him along towards the harsh separation, towards the dreadful wrench, towards that lonely fall into darkness, into the void. The threat will be there at the first glance, the first words, they exchange, it will continue to grow until finally, to cut short his torture, and take his own fate in hand, like a man condemned to die who commits suicide, he will rise all of a sudden before it is time, take leave too abruptly . . . or else, out of cowardice, feeling her embarrassed, impatient eyes upon him, he will do his utmost to put off the reckoning, the fatal moment.

But now he is free, he is the master. He can dispose of his time. He must prepare himself. It's the period of meditation, of purification, that precedes corridas, coronations. No alcohol. Beware of stimulants. One should not force one's luck, cheat, coerce an already propitious fate, that only brings bad luck . . . He must remain in full possession of his faculties . . . Weak tea, at the most . . . or rather, no, just a cup of coffee . . .

As he sits there motionless, he feels it forming inside him: something compact, hard . . . a kernel . . . But he has become all over like a stone, a silex: things from the outside that knock against him strike brief sparks, little light words which crackle for an instant . . . 'How that stove of yours does heat, tell me . . . What make is it? A Godin? They heat like a house afire, those things do . . .' The waiter nods approval, looks interestedly at the stove. No hard kernel in him, that's obvious. Inside him everything is soft, everything is hollow, anything at all, just any insignificant object from the outside fills it entirely. They're at the mercy of everything. He had been like that himself a few moments ago, how had he lived? how on earth do all these people live with that enormous emptiness in them in which, at any moment, just anything at all surges in, spreads out, takes up all the room . . . The waiter stoops down and turns the knob that regulates the draught, stands up again, looks at the stove affectionately: 'Oh, you can say what you want, Godins, there's nothing like 'em, they're as good as a furnace. They never go out. You fill them full at night, in the morning all you have to do is to empty the ashes . . . They'll never make anything better than those things. And to-day the weather is mild, but if you had come when it was really cold . . . it's so warm in here I can never stand a sweater . . . —Oh, you're lucky, I'm always frozen, I could wear two sweaters in mid-summer.—Well, that depends on what work you do. But in our job, we are on the move, running back and forth all day long . . . Oh, I can guarantee you, there's no risk of our getting stiff. It's good for your circulation . . .' Rubbing, merry crackle: 'Oh, with me, it's the same thing whether I move about or not. I've always been like that. Already, when I was a tiny child—no blood in my veins. My grandmother used to tell me even then: Why, you're more sensitive to cold than I am . . . What I need, to feel really well, is the good old dog-days, the Sahara itself . . .'

But time, all at once . . . what time is it, anyway? Time—that couldn't fail, that had to happen to him while he was there amusing himself, watching the crackling sprays of words surge up and fall—time forgotten, released, has taken a leap . . . Only four more minutes, damn it . . . and he's not ready, he would have needed a few seconds more of reflection to prepare himself, he would have needed to pass first through a zone of silence . . . something has been put out of gear in the mechanism he had adjusted so well, he has jeopardized everything through sinful insouciance, unpardonable absent-minded-ness, he's being driven, jostled, he's going to take off badly . . .

Above all, he must not lose his head, better to be a few minutes late than to arrive all over-heated, out of breath . . .

He steps as unhurriedly as he can through the old door-way, walks slowly across the vestibule, opens the door giving on to the courtyard . . .

Tall liveried footmen standing frozen on the steps of the grand stairway, a gold-braided major-domo preceding you slowly over vast expanses of slippery floors, all the display and outer signs of power and glory, all the ceremonial, flaunted hierarchy, etiquette, the conventional, required gestures, had something to recommend them. All that maintained you, guided you, it was less upsetting than this slipshod concierge sweeping out her courtyard, who looks at you furtively, who sees everything, who knows, and answers quite casually: Mme. Germaine Lemaire? Across the courtyard, to the right, first floor; it was less disturbing than the cleaning woman with the tucked up apron who opens the door for you, lets you in with an absent-minded, hurried air, then deserts you, left to your own devices, in the midst of sly threats, of invisible, unforeseeable dangers.

She has real beauty, 'Germaine Lemaire has real beauty,' they're

right, obviously. There . . . in the line of the cheek, the eyelid, the
forehead . . . something which recalls what he had discovered in the
faces of certain pre-Columbian . . . Aztec . . . statues, what he had
taken away from them . . . it's hard to discern, sometimes long
initiation and great effort are required to catch it; a certain austere
strength, a crude grace . . . And that rather weak, rather displeasing
curve . . . meagre . . . vulgar . . . of the nostrils, of the chin, it's
nothing, one need only make a little effort, and the grace, the strength
that he had caught in the faces of the Aztec statues, or were they
Etruscan? he no longer knows, and which inflect the line of the
forehead, of the cheek, must also be made to pass, to flow—the way a
part of the water in a river is turned aside to irrigate arid land—there,
into the chin, the nose . . . they overrun everything . . . and the entire
face . . . how could one mistake it? who would dare deny it?—radiates
a secret, exceptional beauty.

From the effort he has just made to perform this sleight-of-hand
with such ease, such speed, from the certainty he now has of finally
being worthy to belong to the little cohort of the initiated, something
has begun to ooze, it is that same note of annoyance he had heard in
their voices when, in reply to the good people who, like himself at one
time—he's ashamed of it now—expressed naïve surprise, didn't
understand . . . 'Not at all, Germaine Lemaire is a real beauty, how
can you say that?' It's even, in his case, a bitterer, sharper feeling, it's
exasperation, hatred almost, he can't bear, he is ready to exterminate,
the ignorant, the faithless—those repugnant creatures who prefer to
let their idle gaze wallow basely among the insipid curves, the facile
and misleading sweetness of the noses, chins and cheeks of cover-
girls, of stars

But something remains, nevertheless, of his very first impression—
this uneasiness, this painful sensation, he retracts a little, exactly the
way he did the first time he saw her . . . In the corners of the lip which
cuts a little too deeply into the cheeks, which curls up a little too high,
in the movement of that thin mouth, something is creeping, fleeing
. . . he doesn't know what it is exactly, he has never tried to name it,
he doesn't want to, one must not, it's nothing, no one but he sees it,
it's a mirage, an illusion, bred of his uneasiness, it's his own fear
which he projects, his own apprehension which he sees cowering there, hiding . . . he must not let his glance pause, settle there
. . . it should barely graze . . . not see, not think about it any more,
it will disappear . . . There now . . . There is nothing more. It has
vanished.

But how could he not have foreseen it—in fact, he had expected it—it's the lesson his stupid vanity has cost him, it's the lie given once more to his romancing: she's not alone, of course, that would be asking too much, some one is seated beside her, at her feet, that tall, gawky lad with the long, anaemic face, who is encircling his crossed ankles with his hands while he swings delightedly back and forth like a big monkey . . . His deeply set, bright little eyes are watching him as he advances awkwardly . . . And she too is watching him. Her big, limpid eyes are staring at him. A current emanating from her repulses, crushes his thoughts, his words . . . He looks about him . . . help will come perhaps from the outside, from just anywhere, from that big fire blazing in the fireplace in this mild weather, from that lap robe she has on her knees, he clings to that, something is springing up from it, the words are already forming . . . but watch out, they are driven back, dangerous corner, the crime of *lèse majesté*, he's lost if he dares ask her a question as he would just anybody, put himself on the same level . . . she's going to draw herself up with that manner that he has seen her assume, the manner of an outraged empress . . . But again this time, while he is pulling them back to hold them in, the words break away, lurch a bit, then grow steady: 'I hope . . . you are not ill?'

The tall fellow leans still farther backwards and laughs derisively, showing his big teeth, he's in seventh heaven . . . 'Ill? The very idea! The lady has iron-clad health, you didn't know that? Reinforced concrete, I shan't say more. But she loves her comfort, as is well known, and there's nothing she likes so much as to coddle herself . . .' She leans towards him: 'Hold your tongue,' and, with the back of her hand, gives him a little slap on the cheek, while he lifts his elbow in fun, ducks his head . . . The queen's jester, the buffoon jingling his little bells, turning somersaults on the steps of the throne, serving a learnedly dosed mixture of impertinence and provocation, has dared to say, to do, what should have been done . . . She laughs . . . They had both seen, that's certain, his paralysed, over-respectful manner, his fright. The buffoon had sought to bring them into greater relief, in order for her to enjoy them all the more; he had made an insolent display before the poor greenhorn, fresh from the back-woods, ignorant of court customs—of his own complete ease, his off-handedness, his privileges acquired long since, the liberties he may take. He spreads himself. His hands drop his ankles, he deploys his long, lanky body, stands up on his two feet . . . 'Well, with that, I shall be off . . . it's high time . . .' He leans towards her, seated erectly, royally, on her high-backed chair . . . something flits from him to her, something barely perceptible . . . an invisible movement, more rapid, clearer, than words, and which she immediately records: There now, I'll be leaving you to do what you can with this clod, but try to have a

little fun, just the same . . . you'll tell us all about it later . . . we'll
have a good laugh . . . Ah, what's to be done about it, *noblesse oblige*
that's the price of fame, all these avid little fellows who try to come
and rub elbows, who want to glean what they can . . . The favourite,
the fortunate sycophant bends, smiling, over the hand she holds out
to him, straightens up again . . . 'Very well, then, I'll call you tomorrow about that paper' . . . turns round . . .

Not a trace of the buffoon remains in the slightly gawky young man
with the sensitive face and serious, direct expression, who walks
towards him to say good-bye, his hand outstretched . . . no more
jesting, you're allowed to laugh a little, but here we know what
courtesy means, respect for others, the most complete equality,
fraternity, reign, as is well known, in this house. Consideration is
shown to all the foreigners who come here from distant lands, to all
poor pilgrims: 'I'm delighted to have met you. Good-bye, I hope we'll
meet again soon . . . —Oh, yes, I too, certainly, I should be delighted
. . .' He too, shakes hard this firm, helpful, friendly hand, which
clasps his fingers, he holds on to it a second . . . But resolutely,
pitilessly, the hand breaks away.

A moment ago, that malicious joy of the buffoon squatting on the
floor, swinging, showing his big teeth, those secret signs between
them, that current which had passed between them above his head,
had been, nevertheless, security, it had been happiness, compared to
this forlornness—alone here with her. In what moment of madness,
of insane audacity had he let himself be roused by the impulse that
had made him climb to these heights . . . he feels dizzy now, perched
up there on the highest peak . . . one false move and he'll fall, he'll
crash to earth . . . She's watching him, clinging there, not daring to
budge, quite petrified, she must feel like smiling . . . how comical he
is, really . . . she's not accustomed . . . usually the people about her
have stouter hearts, their lungs are more used to breathing this tangy
air. He's so weak, so awkward, he must make her feel sorry for him
. . . how ridiculous he is, how tiresome . . . But there's nothing to be
done about it, she rouses herself, pulls herself together. She must
bear up, set to work. These are weighty obligations. She smiles at him,
makes him a sign with her hand: 'Now then, why don't you come and
sit here, near me . . .' don't be frightened, it's nothing . . . you'll see,
you won't fall . . . 'There now, you'll be more comfortable near the
fire, in this easy-chair . . . It's been an age since I saw you. . .' do stop
looking under your feet, think about something else . . . 'What have
you been doing that's interesting? Tell me . . .' now then, things are
better already, aren't they? feeling calm again? make one more try . . .

'What have you been up to? Has your work been going well?—Well, no, I haven't done very much lately . . .' At the sound of his own voice—the way it used to be when the examining professor had just asked a question and, his head empty and not knowing what to say, he heard himself reply—at the sound of his own voice, like sleeping soldiers who, at the sound of the bugle, jump up, shoulder arms, run, fall in, all the scattered strength in him that had become sluggish, surges up . . . all of a sudden, he feels sure of himself, full of confidence, assurance, free of movement, relaxed . . . 'I must confess to you that I've been very lazy . . .' No cheating with her. No mock triumphs. No constantly threatened victories . . . 'I let myself be led astray by all kinds of idiotic things. I've been stupidly wasting my time . . .' He has nothing to fear, he can allow himself that: she will know how to find what's hidden under the matrix . . . She had been the first to discover him . . . The proof is there, always worn next to his heart: the letter he received from her the first time . . . he hadn't believed his eyes . . . to him . . . it wasn't possible . . . at the bottom of the page, he had not been mistaken, in big letters, it was certainly that: Germaine Lemaire . . . Miracle . . . He knows every word of it by heart . . . Bits of phrases rise up to the surface at any moment, while he's walking along, lost in the crowd, while he listens to people's chatter when, seated in the bus, their empty gaze upon him, he hands his ticket to the conductor. They murmur inside him. He hears their call . . . for him alone . . . they are the secret sign of his preferment, of his predestination . . . 'Well, yes, I've let myself be swallowed up. Upset by just anything. The entire family . . . Fixing up our apartment . . . But I don't know how to defend myself against that . . .' Verlaine and his 'wretched fairy Carrot'. Rimbaud. Baudelaire and his mother, and General Aupick . . . Lazy, childish, wasting their time, ruining their lives . . . the words he has just spoken make them rise up in her right away, she gazes at them . . . they are the models he wants her to draw upon. And she obeys him. He looks, enchanted, at the picture resembling them which he sees in her, his portrait which, he knows, he is sure of it, she is engaged in sketching . . . He leans towards her and looks deep into her grey-green eyes . . . 'What joy, if you knew, what pleasure it is for me to be here with you, in your house.' Now he can do anything he wants. He can strip naked. No more ridiculous fears, no more shame, no thought of his dignity. He can tell her what he wants. They understand each other over and beyond mere words . . . 'It's a long time now since I've told myself stories, you know, those "continued stories" such as adolescents and persons suffering from depression tell themselves, but I did like to imagine myself coming to see you, seated like this near you, talking, very brilliantly, of course . . . they both laugh . . . holding you spellbound. But I didn't very well see what your place was like . . . At that point, I always hesitated. At times . . .' all at once he has the impression—it's very fleeting—that inside her a long, avid arm with grasping fingers is reaching out, he doesn't know very well, he hasn't time to know, how he detected this movement in her . . . and right away, within himself, with the return of a sense of danger, that rapidity of adaptation—he himself is surprised by it . . .

In one second he has given up the idea, all dreams of intimacy are forgotten. Squatting at her feet, he shows her, he spreads out before her, his gifts, his offerings, all he possesses . . . of no great importance, but he's ready to give her everything, she should choose what she wants . . . but what does she want? 'At times—it was the sparseness in your writing, that dry warmth . . . which trembles . . . which made me think of that—I saw you in a big Southern farmhouse with white-washed walls, a large, bare room . . .' It seems to him that the long arm drops, there is something a bit misty in the big eyes . . . right away, he's going to show her, she should be patient, this is going to be better: 'But I was foolish, it's reality, of course, that's in the right. As usual, reality upsets all preconceived ideas, all expectations. Now I see that it's all this—he looks about him—which gives greatest evidence of that molten lava . . . an incandescent stream . . . At times, in certain of your books, there is a flamboyantly baroque note, when you are stirred with enthusiasm, when the thirst for conquest carries you along. There is here, in this clutter of curious, very fine things . . . this sorcerer's mask . . . these fabrics . . . all your Spanish, conquistador side . . . They make one think of the fabulous spoils amassed by a pirate . . . set there at random, neglected . . . I adore that casualness . . . Beside it, all my fiddle-faddling seems so ridiculous, so petty . . .'

She is wearing a pleased little smile . . . 'Oh, you're exaggerating . . . It's simply that things collect little by little . . . souvenirs, a few presents . . . True, I do like to pick up things wherever I can. . . That wicker cage there, for instance, I brought it back from the Canary Islands. This leather bottle was given me by an old peasant in Tibet . . . it's nice, isn't it? We accumulate a lot of things in a lifetime when we continue to live in the same place. And at heart, you know, I'm very much of a stay-at-home. But I'm sure your place too must be charming. I should love to see what it is like. You'll have to invite me one day to come and see you . . .'

It's moving to see her descend the steps of the throne with such simplicity, such modesty, mingle with the crowd, take an interest in each one, ask each one a question or two; bend over graciously to cross the threshold of the most sordid little hovel, the humblest cottage; sit down among the family, gathered round; allow the children's sticky fingers—oh, no, it's nothing, don't scold him—to rumple her silk gown; give a calm glance at the walls covered with vulgar flower patterns, at the colour-prints, at the artificial flowers emerging from Japanese vases won at a street fair . . . at the pottery brought back from Plougastel . . . at the unspeakable leather chairs . . . 'Oh, no, my place is very ugly. You'd be terribly disappointed . . . there are all sorts of presents, each one more frightful than the other . . . But there's no way of getting rid of them. We'd need a fire, an earthquake. And even then . . . the family would see to it that they were all replaced. Because they must have all that, my family must: platters from Plougastel, awful easy-chairs . . . that's the flag they plant on newly conquered territory. Their banner which marks the extent of their empire. As for me, I escaped them, but I have been brought into subjection. And this time, for good and all. I'm occupied, they're building roads, setting up boundary marks, measuring, administering and vaccinating for the welfare of the population . . . But I'm boring you . . .' Useless precaution. Pure coquetry. He has a foot hold, he feels it, he's on his own ground, he's no longer afraid. He rises and starts walking up and down, and she watches him . . . At last . . . he knows that that is what she expected of him, that's the cream of the milk, for her alone, the hidden treasure that she alone has been able to discover, to bring out to advantage, and which, one day, she will reveal to the world . . . Never has he felt freer, more skilful . . . his gestures are sure, elegant: now, look at this. 'Here, as you see, are two leather chairs, quite ordinary in appearance, the English "club" type that exists in certain movie-houses. Well, bloody battles are being fought over them. I'm fighting not to have them in my house as though I were defending my very life. And I'm right. I am, indeed. Because these chairs, we all know what they are. But never a word on the subject. Absolute secrecy. There exists a tacit agreement, we don't speak of them . . . We use all the weapons in our possession, but never an allusion to what they really are: the badge of the order they want to force upon me, of their power, of my submission . . .'

This time, he has found his audience. An audience worthy of him. From his hat come cascading billows of ribbons, objects of every sort, they flow, get out of hand, form enormous piles all round him . . . world is confronting world . . . the angel is combating the beast . . . he brandishes his blade at their common enemy, hers and his . . . now he can amuse himself, take all kinds of liberties . . . he seizes hold of something in the air . . . 'Look . . . take, for instance, my aunt, an old crank . . . she would amuse you no end if you knew her . . . she's a character for you . . . I'll introduce her to you one day . . . You should have seen her when she came to see us. Sweetness itself.

Deeply moved. But her eyes were taking it all in . . .' He imitates her walk: 'The end of her nose moves the way a dog's does, she keeps wiggling it: Why, children, it's as cute as anything, your place is. That towel rack, it's marvellous . . . A quick look at the view out of the windows. Just here there's a smell of heresy. Here, rebellion smoulders. I tease her, I provoke her: Come and look, auntie, isn't it lovely, that view, and those old roofs, in the distance, over there . . . Right away she gets her back up: I think that's what you paid for especially, that view . . . Because the rest, it's very cute, but when all's said and done . . . in a few years, ho, ho, let's hope so, anyway, you're going to be cramped for space. With that she gets a hold over us, my wife and myself. We're caught. We're disarmed. Bound hand and foot in no time. And then she begins to amuse herself a bit, it's too tempting: But you know, children, what you should have? My apartment, why, of course . . . It's exactly what you need . . . We don't dare believe our ears, we tremble, we crane our necks, we stare at her with eyes filled with the most despicable cupidity, we ask her: But auntie, how is that possible? Do you mean it?'

She settles upon him a gaze in which he sees a gleam of recognition, of approval. He comes to a halt in front of her. She can look closely now. He feels this is the moment. Luck is with him. All his gestures are sure, bold, free, he is free, he does what he wants, he is skipping along, brandishing his sword, he's going to dismay the dislocated ranks of the enemy, he charges, nothing can stop him . . . 'But that's finished, you understand. I've had enough. I'm going to break with all that for good. Escape. And you will be the one to have helped me. That's what I came to ask you today. Now I know it, I can't come to terms with all that . . . It's all or nothing . . . Why tell ourselves lies? I'll have to resort to surgery, there's no other way . . . And that means . . .' The telephone rings. She rises, without ceasing to look at him: 'No other way, really? You think so? . . .' She said that a bit mechanically. He has the impression that she has caught hold of just anything, the words he has just spoken, and which were still inside her, and that she is repeating them without knowing very well what she is saying, in order not to interrupt too abruptly his roulades, his serenading . . . She shakes her head, sighs; she is walking slowly, as though the tie by which he is holding her impeded her movements; finally, still gazing at him, nodding impatiently . . . Oh, what a bore, I'm so sorry, how tiresome they are, all those people . . . she slowly stretches out her arm, takes down the receiver: 'Hello . . . Hello . . . Yes . . . When? I'm surprised at that. Why yes, I was in, I haven't moved out of the house. She laughs. Oh, nothing in particular. Same old sixes and sevens. What? her voice grows lower, softer, assumes an intimate, warm tone . . . In a little while? Yes . . . When? In an hour?

Very well. Fine. No, nothing as yet. Oh, we'll talk about that another time. I'll tell you all about it. Don't be late.'

She comes back towards him. But he knows that the play is over. A little belated applause. People are already thinking about getting their coats from the check-room, they must hurry, they will miss the last *métro* . . . 'Yes, well, all that is very thrilling, what you were telling me . . .' It seems to him that she is collecting all her strength to make a final effort . . . 'But personally, I believe, on the contrary that, if I were in your place, I should accept. Only too delighted. I mean it. They ought to be of some use at least, all those people. So take what you want. It's darned pleasant not to live in cramped quarters. And it will take more than that to make a slave of you. We're swallowed up only when we are willing for it to happen. You have to be more cynical than that, since you say you like . . . she looks about her, smiles . . . pirates and conquistadors . . . —Yes . . . after all . . .' he has difficulty in recognizing his own voice. As always, in moments of break-down, of collapse, someone speaks the words for him, saves his face . . . 'After all, you're probably right. But here I am talking away . . . When I'm with you I can't stop, I'm making you waste your time . . . —Oh, I like to listen to your stories . . . you must come again, often . . .' He feels that it would be dangerous to linger, to beg for a few moments more, there's something threatening in her slightly remote, society politeness . . . it's obvious, she's straining at the bit . . . 'Yes, I should love to, if you'll allow me . . .'

When she accompanies him to the door, shakes his hand, he senses in her the warmth, the generosity, the overflow of strength—she's ready to squander it—that come from the feeling that deliverance, freedom, are at hand . . . 'Well, I'll see you very soon, you won't disturb me. So call me one day about this time. I am nearly always in. She sticks her head through the door and smiles at him archly . . . And above all, get to work, do you hear? I'm counting on you, you know. Work hard.'

Astonishing how everything had taken place according to the plan he had drawn up somewhere within himself; how everything from the first moment had converged towards this, towards this disaster, this collapse . . . he is rejected, reduced in rank . . . Ah, it was magnificent, that superiority . . . but how do all these people live? . . . to think that less than two hours ago he was asking himself that . . . How can they live without that hard kernel inside them, that little compact mass, preserved secretly, that certainty, that security . . . The waiter in the café, poor man, so pervious, so soft . . . the stove is not merely an object for his eyes, for his hands, which he must attend to while waiting for the big moments that count, no, things occupy him entirely . . . And he himself, how does he live? that's what they might ask themselves, if they knew, but they're too innocent . . . the bus conductor rushing through the aisle, ringing the bell, calling out the names of the bus-stops, is pure, hard, nothing can scratch him; not a crack between his gesture and himself through which the slightest impurity might enter. Not the slightest trace of an experience of this kind. Never. In none of these lives. You have to be him, possess his exceptional skill, his cleverness, to treat yourself to such pleasures as these. The buffoon must have been amused, so self-assured there, quite at home, well settled in complete security, to see him, like someone descending the moving steps of a Luna Park stairway, reeling, holding on tight, one foot in the air, a haggard look in his eyes . . . Good lesson he gave him . . . the important thing, you see, is not to be afraid. Watch what I do . . . And that hearty hand-shake to mark the nobility of all of them there, their sense of equality, even with regard to him . . . or rather, it meant—an enormous sudden flush submerges him—that hearty hand-shake, that look deep down into his eyes . . . Come, come, pull yourself together, be a man, hang it! Are you so impressed as all that by celebrity, by fame . . .

(Translated by Maria Jolas)

Between Life and Death (1968)

Impossible to make a movement to leave, to show any aversion. Even those who are the closest, those about whom he says that they are on his side, that they belong here, would look upon him severely . . . What's the matter? What is it that disturbs you? I like the way common people speak. I like his rather waggish familiarity . . . his good-natured bohemianism . . . Don't tell me that you still judge people by their accent, the way the English do . . . Even in England, today, these practices . . . But here, among us, people don't have these aversions . . . they wouldn't think of setting up hierarchies, pronouncing exclusions from such signs . . . You are the one who deserves to be banished, excluded . . .

Humbly he tries to correct his faults. They're right, there must be something dubious, something shameful in this aversion. We must crush this in ourselves, we must destroy it, mortify ourselves . . . May the lazy, drawling vowels freely flourish . . . My vaalise . . . We must pass through them without stopping, leap over them without breathing, hold our noses, and look at what is there, behind them . . . and here it is . . . we see the fine-grained leather, shiny with use, silky, the golden gleam of its brass fittings, its thick rounded handle, smooth to the touch . . . Vacaaation . . . and there between the rocks are the emerald coves, the transparent water in which is trembling rippled virgin sand . . . the motionless peaks of pine trees, red suns, green rays . . . 'Yes, vacation time soon . . . The only place I like is the South, the warm sea . . . And you? Where are you going this year?'

But you can't get off so lightly. Pitilessly the lazy, unctuous vowels stretch themselves, spread themselves, wallow over him . . . This vacaaation . . . the short final consonant gives a brief respite, and then it'll start up again . . . the suhhn . . . the seeea . . . the stale-smelling liquid that they disgorge, sprinkles him . . .

Not budge. Not make even a furtive gesture to wipe it off. But afterward, when the torture is over, he can no longer contain himself, he must be assured at whatever cost that he is not alone, that others like himself suffered torture, he must force them with precaution to confess, to join him . . . 'Did you notice his accent? . . . No, don't think that, I have nothing, I assure you, against a slightly waggish accent . . . At times it is charming, good natured, sparkling . . . it has

a sort of corrosive freshness . . . I have a friend, a real Parisian type
. . . But here you sense quite well that there's something special . . .
something ponderous, overstressed . . . like some furtive violence, an
aggression . . . It's as though someone brushed you with . . .'

And they, the way we use salt to take out an ugly wine-spot which
some awkward person has made on the white tablecloth, immediately
they hasten to sprinkle on that the words that will absorb it . . . 'He
comes from humble surroundings. All the more to his credit.' Quickly
they scatter over this patch of sticky tar a few shovelfuls of sand . . .
'Full of complexes. Proud. Somewhat aggressive.' The grains of sand
are falling . . . 'That's frequent. A commonplace. Well known.
Overdoes it to assert himself. Nothing to be shocked at.' There. It's
covered. We can walk over it, straight ahead, go elsewhere, there's
nothing to fear. The disorder has been repaired.

What you must do is not resist, not grow tense, let yourself be invaded
docilely, dilate your nostrils fraternally and take a deep breath, open
your mouth with your head thrown back the way young birds do, and
swallow . . . let the vowels reverberate in your own throat, let them
come out drawlier still, throatier, let them spread out even further, let
them sprawl . . . My vaaaaleese . . . moooonlight fiiiishing . . . And
then laugh, give him a tap on the shoulder . . . You really can be very
funny, you're a scream when you take on that accent . . . You don't
think so? You do, don't you? Near me, near us, all huddled up close
together, all alike, laughing together, surprised, amused, let's take a
look at that maleficent little genie you were harbouring . . . it was
hurting you . . . now you're exorcised . . . it has left you . . . see how
comical it is, the little imp, kicking and writhing there at our feet.

But you might as well try to bring to his senses with friendly back-
slaps and mocking laughter, a sadist in the act of assaulting his victim.
Nothing can force him to leave off . . . Vacaaation . . . it is dragged
about, entirely disfigured, ludicrous, debased, prostituted, an object
the brute uses to carry out his shady designs . . . it must be retrieved,
torn from him, we must dare, face the danger, heroically, with quiet
determination, just blushing a bit, how to keep from it? articulate
each vowel very clearly, reduce it to its normal proportions, restore its
pure outlines . . . Yes. Vacation time. Sea. Fishing . . . See how
pleasing the vowel is when treated this way, the way it's done in any
civilized country, between decent people, with all the consideration
that is its due . . . How it stands there, straight and light, naturally
discreet, modest and proud . . . its extreme clarity, its innocent grace

keep people at a distance, command respect. No one has the right to
cast a slur on that. These are very important things . . . There are
people who, to defend them . . . I know of precedents . . . A certain
poet on his death bed . . . no, not that . . . just a plain man, a man like
you and me . . . they say that on hearing the nun who was nursing him
say collidor, he sat up in bed, and gathering all his strength,
articulated very distinctly: cor-ridor. And then he fell back on his
pillow. Dead. And yet how can one compare the nun's innocent
mistake with the crime you're committing?

But nothing is more dangerous, nothing more excites the torturer's
need to recapture, debase it . . .

   Immediately there it is, in his clutches again, there it is, this time,
dragged still further, in a tighter grip . . . crawling, hideous,
deformed, swollen, bloated . . . You knooow . . . *vay* . . . at last its
tormentor, as though exhausted, reluctantly releases it . . . *cation* . . .
just for a second . . . And then, if you've no objection, my friend, we'll
have to start all over again . . . the *seeea* . . . the *ownly* place I like is
the *Meeediterraainean* . . .

Stop, do you hear! Why do you do that? Where on earth did you get
that accent? You're getting on our nerves. Who speaks like that?
What's it all about, anyway, this imitation-tough accent, of the 1900
apache variety? It's ridiculous, I assure you . . . it's old-fashioned, it's
pretentious . . .

   But right away all of them, even those, above all, those who had
always been so comprehending, so indulgent toward him, rise up in
horror, now they are shouting . . . How do you dare? How can you
allow yourself? You have broken all the bans. Laid violent hands on
something that nobody has the right to touch, something sacred . . .
You followed the traces of what was coming out of there, you dared
proceed to this source in him, accede to the place that has been set
apart in each one of us, from which it filtered . . . that vital spot . . .
you laid violent hands on that, committed that rape . . . See how he's
looking at you now . . . see his startled eyes like those of a mortally
wounded animal . . . —No, that's not true. Nothing inviolate here.
No source that nobody has the right to desecrate. What is coming out
of there is not a pure emanation, a secretion that would seep from his
very depths without his realizing it . . . not even a poison that would
well up in spite of himself . . . there is about it cold determination, a
deliberate scheme to jeer, to demean, to destroy . . . It's an intolerable
aggression, an outrage . . . For less than that a poet sat up on his

deathbed . . . —The proof of premeditation. Furnish proof. We'll
have to have absolute proof, do you hear? Have you got it? —It's a
certainty. —Based on what? —I don't know . . . I sense it . . . You
sense it too, like me . . . —sensations don't count. Nor do
presumptions. It's too serious. We must have unimpeachable proof.
And there never is any. There's always room for doubt. Therefore
you'll have to give in. You'll have to acquiesce. The way we all do.
Nobody can choose.

Nothing escapes him, not the slightest suspicion of a movement, not
the faintest shudder of disgust, of pain, not one immediately stifled
groan . . . he knows he has aimed true . . . he senses deliciously,
without your stirring, in the innermost part of you, something that is
just barely fluttering, timidly struggling . . . and there he presses . . .
there, with complete impunity, he sprawls . . . there his flabby vowels
spread their trembling jellyfish flesh, apply their suckers from which
there oozes a liquid that stings . . . My vaaaaleeese . . . how we blush
. . . hardly . . . we would like to look at the floor, but we don't dare
. . . be good . . . as good as can be . . . no contortions . . . we must
give in, isn't that so? that's all we can do . . .

Yes, you have to resign yourself. They're right. You must grow hard.
Lose that princess-and-the-pea sensitivity. Above all, you have to get
rid of your respect. Of your childish veneration. You can even, the
better to lose them, train yourself to take certain liberties, from time
to time amuse yourself by giving it a slight jostle, stretch it just a little
. . . vacaaation time . . . treat it a bit cavalierly, familiarly, off-
handedly. That might succeed. You can become accustomed to
anything. It's a question of training. You can end up by doing it
naturally, without noticing.
    Then, perhaps, the aggressor, who is never taken in by any tricks,
no longer perceiving anything trembling in you, convinced that you
won't lift a finger to protect it, that you would feel no relief, no sense
of victory if you saw it released and its rights restored, that you are
completely indifferent to its fate, then perhaps he will decide to loosen
his grip, and let it reassume its form.
    It will no longer attract anybody's attention, being, as it is,
naturally discreet, always inclined to self-effacement, to becoming
invisible . . . it will be forgotten.

(Translated by Maria Jolas)

It's Beautiful (1973)

C'est beau (It's Beautiful) was first performed in October 1975 at the Théâtre d'Orsay with the following cast:

HE   Jean-Luc Bideau
SHE   Emmanuelle Riva
THEIR SON   Daniel Berlioux
Voices of MRS. DENNISON, MR. DENNISON and others.
Directed by Claude Régy

HE.   It's beautiful, don't you think so?
SHE *(hesitant)*.   Ye-es . . .
HE.   You don't think it's beautiful?
SHE *(as though reluctantly)*.   Yes . . . Yes . . .
HE.   What's the matter with you?
SHE.   Oh, nothing. What do you expect? You asked me the question . . . and I answered yes . . .
HE.   But the way you said it . . . mere lip service . . . As if it were such a concession. *(Worried.)* You don't like it?
SHE.   Of course I like it, I told you so . . . But just now . . . you really don't want to understand . . .
HE.   The fact is, no, I don't understand . . .
THEIR SON.   Oh, listen, why pretend? You know that's all you'll ever get . . . lip service . . . a dull voice . . . that's all . . . absolutely all, and you know it. Since I'm here . . . And I don't even have to appear, there's no need even to say 'hoo-ooh', there he is . . . It's enough for me to be on the other side of the wall . . . shut up in my room . . . Even on the other side of a cement wall, my very presence would keep her from saying 'it's beautiful' the way you'd like her to say it . . .
HE.   But what's got into you? What's he talking about? Is he crazy?
THEIR SON.   Crazy? Me? Still the same old defensive reflexes, the same evasions, the same disguises . . . To deceive whom? Let's start over again . . . Just to see . . . I'll go to my room . . . And you will repeat it, you will say the way you did before: 'It's beautiful', isn't it? Don't you think so?
HE.   Are you making fun of me! . . . How dare you? You little good-for-nothing . . .

THEIR SON.   There we have it, it's contagious, you too have
caught it. You felt it . . . You're backing down. You don't dare.
The word sticks in your throat . . . It's beautiful. Beautiful.
Beautiful. How beautiful it is! . . . Impossible, isn't it? You can't
do it . . .

SHE.   That's true, he's right. You see yourself . . . you don't dare
. . .

HE.   So you too are going crazy. I don't dare! I can't say 'It's
beautiful', in front of him. Just because he's present, that little ass.
We'll see. Beautiful. Beautiful. Extremely beautiful! Excruciat-
ingly beautiful. Beautiful!

SHE.   Oh, stop, please be quiet.

THEIR SON.   Just to hear him is more than she can bear. That
makes her panic, doesn't it? She would like to stop her ears . . .
hide . . .

HE *(waking up)*.   What's happening anyway? What are we? What
are you talking about? To begin with, who is 'she'? Who are you
talking about? Go on, get out, get going, you're disturbing us.
Have you done your lessons? Remember you have a test to
prepare.

THEIR SON.   Yes, Dad. I've almost finished . . . All that's left is the
end of the Restoration.

Sound of a door closing.

HE *(laughs)*.   Did you see that? 'Who is "she"? Who is "she"?'
repeated firmly and there you have it. He withdrew into his hole.
That's what you call putting someone in his place. The place he
would never have left if he had had to deal with me. Under lock
and key . . . But you, of course . . .

SHE.   Naturally, it's well known that I'm always to blame . . .

HE.   I didn't force you to say it. But to prove it . . . who said, 'Who
is "she"?' Was it you or I? There you were, prostrate . . .

SHE.   That's true. Shall I tell you something? I admired you. I
admired your courage, your strength . . .

HE *(chest out)*.   Oh, that's going a bit far. I'm normal, that's all . . .

SHE.   The fact is that, for a moment, you did weaken, you too were
afraid, admit it . . .

HE.   Afraid? I? You're dreaming . . .

SHE.   But you deserve all the more credit, you know . . . People
who aren't afraid . . . But in your case, I saw it; there, when he
dared you . . . when you grew angry . . . you had to make a great
effort.

HE.   Not at all. Not the slightest. I said it, I shouted it, 'It's beautiful.
Beautiful. Beautiful . . .'

SHE.   Yes, you said it . . . very loudly . . . too loudly . . . there was something overwrought, exasperated about it . . . The old carcass was trembling . . . 'But suppose we should fail' . . . And in spite of everything, in spite of hell and high water, you hung on . . . 'Beautiful. Beautiful. Beautiful . . . for dear life . . . It was terrible . . . I felt like stopping my ears, hiding, as far from you as possible . . . I was about to disown you . . . When suddenly . . . what made you think of it? What presence of mind . . . That was a stroke of genius . . . at such a moment . . . to seize upon that, 'Who is "she"?' Who is "she"?' Marvellous . . . Where did you find it? It had so completely disappeared. 'Who is "she"?' And to have dared to brandish it, to hurl it at him . . . Really, you are wonderful.

HE.   I admit that in the pass we had come to . . . or rather he had come to, it had to be done . . . If you had listened to me . . . when it was not yet too late . . . You remember, I said it to you. You remember? . . . the forbidden words? Words we didn't have the right to use? . . . In fact, I must say that I myself . . . Lord, how silly we were . . .

SHE.   Oh, I'm not so sure . . . Even now, some of those words . . . I couldn't . . .

HE.   Yes, now . . . you remember when he was still a puling, damp, wrinkled infant . . . For the life of you, you couldn't, you would never have dared to say . . .

SHE.   Yes. To say to anybody, even to him: 'dearie'. Or worse still: 'young man' . . . That's true, that shocked me. It seemed to me that it was sort of like saying . . . like saying, 'kike'. Like saying, 'nigger'. Or 'women-folk'. Impossible. No question of it. There had to be perfect equality . . .

HE.   Perfect equality, that's a good one! Equality . . . You're joking. You should say, superiority . . . He was superior to us . . . Entirely composed of exquisite potentialities, of possibilities too numerous to choose from. He was still intact. Before the fall. The falls . . .

SHE *(sighing)*.   Yes, before we had made everything impossible, spoiled everything . . .

HE *(ironically)*.   We? Not so. Not I. It was not I who wrapped him up the way you do a parcel. It was not I who neglected to talk to him or tickle or kiss him enough while I was changing him . . . Not I who made him wait for his feeds . . .

SHE.   Oh, that's not true, I always hurried . . .

HE *(in an awful voice)*.   Don't deny it. How many times I used to hear him bawling himself hoarse . . .

SHE *(upset)*.   Not for that reason . . .

HE *(bantering)*.   Indeed . . . Not for that reason. And when her ladyship tore herself away from those exhilarating conversations

... It was too late ... frustration ... With all its consequences ... Madame may consider herself fortunate. But that's nothing. We can say that we had a narrow escape ... We had luck. 'A break' ... as he says ...

SHE.   Yes. That's true. Lots of luck. Just the thought of what could have happened to us ...

HE.   You mean there were worse things still? More serious crimes? ...

SHE.   Oh, no ...

HE.   There were too. Say it. For a long time I've felt that you were hiding something from me. Admit it. It'll do you good. And me too. It will help me to understand your permissiveness ... to be less exasperated by it ...

SHE *(firmly, taking herself in hand)*.   No ... It's nothing ...

HE.   Go on, try. You'll see, you'll feel better. It must not be so awful ... Look, I'll help you ... You wanted to teach him to be clean? You put him on the pottie ... you made a sort of whistling noise ...

SHE *(horrified)*.   Certainly not! What will you invent next? You remember perfectly ...

HE.   That's true, I do remember ... Perhaps, you took out of his mouth ... while he was asleep ...

SHE.   His thumb? Why, you're crazy. You know perfectly that I never ...

HE.   Well, what then? Darling. Don't torture me. Say it ... let's share the burden of it ... Tell me, what is it?

SHE *(in a whisper)*. Once, before he was born ...

HE.   Oh ... before he was born ...

SHE *(feverishly)*. But it's known now that that matters. People have told me that. People who know. I've read it. It's been scientifically demonstrated. Everything can go back to that ... all the mistakes ... criminal mistakes ...

HE.   Which mistakes? What did you do?

SHE.   Oh, it's too awful ... when I was pregnant ...

HE.   When? In what month?

SHE.   It was at the very beginning ...

HE.   At the very beginning ... let's not exaggerate. ... That's certainly less serious, all the same ...

SHE.   No, apparently it isn't. Some people say it can be even more serious before ...

HE *(firmly)*. Certainly not. I don't believe that.

SHE.   Well, no matter. In any case, it was when he already 'existed' in an embryonic state ... One day ... I had ...

HE.   You had what?

SHE.   I'll never forgive myself. It came over me all of a sudden. A terrible thought . . . All of a sudden. Oh, it's awful; I didn't want him.

HE.   Oh, merely the thought . . .

SHE.   Not merely. Not just a thought that quickly flashes across your mind . . . And even that, how can we know what effect . . . But I even . . . . . . *(pauses)* . . . went so far as to cry . . .

HE.   Oh!

SHE.   Yes. Real tears. That rolled down my cheeks. Imagine! The disturbance for him. The shock . . .

HE.   How awful! All that play-acting . . . when I think of it . . . your ecstasy when you felt him move . . . that beatific look . . . All pretence!

SHE.   Oh, no, don't say that. It was *genuine*. I was happy, happy, happy, happy! There was just suddenly, I don't know how it happened . . . that awful moment . . . Every time I think back on it . . .

HE *(coldly)*.   In any case, what good does it do? It's better forgotten. What's done is done. You can't change it now. He's there. Just as he is. Shut up, under lock and key. Obtuse. *(Becoming more and more enraged)*.—Narrow minded. 'Practical.' Oh, he's no 'dreamer'. No 'aesthete': no danger of that . . . comics . . . detective stories . . . juke-boxes . . . sporting matches . . . a fine product. Bravo! we've reached the point, when he's present, of not being able to say 'It's beautiful . . .' we don't dare listen to a record . . . we're afraid . . . and we have to put up with it. Shall I tell you something? There's only one way . . .

SHE.   No. Not that. That would be useless. You know perfectly well that we wouldn't succeed . . . You would be the one to run and bring him back . . . and everything would start over again . . .

HE.   Never, you hear me. Never! Let him go to the other end of the earth. They can put him in prison . . . In a reform school. Just so he disappears . . . And to Hell with him.

Pause.

SHE.   Oh, after all . . . if you think about it . . . that's going a bit far . . . To have to bear that: just so he disappears! . . . Well, . . . That's how it is . . . You can believe me or not, as you want . . . That's what we've come to!

HE.   What did you say? To whom are you speaking?

SHE.   Be quiet . . . Yes: 'Just so he disappears. And to hell with him' *(In a voice that is not hers)*. Why? What has he done? Is he a murderer? *(In her own voice)*. Oh no . . . He wouldn't hurt a fly. *(Different voice)*. He's a thief? *Her voice* – Oh, no . . . honesty itself . . . *(Different voice)*. A liar? *(her voice)*. No. *(Different voice)*. A pervert? *(Her voice)*. No. No. *(Different voice)*. A feignant? . . .[1]

HE.   What did you say? I heard *'feignant'*. You didn't say that?

SHE *(Defiantly)*.   I did. I did say it. *'Feignant'*. And why not?

HE.   My poor darling . . . You must really be suffering . . . So you've come to this . . . That little good-for-nothing has brought you to this . . . has made you demean . . . lower yourself . . . degrade yourself . . . cheapen yourself . . .

SHE.   Quiet. A little modesty, I beg of you, A little humility. When people come here for a consultation, they must leave their pretensions outside . . . I did say *'feignant'*. You see, ladies and gentlemen, that's the whole point. He can't bear such words as that. *'Feignant'* is forbidden . . .

VOICES.   *Feignant?* Forbidden?

SHE.   Yes . . . You understand? *Fai-né-ant*. That's allowed. That's superior. Airy. Lofty. *Fai-né-ant*. That's 'beautiful'! While *feignant* is ugly. *Fai-né-ant* is beautiful! Beautiful. Beautiful. That's the whole point. . . . You never know how far that can go . . . His contempt and his tyranny. And when the poor child can't stand it any longer . . . When he turns from us . . . his own father goes as far as to wish . . . Oh, help me . . .

VOICES.   If it isn't a shame, to see a thing like that. If that isn't a shame . . . To want to banish that poor child . . . to come to that. You could understand if he were wild . . .

SHE.   No, indeed, that's not the case.

VOICES.   You could understand if he were a crook, or a murderer.

SHE. No.

VOICES.   Let's suppose he took drugs . . .

SHE.   Not so.

VOICES.   Or you could understand if he had the misfortune . . . You'd understand if he were an ungrateful son . . .

SHE.   Not so.

VOICES.   Or suppose you were old . . .

SHE.   No.

VOICES.   Or suppose you were without means and he refused to pay for your food . . . a thing one sees so often these days . . .

HE.   How much longer will that go on? That's enough . . . I can't bear any more. Stop . . .

SHE *(very softly)*.   Watch out, what are you doing? Be quiet. And above all, don't interrupt. It has to unreel. Be patient. You'll see . . .

---

[1] Footnote: Readers and actors will want to use their own term for *feignant* (an uncultured pronounciation for *fainéant*). 'Good for nothin'', 'scrounger' or 'lazybones' are among the possibilities, although the latter does not convey the sense of a slip into an uncultured pronounciation.

HE.   I can't, it's more than I can bear. It gives me the staggers, it nauseates me.

SHE *(whispers)*.   Do be quiet. *(Aloud)*. Continue, pay no attention . . . You see, he's so refined . . . Very exacting. Always so impatient.

VOICES.   If it isn't a shame to see that. Let's suppose he were dishonest . . .

SHE.   No.

VOICES.   Let's suppose he were licentious.

SHE.   No, No.

VOICES.   Let's suppose he were a *feignant* . . .

HE.   Oh . . .

SHE.   No. He's not a *feignant*. He works . . .

VOICES.   If that's not a shame. Not licentious. Not a thief. Not a liar. Not dishonest. Not a drug-addict. Not *feignant*. There are lots of people in your place who would be satisfied. Some who would be proud. And some who would be downright happy. There are some who never hoped for that much . . . Imagine, in times like these . . . with the young people you see nowadays . . . with all those good-for-nothings . . .

HE.   Oh . . . that's enough. Enough. I give in. I quit . . .

SHE.   You're impossible. Wait. And above all, don't rush things . . . You'll see . . . It's coming . . .

VOICES.   When you think that some people have such luck . . . A polite boy . . . A conscientious boy . . . A hard-working boy . . .

SHE.   Oh yes, he's even in advance for his age.

VOICES.   If that's not shameful. They must be spoilt . . . They must be rotten spoilt . . .

SHE. *(ecstatic)*.   Oh yes, isn't that true?

VOICES.   Hard-working . . .

SHE.   That he is . . .

VOICES.   Do you hear that? . . . When I think of all the people who would give almost anything . . .

SHE.   Yes. From that standpoint . . . eh? You'll admit.

HE.   Yes, as regards his studies . . . that's true.

VOICES.   His studies! . . . You'd think they didn't count . . .

HE.   On the contrary. Of course they count . . .

VOICES.   Well, then, what's wrong?

HE *(hesitant)*.   It's . . .

VOICES.   What?

HE *(mild, softening)*.   Oh, it's nothing . . . nothing . . . That's true. Nothing to speak of. Nothing to be anxious about. Nothing to send you looking for trouble. Nothing to make a fuss about . . .

We're the ones . . . we . . . we are spoilt . . . Rotten-spoilt . . . We are crazy.

SHE.   There, you see, darling.

VOICES.   Be careful lest Heaven should punish you. If it should happen . . . May God forbid, let's touch wood . . . Whenever you thought back on it . . .

SHE and HE.   Oh yes, may God forbid . . .

VOICES.   Oh, you see . . . you're tempting fate . . .

SHE AND HE.   Oh no.

VOICES.   You don't know how fortunate you are . . .

SHE.   Oh, yes we do . . .

VOICES.   Of course . . . no need to say it. In reality, you're very proud, aren't you? You wouldn't exchange him for anybody, would you? Admit it. A strapping boy like that.

SHE and HE.   That's true.

VOICES.   Tall, well-built. Sturdy.

HE.   Oh, in that respect . . . I feel like a whipper-snapper beside him.

VOICES.   And already interested, I bet . . . it's not surprising . . . all the girls . . .

HE.   For that matter, there are some already . . . They swarm about him . . . The other day the telephone rang . . . I picked up the receiver and I heard . . .

SHE.   But he would never do anything wrong. When his father spoke to him about it, to warn him . . . He interrupted him. He's very modest you know. With that serious look of his he said: Yes, I agree with you, I know, Dad.

HE.   I myself at that age, was a fool . . . Slightly retarded . . . Always with my nose in a book . . . Or in museums . . . But he . . . Oh, for him, that's certainly true, such things as that bore him . . . he doesn't like them . . . what he wants are comic strips . . . television . . .

VOICES.   After all, he belongs to his time . . . that's normal, he's like everybody else . . .

HE *(anxious)*.   Everybody else?

SHE.   Oh. You're not going to start again? You're not going to have another attack? . . . *(Loudly)*. Yes. He's like everybody else. Today everybody his age is like him. Don't make that face, I beg of you . . . Don't bristle up like that. Come on, repeat after me: 'Everybody' . . . Practise it . . . You'll see, it'll go better . . . Repeat: 'Everybody does it. Everybody says it. All young people are like that. We are like everybody else . . .'

HE *(in a weak voice)*.   Everybody does it . . . all young people . . .

SHE.   All young people prefer the comics.

HE. All . . . young people prefer . . .

SHE *(severely)*. Come on! . . . the comics.

HE. The comics.

SHE. Juke-boxes. Pin-ball machines.

HE. Juke . . . Yet there are some . . . even among the young people . . .

VOICES. Oh, my poor friend, you're talking about exceptions. They only confirm . . .

SHE. Why, of course. All you need to do is look about you . . . even among the most brilliant specimens: graduates of the very best universities . . . the Aubry boys, or the Jamets . . . And yet, it's as I tell you . . . 'The Wizard of Oz'. 'Lucky Luke', 'Asterix', are their favourite reading. Their father . . . who would have the right to demand more of them . . . oh, he just laughed, he thought that was alright . . .

Pause

HE *(firmly)*. It's finished. Ended. Thumbs down. I don't want to play any longer.

SHE. What's the matter with you?

HE. What's the matter with me is that you have made a mistake. A fatal mistake.

SHE. What mistake? with him again? Diapers again? Bottles?

HE. No, a mistake, here and now, with me. You did. You changed games. Without letting on. But I saw it. You had to drag in old man Jamet. And the Aubry boys. Now I am going to ask you to let me have Mrs. Dennison, . . . and Mr. Dennison . . . Absolutely, I want both the father and the mother . . .

SHE. What?

HE. Yes, give them to me. Come on, give them here. And now, the daughter and the son. Yes, Dennison. The entire family.

SHE. What will you do with them?

HE. You'll see. I need them. And the Herberts as well. All of them, father, mother, son, grandson. Give them here. And the Charrats. The entire family. I could ask you for others . . . but for the time being, they will be enough for me.

SHE. I don't understand a thing . . .

HE. Wait, you'll understand. Now let yourself go. Repeat after me: say, 'It's beautiful'.

SHE. Oh, what for?

HE. Repeat it, I tell you. I myself was very patient a while ago. Repeat after me: 'it's beautiful'.

SHE *(wearily.)*. 'It's beautiful'.

HE. Repeat: 'It's beautiful are words that we do not dare to use in the presence of our own child.' And now you're going to see, screw up your courage.

SHE.   It's beautiful are words that we do not dare to use in the presence of our own child. And now you're going to see . . .'

HE.   No, not that . . . not 'and now you're going to see', that was spoken to you.

SHE.   And all the rest was spoken to whom?

HE.   To the Dennisons, the Herberts, and the Charrats . . .

SHE.   Oh listen, how silly we must look! They're going to think we're completely mad.

HE *(nostalgically)*. Mad . . . *(Sighing)*. Fit to be tied. If only you were right. If only it were possible . . . Personally, that's all I ask. Unfortunately, there's little chance . . . Come, brace up. Let's repeat it. But just a second, so I can gather my strength . . . There, I'm ready. Let's start.

SHE and HE.   'It's beautiful' are words that we do not dare to use in the presence of our child . . .

HE.   You understand? The words 'It's beautiful' don't come out. *(Aside)*. Oh, God, spare me, I haven't the heart . . . . *(Becoming firmer.)* Yes, you see . . . 'It's beautiful', when said in his presence, makes us tremble, makes us panicky . . . There we have it. I've said it . . . now, in a second, the Dennisons, the Charrats . . .

SHE.   What will the Dennisons and the Charrats, who are perfectly healthy, normal people, take us for? They've never seen such madness, have they?

HE.   No, darling. You know perfectly that they haven't. Let's not have any illusions . . . Take your courage in both hands. The shock will be great. Worse than anything I imagined. Anything I might have feared . . .

SHE.   What is it? You're killing me . . .

HE.   It's frightful. In a twinkling. In a split second. Right away. Without hesitating. As though it were the most natural, the most commonplace thing, they understood . . . Not the slightest surprise. With a pitying look: *(imitating someone's voice)*. 'Oh how sad that is . . . It's really a great misfortune . . . People before whom one doesn't dare to say 'It's beautiful'.

MRS. DENNISON'S VOICE.   I flee them like the plague . . . But then, when it's a question of your own child . . .

MR. DENNISON'S VOICE.   It's a misfortune . . .

HE. *(toneless voice)*.   You think so?

THE DENNISON and OTHER VOICES.   Of course we think so.

HE.   But why, really, why? I never have quite understood . . . I tell myself that I'm mad. Explain it to me . . .

VOICES.   Explain it to you? What's the use? Why turn the knife in the wound?

HE.   Do, I beg of you, do turn it. I want to know. It's perhaps not for the same reasons, that you and I . . . We may not be thinking about the same things . . .

VOICES.   Alas, we are, my poor friend, what else do you expect us to be thinking about? Shall we tell you?

HE.   Yes, do. Tell it . . .

VARIOUS VOICES.   You must really be in a very bad way . . . you're in a panic, you're afraid, because you sense an insulting barrier . . . a vile contempt . . . a furtive threat . . . which those people cause to weigh on everything that matters, they debase and level everything, everything that makes life worth while . . . *(Becoming excited)*. You're ashamed before them of profaning. . . you feel you want to withdraw from their contact . . . to put things in safe keeping . . . above all, they must not be provoked . . . they must not come too close . . . in fact, just to think about it . . . horrors . . . why talk about that? Nobody mentions it out of embarrassment . . . or out of just plain decency . . . But who doesn't feel that?

SHE.   Who? Why, most people. Healthy people. Normal. Strong, whose heads are well screwed on their shoulders. Their hearts in the right place. Thank God there are some people like that. Adults. Hardened. Whom life had confronted . . . to whom it has taught something more than the refinements of this spoilt, dissolute, rotten lot . . . A threat? Bad luck . . . a misfortune . . . to have had him . . . to have a son like him . . . But it's almost unbelievable . . . *(Imitation)*. Is he a murderer? Of course not. *(Imitation)*. A thief? A liar? No. *(Imitation)*. A pervert? No. *(Imitation)*. A feignant? . . . *(Weeps)*.

THE DENNISONS' VOICES.   Ah, my poor friends, so you've come to this . . . Asking for help . . . going to consult healers, bonesetters . . . writing letters to the agony columnists . . . Who could throw the first stone at you? . . . In desperate cases, what will one not do? We ourselves if, by ill luck, such a thing had happened to us with Jack or Peter . . . They, thank heaven, up till now, are always poking about . . . as soon as they have a free moment . . .

HE *(avid)*.   Yes, isn't that so? In books? Museums? At all the exhibitions? Good records . . . Art books. Yes, the way I used to be . . . But you know, at times, I wonder . . . I don't mean to offend you . . .

VOICES.   What is it? What is it you wonder?

HE.   Well, if there wasn't perhaps in that, a certain something that was lacking . . . yes . . . a certain vitality . . . Our son, you know, a stalwart fellow. Bursting with health and youthful strength. Not a little old man the way I was at that age. He's got a good head. A strapping physique. Already interested . . . he is that . . . *(laughter)* quite a heart-breaker. *(Chuckles)*. Of course we ourselves never mix in . . . Besides, he has already reached a stage of maturity . . . that is astonishing for his age . . .

SHE.   A very open mind. He never lets himself be taken in . . . No authoritative arguments go with him. He sifts everything through a fine sieve.

VOICES.   Well, then, what are you complaining about? What is it that makes you suffer? Everything's fine. You can be satisfied. Proud. Let's all be happy in our way.

HE *(worthy)*.   Yes, you're right. We were wrong.

SHE.   Excuse us. Yes. Let's all be lucky in our way.

Silence

HE.   Did you hear that pitying tone . . . As though they were speaking to feeble-minded people . . .

SHE.   Yes. But admit it was coming to us. Just imagine! And you reproached me with lowering myself! You can say that you baited them . . . *(imitating them.)* I do feel sorry for you . . . such a demeaning contact . . . one would like to hide everything . . . everything that 'matters' . . . simple decency – shame on you – keeps people from talking about those things . . . How awful if such a misfortune . . . if that had happened to us . . . if our Jack or our Peter . . . But in front of them *(gradually changing her tone)* no danger, in front of them, we can say 'It's beautiful'. We can swoon. Kneel down . . . All together. The whole family. Bow our heads at the same time . . . There's no danger that they would raise theirs . . . No, quite so. No danger. Not like in our family . . .

she knocks on the door

Come in, darling, come on in here with us . . .

What have you been doing? Did I interrupt you? Come in, do, just for a minute . . .

THE SON.   Yes, mama. What's the matter?

SHE.   Well, darling, I just wanted to ask you . . .

THE SON *(a bit excited)*.   Yes, I've finished. All I have to do now is to make a summary . . .

SHE.   No, no, that's not what I wanted to speak to you about . . .

THE SON. ˙ Well, then . . . What was it?

SHE.   Don't look like that . . .

THE SON.   Like what?

SHE.   Don't make that baby-face.

HE.   Oh, you do have some good ones! What do you expect? Do you

think you have a magic wand that can transform the swan into
Prince Charming, or the frog into a beautiful princess? You know
quite well that I put a spell on him.

SHE *(to her son)*.   Do you understand what your father's saying?

THE SON.   No, mama.

SHE *(begging)*.   Of course you understand . . . You're pretending
you're stupid . . .

THE SON.   Certainly not . . . Really . . .

HE.   You may be sure that now, no matter how you try . . . I told
you that before, I put him in his place . . . I locked him in. Who's
'she'? You thought that was fine. You admired my presence of
mind, my courage . . . Now you'd like him to come out. You have
to decide what you want. Would you like for him to begin again?

THE SON *(with a naive expression)*.   For me to begin what again?

SHE.   Why, darling, you know perfectly . . . I would like for you to
be again the way you were a little while ago . . . when you
understood everything better than we did, when you sensed
everything so clearly . . . we were the ones who were like children
. . . when you yourself said, you remember, that we didn't dare to
utter . . . to say: 'It's beautiful' . . . simply because you . . .
because you were present . . . You are so sensitive, so keen . . . All
those things, for you too, when you feel like it . . . nothing can be
hidden from you, it's impossible to astonish you . . . you have such
clear-sightedness, such a free mind . . . I wish the same for the
people . . .

THE SON.   But you were so frightened. And dad was furious . . .

SHE.   That was ridiculous. I'm sure he realizes it now . . . he should
have let you explain yourself, assert yourself . . . And he, with his
'Who's she?', that was not intended to crush you, you know . . . I
know him . . . he couldn't help it . . . a simple reflex . . . 'who's
she'? . . . out of habit. Out of conformity. So old-fashioned.
'Who's she?' I ask you, after all, Such trifles . . . Where did he get
that . . . when we were there, all three of us, in one of those rare
moments when finally . . . it's marvellous . . . all of a sudden . . .
it's like a rift in a cloud . . . We were finally about to experience
something . . . between ourselves . . .

HE.   Oh listen, stop. Don't you think you've had enough? You want
more? . . . You have only yourself to blame . . . I warn you. Don't
expect me to come to your rescue . . .

SHE *(uplifted)*.   No, no, I'm not counting on it . . . I won't need it
. . . *(to the son)*. Listen, darling, I beg of you, tell me, tell me . . .
don't refuse . . . tell me . . . just why . . . why, do you think, tell me
. . . when you are present, even on the other side of the wall . . . as
you expressed it so well . . . we can't . . .

THE SON *(airily. Very much at ease).* Ah, that, it's true, you see yourself, even now, in the midst of all these effusions, you stop, you don't dare . . .

SHE *(taking herself in hand).* But I do dare, you see: 'It's beautiful'. And I'll even show you. I'll drag it out . . . look, watch me, before you. And I'll say—do you hear me? 'It's beautiful . . .' And I'll ask you, you too: Don't you think so?

Silence

. . . Well, say something!

THE SON. Well, there's nothing to be done about it . . . I can't help it . . . I cringe. In a moment *(in a jokingly terrible voice).* I'm going to secrete, the way an octopus does . . . black ink will spread over everything . . . Look at dad, he's already all doubled up . . .

HE and SHE *(toneless voices).* Don't you think that's beautiful? You hate that? . . . all that . . .

THE SON *(condescendingly).* No, of course not . . . that's not the question . . .

HE AND SHE *(with hope).* Not the question . . . Oh, darling, what is it then?

THE SON. It's . . . It's . . . but it embarrasses me to say it to you . . . It's going to shock you.

SHE. No, no, I beg of you, say it . . .

THE SON *(hesitant).* Well, it's that expression: 'It's beautiful' . . . that ruins everything for me . . . it's enough for that to be plastered on anything whatsoever, and right away . . . everything seems like . . .

SHE. Yes . . . I believe I see . . .

THE SON. Yes . . . you do see . . .

SHE. I understand . . . it becomes conventional . . . doesn't it?

THE SON. Yes, I suppose so . . . Commonplaces of that kind, as soon as you apply them . . .

HE and SHE *(full of hope).* Yes. One shouldn't, you're right. It's a sort of facility. Conformity.

THE SON. Yes, that's it . . . I have a horror of . . .

SHE *(aroused).* Yes, you, you have too much respect for things like that . . .

THE SON *(irritated).* Ah, there we are. Now it's respect. Always those words.

SHE *(humble).* Excuse me . . . I meant to say that the thing itself . . . on which we plaster the words . . . and which you don't want to see flattened out, isn't that so? or banalized . . . but the thing itself, it . . . you . . . you . . . after all . . .

THE SON. Why yes, mama, of course . . .

SHE *(to the father).* You see how mistaken we were. How little we knew our own child . . . That's true, they are the ones we know least well . . . He doesn't at all hate . . . He likes, you see . . . well, 'likes' is an unsuitable word . . . forgive me . . . we are so awkward . . . oh, well . . . I mean to say that what your father was showing me a while ago, this engraving . . . you, too, if you would look at it without anybody saying a thing, you too . . .

THE SON *(reassuring)*. Why yes, I too, of course . . .

HE.   You too? Eh? You think so? You don't think that it's . . .

SHE *(panicky)*.   Oh no, stop, be careful . . . don't begin again . . . not those words . . . which are so conventional . . . sclerotic . . . emphatic . . . you see, darling, I believe that I understand . . .

HE.   Alright, alright, granted . . . since he's so refined . . . *(delighted)* so delicate . . . But after all, it's, isn't it? . . . don't you think so? . . .

Whistle

THE SON.   Yes. It's pretty nifty, that I'll grant you.

HE *(delighted)*.   Nifty. Nifty. Nifty. I shouldn't have thought of that. Nifty. Now I'll know. One word is enough! . . .

SHE *(feverish)*.   Yes, for everything to change . . . for real understanding for it to be possible yes, isn't that so?

HE.   Watch out. You get carried away every time . . .

SHE.   That's not so, I'm not carried away . . . *(Feverishly, as though about to explode and pour forth)*. Listen, darling, I've always known this, always felt it, we are so like each other . . . it wasn't possible . . . now, isn't it so? I can say it to you, share . . . you remember? like in the old days . . . when you were little . . . when you yourself came to show me . . . now we'll go . . . we won't? that doesn't tempt you? You'd rather go all by yourself . . .

THE SON.   Go where?

SHE.   Why, you know, I spoke about it the other day . . . something . . . no, don't worry, I am careful . . . something that should not be missed, you'll allow me to say that . . . for me it was a shock . . . an event . . . that exhibit . . . But perhaps you have already seen it? . . . No? very well, it's not that . . . What's the meaning of all this supervision? . . . very well, let's leave it . . . but I'd like to show you . . . look . . . no not at that . . . not reproductions . . . *(coaxing)*. You'll see, be patient . . . or rather you'll hear . . . . . .

A few measures of Boucourechliev.

No . . .

HE *(Whispers)*.   You're crazy . . .

SHE.   Yes, that's not it . . . wait . . .

A few measures of Webern.

No, not that either . . . But I know what . . . I think that this time . . .

Mozart, for longer.

HE.   Oh, that'll do. *(He turns off the record.)*

SHE *(tearful)*.   But why did you do that? We were listening so intently . . . It penetrated . . . it filled everything . . . it was . . .

HE.   Nothing. It bores me stiff.

SHE.   It bores you stiff?

HE.   Yes. I think it's boring . . .

SHE.   You do? You don't think that it's . . .

HE.   That it's what?

SHE.   That it's . . . well, pretty nifty . . .

Silence

But what's happening?

HE.   What's happening is that that bores me . . . What's happening is that I don't want . . . now now.

SHE *(weeping)*.   Oh . . .

HE.   Not as long as he's here . . . it doesn't penetrate . . . I cease to hear anything. I don't feel anything . . . everything is shrouded in black ink . . . Quick, help! . . . help me, please . . .

THE SON *(very calm and a bit condescending)*.   Alright, oh, alright. I'll go. Calm down a bit . . . It's not about all that, but a while ago Mr. Bertrand called. I answered . . . He'll call back . . .

HE *(relieved)*.   At what time?

THE SON.   I said you'd be home after eight o'clock . . .

HE.   Why eight o'clock? . . . When I had said that I would be back at the latest . . .

THE SON.   Excuse me, you didn't say it to me . . .

SHE.   No, you said it to me . . .

HE.   No, to him.

SHE.   No, to me.

THE SON.   So you see.

HE.   In your defence, your mother would say anything . . .

THE SON.   No. You know perfectly well that she never lies.

HE.   Are you giving me a lesson? And besides, who are you talking about? Who is 'she'?

(Translated by Maria Jolas)

CLAUDE SIMON

Some forty years ago Claude Simon published his first novel and was hailed by the critics as a writer of great promise. Born by a curious coincidence in the same year as Albert Camus (1913), he took much longer than Camus to fulfil this promise. It was not until 1960—the year Camus died—that Simon published the novel which was to ensure that he would dominate French literature of the sixties and seventies as Camus had dominated that of the forties and fifties. This book, *The Flanders Road*, developed in a highly original fashion a moment lodged in the consciousness of the narrator: the sight, sound and smell of a brief but unforgettable incident which took place during the Battle of the Meuse in 1940. James Joyce drew on the events of a single day to create *Ulysses*; in *The Flanders Road* Simon expanded a mere ten minutes or so of real time into a complex and powerful work of fiction.

By the time Claude Simon reached artistic maturity, the stance and manner of Camus and Sartre had been superseded by the very different mode of the *nouveau roman* as developed by Robbe-Grillet and his colleagues. Simon soon took his place among the exponents of this new method of fiction-making, and is now held by many to be its greatest and most powerful talent. For when all is said and done, the only justification for fictional experiment, for the restless dissatisfaction with pre-existing forms and modes of expression, must be the more precise and exact formulation of what Claude Simon calls, in the dedicatory note in *La Corde raide* (1947), 'la tragica i dolorosa inquietud', in so far as this 'anxiety' besets mankind at every moment. For Simon eschews two extremes, set out on the one hand by Alain Robbe-Grillet when he says that by repudiating communion with the world of things man can escape tragedy, and on the other by George Steiner who has drawn attention to the tempting blandishments of what he calls in an arresting phrase 'the suicidal rhetoric of silence'. Simon has not succumbed to this rhetoric; nor has he fallen either for Robbe-Grillet's easy optimism. 'Life is tragic for Claude Simon,' writes Laurent LeSage, 'because human existence counts for so little in the universal order of things,' and he compares Simon's vision to that of Ecclesiastes. There is in both works, LeSage argues, a clear perception of the essential vanity of human activity coupled with a strangely satisfying emphasis on the cyclical perenniality of the natural world in which 'to everything there is a season . . . a time to be born, and a time to die' (Eccl. iii. 1–2). And Jean-Luc Seylaz has drawn attention to a fertile paradox in Simon's fiction between an impulse towards complete reconstitution and a tendency to nihilistic destruction, and between a powerfully evocative vision and hesitations about the solidity of things.

It is this dual perception which drives Claude Simon to write novels in a vain (though for us fortunate) attempt to reconcile the conflict between the sceptical pessimism of the intellectual and the confident optimism of the artisan, between the Diogenes and the Daedalus aspects of his nature. It is this which causes him willy-nilly to explore the major permanent themes of the western novel in the wake of his masters, Dostoyevsky and Conrad. In *The Flanders Road*, for instance, Pierre reacts in a characteristically intellectual fashion to the news of the destruction of the 'most precious library in the world' by writing to his POW son Georges in Germany that 'all of this is infinitely sad.' To which Georges replies, shrewdly enough, 'that if the contents of the thousands of books in that irreplaceable library had been impotent to prevent things like the bombing which destroyed them from happening, [he] didn't really see what loss to humanity was represented by the disappearance of those thousands of books and papers obviously devoid of the slightest utility.'

We can be sure that this debate, between Pierre the professor and the son whose interests revert to those of his illiterate peasant ancestors, is one which Claude Simon conducts with himself. On the one hand, as a man of extensive culture, he regrets the loss of the books in the Leipzig collection, as does Pierre; on the other hand, with Georges, he is conscious of the fact that words merely serve, 'like those vague sugared pellets disguising a bitter medicine for children' to conceal from our awareness 'the whole dim and blind and tragic and banal imbroglio' of life.

Tragic, yet banal: this sums up a lot in Claude Simon's attitude to human existence. *The Palace* (1962), being about a political catastrophe, the Spanish civil war, concentrates on the images of disaster such an event throws up, 'the eternal and unchanging scenes of all catastrophes and all migrations'. One of the characters, the American, imagines that a dead child lies putrefying in the sewers of Barcelona wrapped in newspaper, a 'shroud of words', and later the Student contemplates in the republican headquarters 'the bureaucratic accumulation of paper which always manages to soak up all violence and every act of revolt'. Unavoidable in its ordinariness, commonplace in its inevitability: this is the nature, for Claude Simon, of the story of this failed revolution, and the true meaning of the dictionary definition of the word, 'revolution', quoted in the epigraph to the whole novel, as the locus of a moving body which, describing a closed curve, successively passes through the same points. The revolution, in other words, is cyclical like the rest of life. This notion, profoundly held by Claude Simon, is encapsulated in the brilliant image which closes the novel, that of children's coffins, a grotesque juxtaposition of birth and death, beginning and ending, renewal and decay.

Histoire (1967), his next novel, deals not with a political disaster, but with the break-up of a family and its fortunes. One can hear in the novel the murmurings of the old women, for whom 'all events, happy, unhappy or neutral occasions, Maman's illness, the bad harvests, the engagements of granddaughters, the trips, the suspicions about the estate-manager, births, deaths, misalliances, the wild oats of their children, the bankruptcies, were indiscriminately reduced to those snatches of desolate sentences, those commentaries hanging in the motionless air like those vibrations which persist long after the bells have stopped ringing . . .' Such familiar (and familial) catastrophes exist to demonstrate that 'at any moment the ordered and reassuring world can suddenly capsize . . . disclose the hidden surface in order to show that its other side is no more than a simple heap of garbage'.

The sense of the epigraph to *Histoire*, a quotation from Rilke to the effect that we are perpetually engaged in organizing a chaos which engulfs us continually until we fall apart ourselves, recurs in *The Battle of Pharsalus* (1969), in a passage which contemplates an abandoned McCormick reaper; but if the machine (and man who makes it) is destined to decay and corruption, the same is not true of the natural world, as *Triptych* (1973), makes clear, in speaking of 'the imperious, incessant circulation of the sap, the secret mutations of matter, the manifold breathing of the earth at night'. Once again we find dominant the characteristically Simonian notion of cycle, of decay and regeneration: of tragic paradox, in fact, at the very heart of things.

Indeed, a tragic sense of history, of the self, of human tenderness—in *Conducting Bodies* (1971), for instance, the woman says of her doomed affair, 'We knew it from the start; all through the night we've known it'—pervades, even saturates Simon's world. Life's complex ironies are laid bare: the name of the battlefield of Pharsalus, which changed the destiny of the world, can today hardly be deciphered on the signposts in Thessaly, for instance; or a lost ring, the source of so many tragic misunderstandings in *Le Sacre du Printemps* (1954), is found buried in a pocket where it had lain all the time. These examples, macrocosmic and microcosmic respectively in significance, are typical of the way Simon highlights the vanity of human wishes. This might be melodramatic, romantic in the bad sense, were it not brushed with a hint of comedy; and it is not a cruel form of humour but, rather, a compassionate one. Those children's coffins, which I referred to earlier as constituting the final image in *The Palace*, are described by the narrator as 'absurd' (*dérisoires*). It is not that Simon considers children's coffins to be ridiculous in themselves; such an opinion would be callous and in poor taste. It is simply that objects such as these, which throw into sharp focus the cruelty and sadness of our condition—in this case, that children, so close to birth, do also sometimes die—are often so pathetic as to be comic, like the oppressed populations of Spain who are described as 'serious, taciturn, proud, humiliated and grim' (*The Palace*), or like the grotesque detritus which lines the roads in the wake of a tragic retreat such as that portrayed in *The Flanders Road*.

(J.F.)

The Flanders Road (1960)

As Claude Simon himself has pointed out, there is a hierarchy of events in this novel, the one enclosing the other, with the military ambush in the centre, the horse race which de Reixach loses outside that, and his death forming the outer core of the onion (or, to use Simon's own analogy, the outer edge of an artesian basin). The cut from the race to the battle (at the heart of the book) occurs at 1.00 on p. 97 of the present extract, and the return from the battle to the race at 1.00 on p. 103. The extract also touches on George's later experiences as a POW, and other topics are brought in by the familiar Simon device of associative thematic links.

And then as motionless as a statue. And then Corinne,[1] too, as motionless as a statue, trying with the same eagerness to see what was happening behind the little wood, saying without opening her mouth or turning her head or raising her voice, exactly the way she had argued with de Reixach[2] a little earlier: 'Damn flunkey.' And he so to speak totally absorbed in the huge binoculars and probably not even hearing her, or perhaps realizing that she was talking to him but not even bothering to listen, to try to understand, saying: 'Yes, that was a nice break, yes, that's it, that's it, you have to . . . Yes: she's, she's going . . .', and around them the calm uproar of the crowd, the last bettors flowing back toward the rail or climbing into the grandstands like a slow black tide, although most of them were running, but already not looking in front of them, all with their heads turned toward the little wood, the heads of the ones who were running facing the same way as the heads of the ones already sitting in the stands or standing on chairs dragged out into the paddock: the painted porcelain heads of mannequins surrounded by photographers, the wrinkled and papery heads of old colonels under their gray derbies, the heads of millionaires with their horse-dealer's look, merchants or distillers or money salesmen from father to son, usurers, owners of horses, of women, of mines, of whole districts of houses, of slums, of villas with swimming pools, of chateaux, of yachts, of skeletal Negroes or Indians, of big or little slot machines (from the ones six

---

[1] De Reixach's young wife.
[2] An aristocratic officer to whom the novel's hero, Georges, is distantly related through his mother.

stories high made out of stone, concrete and steel to the trash made out of painted tin and reflectors the color of gumdrops): a species or class or race whose fathers or grandfathers or great-grandfathers or great-great-grandfathers had one day found a means, by violence, trickery or constraint exercised in a more or less legal fashion (and probably more than less, considering that right, law is always only the consecration of a state of force) of amassing the fortunes they were now spending but which, by a sort of consequence, a curse attached to the violence and the trickery, condemned them to find growing round them only that fauna which is also trying to acquire (or to profit by) those very fortunes (or merely fortune) by violence or trickery, and whom the former managed to jostle (breathing the same air, trampling the same dusty gravel, as if they had been assembled in the same salon) without even seeming to notice their presence, nor even—perhaps—to see them: the heads of the bettors with dubious occupations, with dubious collars, with dubious faces, with hawks' eyes, with hardened, pitiless, frustrated faces gnawed, corroded by passion: the North-African workers who paid almost the equivalent of a half-day's work for merely the fond privilege of seeing up close the horse on which they had bet their week's pay, the pimps, the peddlers, the tip-sellers, the grooms, the chauffeurs, the concession-aires, the old baronesses, and the ones who had come only because it was a beautiful day, and those who would have come anyway, trampling in the mud and shivering in the drafts, if it had rained spears, all huddled now in the stands with the sculptured gingerbread floating in the sky with the whipped-cream clouds, motionless, like meringues, that is, swollen, puffed up on top and flattened underneath as if they had been set on an invisible sheet of glass, neatly aligned in successive rows which the perspective brought closer together in the distance (like the trunks of trees along a road) to form, far away, toward the misty horizon, above the tree tops and the delicate factory chimneys, a suspended, motionless ceiling, until when you looked more carefully you realized that the whole drifting archipelago was imperceptibly sliding, sailing over the houses, the incredibly green turf, the little wood to the right of which the horses appeared at last, heading now toward the gate: no longer one, three or ten but, with the varicoloured and motley patches of the silks, the undulating tails, the arrogant gait of the animals on their tiny legs no thicker than twigs, a medieval apparition, a brilliant group in the distance (and not only in the distance, at the end of the turn, but as though advancing so to speak from the depth of time, across the brilliant fields of battle where, in the space of a sparkling afternoon, of a charge, of a gallop, kingdoms and the hands of princesses were lost or won): then Iglésia[3] saw him, he told them later, separate,

dissociated by the binoculars from the anonymous motley of the
colors, on that filly like a streak of pale bronze, and wearing the
black cap and that bright pink silk bordering on mauve that she had
somehow imposed on both of them (Iglésia and de Reixach) like a
kind of voluptuous and lascivious symbol like the colors of an
order or rather emblems of functions so to speak seminal and
turgescent, able to make out between the two (between the silk and
the cap) that perfectly inexpressive face, apparently empty of
emotions and of thoughts, not even concentrated or attentive: merely
impassive (Iglésia thinking, saying later: 'Well good God he could
have let me ride. It was to prove something, hell! What did he expect?
That after that she wouldn't sleep with anyone but him, that she'd go
without being screwed by the first man to come along simply because
she's seen him on her back? But if it hadn't been me it would have
been the same. Because she was in heat. And the weather didn't make
it any better. So even before she started she was soaked to the skin!
. . .') able to see as if he had been only a few yards away the filly's neck
covered with a grey lather at the place where the reins rubbed it, the
group, the hieratic and medieval group still heading for the stone
wall, having crossed the centre of the figure eight now, the horses
hidden again up to the belly by the border hedges, half disappearing
so that they seemed cut off half way up, only their backs still visible,
seeming to slide along the field of green corn like ducks on the
motionless surface of a pond, I could see them as they were turning
right he at the head of the bunch as if it had been July Fourteenth one
then two then three then the whole first group then the second the
horses calmly following each other like those petticoat horses
children used to play with those aquatic animals floating on their
bellies propelled by visible webbed feet flipping slowly one after the
other with their identical arched chess-piece necks their identical
riders with their identical arched bodies swaying half falling asleep
probably although it had been daylight for some time the sky pink
with dawn the countryside still half alseep too, there was a kind of
vaporous moistness there must have been dewdrops clinging to the
blades of grass which the sun would evaporate I could easily
recognize him in the distance out ahead by the way he had of sitting
straight up on his saddle contrasting with the other limp figures as if
for him fatigue simply didn't exist, about half the squadron caught
when they flowed back toward the crossroads like an accordion as
though under the pressure of an invisible piston pushing them back,
the last ones still advancing while the head of the column somehow

---

[3] De Reixach's jockey and Corinne's lover; later a cavalryman in Georges's
unit, and a fellow POW in Germany.

seemed to retract the noise coming only afterwards so that there was a moment (perhaps a fraction of a second but seeming longer) when in the complete silence there was only this: the little petticoat horses and their riders thrown back in disorder, one against the other, exactly like chess pieces collapsing in a row the sound when it came with that slight delay in time with the image itself exactly like the hollow sound of the ivory pieces drumming falling one after the other on the chessboard like this:tac-tac-tac-tac-tac the bursts of gunfire superimposed accumulating apparently then on top of us the invisible plucked guitar strings weaving the invisible chain of deadly silky torn air also I never heard the order shouted seeing only the bodies in front of me collapse closer and closer while the right legs moved one after the other over the rumps like the pages of a book flipped backward and once on the ground I looked for Wack[4] to hand him the bridle at the same time that my right hand was struggling behind my back with that damn rifle hook then it came on us from behind the thunder of hoofs the galloping of wild horses riderless now eyes huge ears flat stirrups empty the reins whipping the air twisting like serpents and two or three covered with blood and one with his rider still on his back screaming They're behind us too they let us get through and then they, the rest of his words carried away with him leaning over the neck his mouth wide open like a hole and now it was no longer with the rifle hook that I was struggling but against that nag trying to break away head high neck stiff as a mast the pupil entirely blank as though she were trying to look behind her ears stepping back not by fits and starts but so to speak methodically one foot after the other and me pulling at her hard enough to tear off her jaw saying All right All right as if she could even hear me in that racket gradually shortening the reins until I could reach her neck with one hand patting her repeating All right All right Theeeeeere . . . until she stopped, standing motionless but tense strained trembling in every limb her hoofs stiff and wide apart like stilts and probably there had been another order shouted while I was struggling with her because I realized (not seeing because I was too busy watching her but sensing, divining) in that disorder that uproar that they were all remounting getting close to her then (still as stiff as strained as if she had been made out of wood) as gently as possible watching carefully in case she kicked or reared or broke into a gallop just when I would have a foot in the stirrup but she still didn't move just trembling where she stood like a motor idling and she let me get my foot in the stirrup without doing a thing, only when I seized the pommel and the cantle to lift myself up the saddle turned over, I was expecting that too for three

[4] Another cavalryman.

days I had been trying to find a girth to exchange for this one that was
too long for her after I had had to leave Edgar behind but you can't
get a thing out of those peasants it was as if asking them to switch
girths was trying to rob them and Blum's[5] was too long too so it was
really the perfect moment for a thing like that to happen to me when
there was shooting on all sides at once but I didn't even have time to
swear not even enough breath not even enough time to get out a word
just enough to think of it while I was trying to get that damn saddle on
her back again in the middle of all those men who were passing
around me at a gallop now and then I saw that my hands were
trembling but I couldn't stop them any more than I could stop her
body from trembling I stopped trying I began running alongside her
by the bridle she starting to canter with the saddle now almost directly
under her belly among the horses—with riders or riderless—that were
passing us the deadly network of plucked guitar strings stretched like
a ceiling over our heads but it was only when I saw two or three fall
that I realized that I was in the ditch of the road while they were too
high on horseback so they got shot down like ninepins then I saw
Wack (things happening paradoxically enough in a kind of silence a
void in other words the sound of the bullets and the explosions—they
must have been using mortars now or those little tank cannons—once
accepted admitted and somehow forgotten neutralizing themselves
somehow you heard absolutely nothing no shouts no voices probably
because no one had time to shout so that it reminded me of when I
was running the 1500: only the whistling noise of the breathing the
swearing itself choked before it came out and then came a jostling as if
the lungs were seizing all the available air to distribute it through the
body and use it only for useful things: looking deciding running,
things consequently happening a little as though in a film without its
sound track), I saw Wack who had just passed me leaning over the
neck of his horse his face turned back toward me his mouth open too
probably trying to shout something which he didn't have air enough
to make heard and suddenly lifted off his saddle as if a hook an
invisible hand had grabbed him by his coat collar and slowly raised
him I mean almost motionless in relation to (I mean animated by
almost the same speed as) his horse that kept on galloping and me still
running although a little slower now so that Wack his horse and I
comprised a group of objects among which the distances were
modified only gradually he being now exactly over the horse from
which he had just been lifted wrenched slowly rising in the air his legs
still arched as though he were still riding some invisible Pegasus who
had bucked and made him fall slowing then and somehow making a

[5] Like Georges, a French POW in a German camp after the fall of France in
1940.

kind of double *salto mortale* on the spot so that I saw him next head down mouth still open on the same shout (or advice he had tried to give me) silent then lying in the air on his back like a man stretched out in a hammock and letting his legs hang down to the right and left then again head up body vertical his legs beginning to come together hanging parallel then on his stomach arms stretched forward hands open grabbing snatching something like one of those circus acrobats during the seconds when he is attached to nothing and liberated of all weight between the two trapezes then finally the head down again legs apart arms outstretched as though to bar the way but motionless now flat against the roadside slope and no longer moving staring at me his face stamped with a surprised and idiot expression I thought Poor Wack he always looked like a fool but now more than ever he, then I no longer thought, something like a mountain or a horse falling on me throwing me to the ground trampling me while I felt the reins wrenched out of my hands then everything went black while thousands of galloping horses went on passing over my body then I no longer even felt the horses only something like a smell of ether and the dark my ears buzzing and when I opened my eyes again I was lying on the road and not one horse and only Wack still on the slope head down still looking at me his eyes wide open with that shocked look but I was careful not to move waiting for the moment when I would begin to suffer having heard somewhere that the worst wounds create a kind of anesthesia at first but still feeling nothing and after a moment I tried to move but nothing happened managing to get onto my hands and knees my face toward the ground I could see the earth of the road the stones looking like triangles or irregular polygons of a slightly bluish white in their matrix of pale ochre earth there was something like a carpet of grass in the centre of the path then to the right and the left where the wheels of the cars and carts passed two bare ruts then the grass growing on the sides and raising my head I saw my shadow still very pale and fantastically elongated thinking Then the sun's up, and at that moment I was aware of the silence and I saw that just beyond Wack there was a man sitting on the roadside: he was holding his arm a little above the elbow his hand hanging all red between his legs but it wasn't a man from the squadron he said They've got us, I didn't answer he stopped paying any attention to me and went on looking at his hand, in the distance there were still a few bursts of gunfire I looked at the road behind us in the direction of the crossroads I saw brownish-yellow heaps on the ground that didn't move and horses and near us a horse lying on its side in a pool of blood its legs still twitching feebly, spasmodically then I sat down on the slope beside the man thinking But it was only just dawn, I said What time is it, but he didn't answer then there was a burst of gunfire very close this time I threw myself down into the ditch I heard the man say They've got us again, but I didn't turn around I crawled down the ditch to where the slope stopped and after that I began running bent double to a grove of trees but no one fired and no one fired when I ran from the grove of trees to a hedge I crawled through the hedge on my belly pulling myself out the other side by my hands lying flat until I managed to catch my breath again there wasn't any more firing now I heard a bird singing the shadows of the trees grew longer ahead of me across the meadow I crept on all fours along the hedge perpendicular to the shadows of the trees until the corner of the field then I began climbing up the hill on the other side of the meadow still on all fours against the hedge my shadow in front of me again now and when I was in the forest walking among the flakes of sunlight I was careful to keep the sun in front of me calculating as the time passed that I would have to keep it in front of me and slightly to the right at first later on to the right but still ahead of me, there were cuckoos in the forest other birds too I didn't know their names but especially cuckoos or maybe it was because I knew their name that I noticed them maybe too because of their more characteristic cry the sun through the leaves cast my leafy shadow that moved on ahead of me then slightly to the right, walking a long time without hearing anything except the cuckoos and those birds whose names I didn't know, finally I got tired of walking through the woods all the time and followed a path but my shadow was on my left then, a moment later I found a path that crossed it I took that one and my shadow was ahead of me again and to the right but I calculated I should follow it longer than the first one to compensate for the digression I had had to make and then I was hungry and I remembered the piece of sausage I was carrying around in my coat pocket I ate it while I was walking I ate the skin too down to the stub knotted by the thread I threw that away then the forest stopped collided so to speak with the empty sky opening on a pool and when I lay down to drink the little frogs jumped in they didn't make any more noise than big raindrops: near the edge where they had jumped in a tiny cloud of gray mud hung in the water then dissolved between the reeds they were green and no bigger around than my little finger the surface of the water was covered with little round pale-green leaves about the size of confetti that was why it took me a moment to realize they were coming back I saw one then two then three breaking the pale green confetti letting just the tips of their heads stick out with their bulging eyes like pin-heads staring at me there was a faint current and I saw one drifting slowly letting itself be carried between the archipelagoes of agglutinated confetti the same colour as it was it looked like a drowned man its arms outstretched the head half out of the water the delicate little webbed hands open then it moved and I didn't see it any more I mean I didn't even see it move, it simply wasn't there any more except for the tiny cloud of mud it had stirred up, the water was viscous with a viscous fishy taste I pushed aside the little confetti when I drank being careful not to drink the mud my face raised among the reeds and the broad lance-shaped leaves then I stayed there sitting at the edge of the woods behind the thickets listening to the cuckoos calling to each other among the silent tree trunks in the spring green air looking at the road that followed the pond and then skirted the trees from time to time a fish jumped with a plop I never saw one, only the concentric circles growing wider and wider around the place where it had jumped once some planes passed over but very high in the sky I saw one or rather something a silver point hanging motionless sparkling a fraction of a second in a blue hole between the branches then disappearing their noise seemed to be suspended too vibrating in the light air then it gradually faded and again I could hear the delicate rustling of the leaves and again the song of a cuckoo and a little after at the turn of the road two officers came out walking their horses but maybe they didn't know there was a war on they were walking calmly in step chatting when I saw they were wearing khaki and not green I stood up thinking of the face they would make when they saw me and when I told them that the panzers were strolling up the road six or seven kilometers from here probably someone had forgotten to warn them I stood up in the middle of the road in the woodland peace where I could still hear the cuckoos and occasionally the sudden invisible and lazy leap of a fish out of the unalterable mirror of the pond then I thought Good God good God good God good God, recognizing him recognizing the voice that reached me now or rather that fell on me arrogant distant calm with something playful almost gay in it saying So you managed to get out of it too? saying as he turned toward the short second-lieutenant You see they're not all dead There are still some who got out, saying again in my direction Iglésia's leading two horses You take one, I could hear the water murmuring where the pond made a little waterfall the rustling of the leaves stirred by the imperceptible breeze, on a level with my eyes I saw the knees press almost imperceptibly and the horse start forward passing in front of me the boots sparkling the mahogany flanks covered with dried sweat the rump the tail then again the calm pond across which the breeze stirred the broad lance-shaped leaves with a papery rustle his voice as he moved away reaching me again (but it was not me he was talking to now he had resumed his conversation with the short second-lieutenant and I could hear him slightly bored distinguished nonchalant) saying: . . . bad business. Apparently they use those tanks as. . . , then he was too far away I had forgotten that such things are merely called a 'business' the way you say 'that business' when you mean 'fighting a duel' a delicate euphemism a discreeter more elegant formula well so much the better not all was lost since we were still among well-bred people say don't say, example don't say 'the squadron has been massacred in an ambush', but 'we had a bad business outside the village of' then Iglésia's voice and his clown's face looking at me with his round eyes his offended impatient and vaguely reproving expression saying Then you're riding yes or no? All the time I've been dragging these two nags behind me, it isn't funny I can tell you! I got in the saddle and followed them I had to trot to catch up with Iglésia then I slowed the horse down to a walk I could see him from the back now with that little second-lieutenant beside him walking calmly the horses moving with that tremendous slowness, that complete absence of haste that you find only in those beings or things (boxers, serpents, planes) capable of striking, moving or changing position with lightning-like speed, the sky, the calm cottony clouds still drifting by at a speed that was also almost imperceptible in the opposite direction (so that between the graceful, medieval and elegant silhouettes that kept advancing toward the right where, with his whip in his hand, the starter was waiting for them, and the clouds, one of those infuriating slowness contests seemed to be in progress, a demonstration in which each entrant vied with the rest for majesty, unconcerned with that feverish and futile impatience that made the crowd seethe: the stiff, delicate and foolish thorough-breds, capable not of reaching but of becoming in the wink of an eye something not released at a tremendous speed but which would be speed itself, the slow clouds like those proud armadas apparently resting motionless on the sea and which seem to move by leaps and bounds at a fantastic speed, the eye exhausted by their apparent immobility abandoning them, discovering them a moment later, still apparently motionless, at the other end of the horizon, thus covering fabulous distances while beneath them, tiny and ridiculous, parade cities, hills, woods, and under which, without their ever seeming to have moved, still majestic, puffy and imponderable, still other cities, other woods, other absurd hills would parade, long after the horses, the public had abandoned the racetrack, the grandstand, the green turf speckled and soiled by the thousands of betting tickets lost like so many tiny still born corpses of dreams and hopes (the marriage not of heaven and earth but of earth and man, leaving it soiled by the persistence of that residue, of that kind of giant and foetal pollution of tiny furiously torn scraps of paper), long after the last horse had kicked up the last clod of the turf and had left, surrounded by more servants, more attentions, precautions and care for its nerves than a movie star, and the echo of the last and furious cries had fallen over the silent stands abandoned to the clean-up crews, no longer echoing save to the faint and prosaic rustle of the brooms), Corinne no longer watching what was happening at the end of the turn, stamping furiously again, saying: 'Couldn't you stop watching for a second? Do you hear me? There's nothing to see now. They're going back to the gate. They . . . Do you hear me, or don't you?' and he reluctantly taking the binoculars away from his face, turning his great fish eyes toward her, the lids blinking, the pupils cloudy, a little blurred from the effort he was making to focus at this proximity, saying in his frail, timid, whining voice: 'You . . . You shouldn't have. He . . . ,' his voice dying away, swallowed up, submerged (beneath the brutal and piercing ringing of the bell) by the kind of long sigh rising from the relieved crowd, swooning and voracious (not exactly an orgasm, but somehow a pre-orgasm, something like the moment when the man penetrates the woman), while far in the distance, they could see now a kind of elongated and motley blur moving quickly across the turf, at the level of the ground, the horses shifting without transition from their casual semi-immobility to movement, the bunch running fast without fits and starts, as though it were mounted on a wire or on rollers, like those children's toys, all the horses soldered together in a single block cut out of a piece of cardboard or painted tin that was being slid along the slot arranged for this purpose in a *trompe-l'oeil* painted and varnished landscape, the jockeys all leaning forward at the same angle, the horses hidden up to the belly by the border hedges: then they came out onto the junction of the track and for a moment you could see their legs coming and going fast, like compasses opening and closing, but always to the same mechanical, regular and abstract rhythm of a spring-operated toy; then again there was nothing else to see, behind the little wood, except for the silks passing behind the tree trunks the branches like a handful of confetti and which seemed—perhaps because of their material, their brilliant colors—to gather up, to concentrate in themselves all the sparkling light of the dazzling afternoon, the tiny pink spot (and yet under which there was a man's body, the flesh, the tense muscles, the tumultuous afflux of blood, the organs abused and forced) in fourth position:

'Because after all he knew how to ride. Have to give him his due: he knew what he was doing. Because he had got off to a damn good start,' Iglésia told them later; now they were crouching all three of them (Georges, Blum and he: the two young men and that Italian (or Spaniard) with olive skin and who himself had almost as many years behind him as the first two together, and probably something like ten times their experience, which must have made about thirty times that of Georges because despite the fact that he and Blum were both apparently of the same age Blum possessed by heredity a knowledge (intelligence Georges had said, but it wasn't only that: still more: the intimate atavistic experience, which had passed to the reflex stage, of human stupidity and wickedness) of things that were worth a good three times what a young man of good family could have gained from the study of the classical French Latin and Greek authors, plus ten days of combat, or rather of retreat, or rather of a chase, where he—the young man of good family—had played the role of the game), all three, then, as different in age as in origin collected here from the four corners of the world ('All we need is a Negro,' Georges said. 'What have we got already? Shem, Ham and Japhet, but we needed a fourth; we should have invited him: after all, it was harder to find this mess and bring it all here than to take off a wristwatch!') crouching in that corner of the still unfinished camp behind piles of bricks and Iglésia cooking over a fire something they had stolen or bartered for (this time a part of the contents of a sack of flour Georges had received in exchange for his watch—the one that had been given to him by his two old aunts Marie and Eugénie[6] when he had been awarded his first diploma—from, as it happened, a Negro—a Senegalese from the Colonial Regiment—who himself had pinched it God knows where (as had been pinched God knows where and brought into the camp God knows why—to what end? probably on the off chance, for the superstitious pleasure of stealing, possessing and keeping—everything that could be found to sell, to buy or to barter, that is almost anything, the whole stock—and even more—of a department store, notions counter, antiques and staples included: not only useful or edible things—like the sack of flour—but even things without utility and even bothersome, and even incongruous things, like women's stockings or books on philosophy, false jewels, tourist guide-books, obscene photographs, parasols, tennis rackets, agricultural pamphlets, loudspeakers, tulip bulbs, accordions, bird-cages—sometimes with the bird inside—, bronze Eiffel towers, clocks, preservatives, not to mention of course thousands of watches, chronometers, pig-skin, crocodile or vulgar leather wallets that constituted the common coin of this realm, objects, relics, spoils painfully lugged kilometer after kilometer by hordes of exhausted and famished men, and hidden, concealed from searches, preserved despite prohibitions and threats, reappearing incoercibly for furtive, clandestine, feverish and hard bargainings whose object was most often not so much to acquire as to have something to sell or to buy), which, given the value of the watch, set on the pancake (for that was what Iglésia was making, pouring out on a piece of rusted iron the

[6] characters who figure prominently in Simon's preceding novel, *The Grass* (1958).

paste made of water, flour and a little of that coal-oil margarine distributed to the prisoners in tiny slices), a price which no proprietor of a three-star restaurant would have dared ask for a serving of caviar,—so all three of them (one crouching, the other two keeping watch), like three famished vagabonds in one of those empty lots on the outskirts of cities . . .

Translated by Richard Howard

Histoire (1967)

The 'trigger' which starts this novel off is not, as in *The Flanders Road*, a supposedly historical event, but a collection of postcards which the hero-narrator (who is not named but who is related to the same family as Georges was) finds in an old family chest he is forced to sell to pay his debts. He is particularly moved by a card which his mother, recently pregnant with him, sent home from her honeymoon trip on the eve of World War One. It is this card which provides the poignant note on which the novel, and our extract, ends.

(J.F.)

fool to send her that card VISTA PANORAMICA imagining what not daring to put Baronne de Reixach simply Madame and not the particle I suppose she would have found that simply repugnant but he only pensive asking me what kind of weapons they had knowing himself to be already dead perhaps or perhaps having already decided to die in that old-fashioned way he too brandishing a ridiculous weapon doubtless preferring that more elegant means than a revolver or swallowing

but really everyone uses them everyone takes it's for exams everyone

well you will not and that's all there is to it

don't shout like that stop shouting what's the matter with you stop shouting like that you

suddenly he turned his back on her crossed the room and walked out

really what's the matter with him? Corinne said She turned toward Grand-mère What's all the fuss about a few

all right now Grand-mère said

what's Now why are you crying

I'm not crying

you're not crying?

you know when I have a cold my eyes water

since when do you have a cold? Now what's this . . . She knelt down

in front of Grand-mère Now you better tell me what all this is about
what is it

nothing Grand-mère said Kiss me

but what

darling Grand-mère said never take those things or anything like
them again it ruins your health

but I have my exams in two weeks sometimes I study all But what's
going on here

where did I put that handkerchief Grand-mère said I'm not crying
Grand-mère please

go get a handkerchief in my room please go on You know where
they are in the top drawer of the chest

Grand-mère

run darling please go now be nice

she stood up stared at Grand-mère without a word then bent
forward and kissed her For a moment they stood there in each other's
arms then she turned and walked out of the room Grand-mère and I
were left alone I didn't move but went on turning the pages of
Illustration VISIONS OF THE FAR EAST Japanese Women
Dancing the first two on the right apparently wrestling facing each
other leaning toward each other arms outstretched foreheads bound
with white ribbons four others standing behind the one on the left
each with her hands resting on the kimono sash of the one in front of
her each leaning a little to one side as though to get a better view of the
two wrestlers the kimonos striped or decorated with large patterns or
scattered with tiny flowers breasts almost bluish in the shadow
between the coral folds they parted

so pretty?

MILANO. Palazzo Brera. Mantegna. Pietà: lying in a fore-
shortened position a shroud covering him only to the waist the folds
of the material running flat first over the slab on which he is lying then
rising over the body, mounting obliquely passing over the flat belly
then down again, flat again on the slab, and finally falling in vertical
folds on the other side the pierced bare feet sticking into the
foreground parted in a V so that the belly over which it swells a little
appears a slight bulge over the sex the shroud sinks between the two
legs forming first a narrow valley which widens though it touches the
slab only when it is quite close to the feet in the rather wide interval
between the ankles

detecting faint moist sounds as if she were swallowing I didn't look
up I could hear it streaming the silence flowing not knowing what to
do in order not to see her Corinne didn't come back down After a
moment Grand-mère said My darling

yes Grand-mère

would you . . . Her voice cracked stopped I could still hear the same tiny sounds She was sitting near the window her back to the light It had always been her chair her place near the window knitting or reading her mail her letters

reading My dear Maman we've been here an hour We won't be going ashore until after lunch it's already ten o'clock and we don't leave until four Life on deck moreover is fascinating there are all kinds of people selling things and native children shouting and diving off the deck for pennies Henri and I send a thousand kisses

Life on deck Already affectedly talking in maritime terms A little like argot An initiate Vague and piquant impression Calculating the effect made on the family her friends to whom Grand-mère would read the . . . Or perhaps out of love . . . Dissolving uniting or rather identifying herself with him who was accustomed to those steamers to those cargoes of colonials of moustachioed and malarial officers with their linen tunics their accordion-wrinkled trousers arrogant susceptible with their dry faces their black hair like some kind of wading bird and she gently fanning herself half stretched out in a chaise-longue on the promenade deck in the shelter of the canvas awning being told that because he had forgotten to wear his pith helmet crossing the Red Sea a passenger had died on the spot her own embellished with one of those light gauze scarves spinach-green or pink carelessly knotted Eyes half-closed radiant content Fanning herself Lazily watching the naked little black boys their bodies shaped like lima beans with protruding buttocks and bellies Tiny monkeys Would you like to see them dive? Cool sounds of the water splashing They say that sometimes a shark secret smooth shadow sliding motionless under the transparent gray-green surface and the jonquil network of shifting sunshine through the water playing over . . .

do you want me to get your handkerchief I said

my darling she said you're . . . yes that's sweet thank you

I stood up and walked to the door

my darling she said

I turned around

would you . . . It's almost time for her lesson Tell her it's almost time she was

I opened the door

just knock don't go in Tell her it's almost time she

she had locked herself in I knocked no answer

why didn't you bring down her handkerchief do you hear me Grand-mère says it's almost time for your

go away

did you hear me you've got to

leave me alone
Corinne
go away you hear me leave me alone leave me alone all of you leave me alone

I stood there a moment in the hall I could hear vague muffled noises in the pillow she must have been lying on her bed Once or twice more I tried turning the handle Corinne! She kept silent I left It was only Maman who could get anything out of her But already too sick by then stuffed with morphine she slept almost all the time out of reach then having already endured everything somnambulistic and serene perhaps having reached (or returned to) an eternal felicity among the curving palm trees interlacing swaying their pendent crests against the pale sky pale mountainsides ringing a gulf of pale water a group of figures with black faces dressed in white shirts and trousers and with broad hats two of them on the right holding little donkeys by the bridle among the patches of sunlight and shade and pasted on the right of the second little donkey the eternal bald and crowned profile olive-green this time and framed with the caption POSTAGE repeated on the two vertical strips on each side of the medallion the imperial crown overlapping the word SEYCHELLES the caption of the card in tiny red letters running among the shadows the sand the sparkling vegetation what happiness what a dream: FELICITE ISLAND—COCONUT OIL-MILL and on the back the jagged arrogant handwriting as rigid in pleasure in voluptuousness as in the years of virginity overlapping the printed letters (CARTE POSTALE—POST KARTE—POST CARD—TARJETA POSTALE, Published by Mr. S. S. Ohashi, Seychelles—Printed in Germany):

Dear Maman
We're at Mahu now and it's raining torrents. I'm writing you from the shop of some sort of merchant. It's too bad about the weather, for the stop here would have been so pretty. This magnificent tropical vegetation enchants me. I won't mail a letter here because they say it would only leave later from Diego. Henry is fine and sends his love and kisses with mine

the rain falling overwhelming echoing and gray on the palm trees the opal gulf the little donkeys the men with their ebony faces their soaking shirts and trousers gray now sticking to their skinny limbs with those paler folds winding interlacing like a network of roots the warm rain it's too bad the torrential sound the huge drops on the leaves taking refuge in the shop of some kind of merchant probably the one who had sold her the postcard a Mr S. S. Ohashi with yellow skin watching her writing on a corner of a table or the counter the lady bending over, her mysterious bust of white flesh swathed in lace

that bosom which already perhaps was bearing me in its shadowy
tabernacle a kind of gelatinous tadpole coiled around itself with its
two enormous eyes its silkworm head its toothless mouth its
cartilaginous insect's forehead, me? . . .

(Translated by Richard Howard)

Triptych (1973)

Claude Simon's most recent novel is based to some extent on childhood memories of the Jura mountains in Eastern France, where one branch of his family lived.

In *Triptych*, three separate and distinct stories are told, not consecutively as in Flaubert's volume *Three Tales*, but concurrently, with little to indicate that the text has switched gear. The unprepared reader is all the more likely to be misled, because the book is divided into three parts; but these are purely arbitrary divisions and bear no relation to the subject matter, the divisions being made simply to divide the text into three parts, and thus make the book resemble a triptych (as in painting), physically as well as metaphorically. The reconstitution of the various events is provoked and pressed forward by generative elements, and the text shunts off along this track or that solely according to the principle of association. We usually know where we are, or rather which story we are in, by sounds which are reported and which serve as a kind of signature tune. In the case of the tale set in a wooded river area in the country, it is a church bell, and the sequences dealing with the wedding in an industrial suburb are marked by references to the noises made by a nearby railway junction.

The stories making up the 'triptych' can even be told in reverse, like a film run backwards through the projector; the narrator imagines the reader doing the same, coming back in search of a passage misread or not paid proper attention to. In this novel, the reader is addressed not by a narrator so much as by the text itself. The narrator has become coextensive with the author; but in the process the author himself is fictionalised out of existence, and the text is, in a literal sense, its own generator.

It might even seem to be frankly itself as a stylistic rag-bag. Parts of it are written in the earlier Simon manner (with participles, parentheses and elaborate analogies), but other sections read like pastiche of Robbe-Grillet, with the same dead-pan pseudo-scientific precision in descriptions, the same painstaking, gradual reconstruction scenes whose initial innocence quickly evaporates before the all-pervading menace of the situation which is ultimately revealed. The tone is distinctly cool, even bland; perhaps surprisingly, *Triptych* turns out to be a powerfully erotic book, though hardly a titillating one. Simon's vision of sexuality is that it is a tragic, not a joyful activity. He associates the paroxysm which terminates every embrace with the last spasm of death: the two capital experiences of the human body—coitus and agony—are so closely related that sex can hardly ever be happy: it merely serves to emphasize the transience of human beings compared with the permanence of nature. In *Triptych* eroticism—and there is a lot of it—is truly desperate; the visceral, abundant, organic world of this book is haunted by the tragic awareness that man, imprisoned in duration, subject to the incoherent dilapidations wrought by time, tries in vain to free himself from chronology through the medium of erotic transcendence. But one glimmer of hope is left for the reader: he is privileged to contemplate the work of art which seals as it magnificently repudiates our irremediable and ineluctable failure to overcome time.

In this extract, taken from near the end of the novel, we start with the suburb scene (though with some interference from an 'esplanade' episode), then move to a country barn where a couple make love, and in the last sentence jump to a cinema screen which soon after the end of the excerpt projects images of a circus turn.

(J.F.)

Finally the moon-faced mask moves again, and stepping over the border of boxwood around the esplanade, the young man unsteadily makes his way toward the terrace. As he comes forward into the light, his wan face seems to grow paler still, at the same time taking on a greenish tinge which makes the trickles of dried blood on it appear almost black. Black trickles also stain the rumpled front of his shirt, the buttons of which have been torn off. The other end of the bow tie hangs out at his back, between the collar of his shirt and the collar of his tuxedo jacket, dangling down over the latter. Despite the precautions he is taking, the gravel crunches beneath the young man's feet, but no light appears in any of the windows. The diffuse light of the city illuminates the ceiling of low clouds drifting rapidly along above the network of criss-crossing black branches, the highest of which sway back and forth and bump together. From time to time the sound of a locomotive whistle or dull rumblings is carried on the wind. Once the shadow of the south slope has covered the barn, the half-shadow inside has grown darker and darker. Sitting up, her torso erect, her two legs pressed together and bent at the knee, the girl rearranges her rumpled hair, searching round about her on the old army overcoat for the hairpins with scalloped sides which she slips between her lips before taking them out one by one to pin down her straggling locks. Her movements reveal the tufts of hairs in her armpits stuck together with sweat, and her breasts sway slightly. The man with the curly hair is still lying on his back, his slightly parted legs stretched out, hampered by his blue cotton duck pants pulled down to his knees, forming accordion pleats above his black rubber boots streaked with grayish trickles of mud. His limp member is lying on its side, stretching across his groin and partway up the top of his thigh. His left arm idly circles the girl's waist and his hand mounts and descends along her side, caressing her hip, slipping one finger in the fold of her waist, then mounting again from time to time to her breast, the knuckles lightly touching its tip. Letting go of her hair, the girl's left hand descends, grasps the man's hand, and pushes it away from her body. The moment she lets go of it, however, it alights on her body once again, the girl pushing it away this time with a brusque gesture, and then, lowering her other arm and leaning on it, she shifts her buttocks, her head lowered now, searching around again on the army coat for the hairpins that have fallen out of her lips, protesting, still trying by means of little annoyed slaps to push away the hand, the back of which is now rubbing back and forth across the nipple of her right breast. In this new position, the entire weight of her body is resting on her right buttock and her right thigh lying flat on the floor, her two legs pressed together and bent to one side, the line of her spinal column forming a curve that begins at her lower back and rises almost vertically between her shoulder blades, the skin at her waist above her jutting hip forming three folds, and the bottom of her buttocks having turned a rosy pink beneath the weight of her body in the previous position. Against the body that glows luminously in the denser and denser shadow, the hand caressing it appears almost black. For a moment, taking advantage of the fact that the girl is busy fumbling about for her hairpins, the man brushes his hand back and forth across the curve of her breast more insistently, as though to test its elasticity, the supple flesh forming a slight hollow as the hand passes over it and then bounding back as the tip of the nipple gradually grows hard. As though possessed of a life of its own, the man's member lying across his groin begins to stir, animated by faint little quivers that cause it first to roll over the top of his thigh and then to swell and harden, gradually growing longer in a series of minute jerking motions. Encircled by the wrinkled crown of the foreskin, the pink tip of the glans appears, pierced with its little blind eye. Abandoning the breast, the hand brusquely buries itself between the girl's thighs pressed close together, attempting to thrust itself between them, fumbling about in the hairs, the girl giving a start and saying No, that's enough, drawing her buttocks back with an abrupt motion, rising up on her knees, stretching one arm out toward her clothes hanging on a part of the tractor that juts out, the man's two dark hands darting out and coming together around her hips at the same moment, the man's arms thrusting sideways with such a violent motion that it causes the girl to fall over on her side, the two bodies collapsing one on top of the other, the girl pushing the man's shoulders away with her outstretched arms, arching her back, the man's hands, taken by surprise by the suddenness of the motion, moving apart, letting go, the girl leaning on her extended right arm, bending her left leg back, then her right, then crouching on her knees with her buttocks thrust out, and finally standing up, the man's two hands, looking light-colored now against the black stockings, seizing her by the ankles and pulling her brutally off-balance, so that she topples over, as though mowed down by a scythe, on all fours on top of the torso of the man, who, taking advantage of her position, roughly pulls her knees apart and buries his head between her thighs, his rod, once again stiff and erect, now jutting out at an acute angle to his belly, with bluish veins snaking beneath the delicate skin of the sheath, the girl's protests dying away little by little, being gradually replaced by the sound of her breathing, growing faster and faster, her body inertly yielding, with only her haunches and her back swaying back and forth in faint undulations corresponding to the movements of the dark curly head of hair, like a ball between the phosphorescent thighs. The surface of the screen is separated lengthwise by a white, slightly curved band, dividing it into two unequal parts.

(Translated by Helen R. Lane)

MARGUERITE DURAS

Marguerite Duras was born in 1914 in Indochina where she was educated until the age of eighteen. Until 1941 she worked for the Colonial Ministry, publishing her first novel *Les Impudents* in 1943. A member of the Resistance, she joined the Communist Party in 1945, leaving it ten years later because she found party discipline incompatible with literary creativity. Since then she has written novels, stage- and the screen-plays, often reworking the same story for different media. Her special technique is to give the reader an insight into emotion and behaviour by oblique comparison to a totally different event with which the reader will more easily identify, or through describing behaviour where her characters give themselves away. She formally identified herself with the *Nouveau Roman* by insisting that *Moderato Cantabile* (1958) should be published by *Les Editions de Minuit*, but she has since fluctuated between insistence on her individuality outside any school and her desire to identify with this group.

In *The Square* (1955), a travelling salesman and a housemaid meet in a public park. They describe their lives to each other and their shared loneliness turns to warmth with the possibility that they might meet again. In her short novel *The Afternoon of Monsieur Andesmas* (1962) an old man Monsieur Andesmas is waiting on a hot afternoon for the visit of an architect who is to make an addition to the house which he has built for his daughter. But the architect never comes and M. Andesmas gradually realizes from the bits of news that reach him and the sounds coming up from the village that he will not come that afternoon, that he is in fact with his daughter, and a sadness descends upon him as he begins to realize that he is forgotten, and will soon be totally forgotten, as his end is near. In this beautiful novella Marguerite Duras brings her particular technique to an astonishing fulfilment, conveying the loneliness of old age and the presence of death through the description of a hot summer afternoon in the Mediterranean and the thoughtless gaiety of the young. In *Moderato Cantabile*, which Peter Brook filmed, she portrays an affluent but bored housewife who having witnessed a *crime passionel*, the killing of a young woman by her lover, compulsively returns day after day to the scene. She meets one of her husband's factory workers and questions him about the crime until he is forced to speculate about the lives and motives of the protagonists. As he falls in love with her, it becomes apparent that her fascination is with the killing and that she is inviting him to re-enact the crime. In *Ten-thirty on a Summer Night* (1967) another wife identifies in her mind the realization that her husband is starting an affair with her best friend with the discovery that a wanted criminal is hiding on the rooftop near her. Her efforts to hide and protect the criminal are part of the need to protect her own emotions.

In the cinema there has been a political edge to Marguerite Duras's scenarios. In *Hiroshima, Mon Amour* (1960) she contrasts the horror created by the first atom bomb with the smaller but no less poignant tragedy of a love affair between a young French girl and a German soldier that inevitably ends in disaster. In *Une Aussi Longue Absence* (1961) she obliquely expresses her hostility to the Algerian war, successfully evading the censorship of that time by centring her pacifist sentiments around the plight of a casualty of the last world war. More recently she has concentrated on the theatre and has made her own films. Through both media she explores the nuances of love, memory and human weakness with a perception which is always highly original and ambiguous. Although she is closely associated with the women's liberation movement in France and has always been politically active, her work is not overtly militant but an attempt to understand and convey understanding. Notable among more recent work are the film *India Song*, originally written as a play for Peter Hall, in which far away past events in Asia dominate the conversation and contrast totally with an all night dancing party in a French house that the camera shows us; and the play *Eden Cinema* where she portrays the mutual frustrations of a colonial mother struggling against inhospitable soil to support herself, and those of her daughter whom she wishes to drive into the arms of a rich landowner against her wishes. The part of the mother has been one of the most triumphant of the many remarkable characterizations of Madeleine Renaud, who has a special sympathy with this period and style of literature.

Although Marguerite Duras disclaims the intellectual outlook of the *nouveau roman* and brings a poetic approach to her work that subtly enables us to realize the stresses and events that have made her characters what they are—her work stands out in sharp contrast to the psychological puzzles of Robbe-Grillet's work and the manner-ism of Nathalie Sarraute—her technique is nevertheless intellectually conceived. It is the easier readability, the warmth, and perhaps above all the appeal to women readers that accounts for the greater popularity and larger sales than can be claimed by any other writer presented in this volume. She also has a cinema public.

The two extracts from her work given in this volume are from *The*

Square and *Moderato Cantabile*. There are only two characters in the novel (which many people know from its stage version), a travelling salesman and a young girl who works as the companion, nanny and maid of all work in a household where she is extremely unhappy. They meet in a park, talk a while and separate, having described their lives. The man talks of his life, remembering the blissful place by the sea that has remained in his memory, but which in the author's description describes happiness.

The other extract, a chapter from *Moderato Cantabile*, describes a dinner party. Anne Desbaresdes, having spent the afternoon in the café where she witnessed the crime in question, and having drunk too much while interrogating the workman whom she now daily meets there, has to cope with a formal dinner, while outside the workman roams around, hoping for a glimpse of her. It is a chapter that enables the author to portray devastatingly a milieu from which she once escaped, while conveying her heroine's increasing death wish.

(J.C.)

The Square (1955)

'I should like to tell you how I went into that town, after leaving my suitcase at the hotel.'

'Yes I should like to hear that. But you mustn't worry on my account: I would be most surprised if I let myself become impatient. I think all the time of the risk I would run if that should happen and so, you see, I don't think it will.'

'I did not manage to leave my suitcase until the evening. . . .'

'You see people like me do think too. There is nothing else for us to do, buried in our work. We think a great deal, but not like you. We have dark thoughts, and all the time.'

'It was evening, just before dinner, after work.'

'People like me think the same things of the same people and our thoughts are always bad. That's why we are so careful and why it's not worth bothering about us. You were talking of jobs, and I wonder if something could be called a job which makes you spend your whole day thinking ill of people? But you were saying it was evening, and you had left your suitcase?'

'Yes. It was only towards the evening, after I had left my suitcase at the hotel, just before dinner, that I started walking through that town. I was looking for a restaurant and of course it's not always easy to find exactly what one wants when price is a consideration. And while I was looking I strayed away from the centre and came by accident to the Zoo. A wind has risen. People had forgotten the day's work and were strolling through the gardens which, as I told you, were up on a hill overlooking the town.'

'But I know that life is good. Otherwise why on earth should I take so much trouble.'

'I don't really know what happened. The moment I entered those gardens I was a man overwhelmed by a sense of living.'

'How could a garden, just seeing a garden, make a man happy?'

'And yet what I am telling you is quite an ordinary experience and other people will often tell you similar things in the course of your life. I am a person for whom talking, for example, feeling at one with other people, is a blessing, and suddenly in that garden I was so completely at home, so much at my ease, that it might have been made specially for me although it was an ordinary public garden. I don't know how to put it any better, except perhaps to say that it was as if I had achieved something and become, for the first time, equal to my life. I could not bear to leave it. The wind had risen, the light was honey-coloured and even the lions whose manes glowed in the setting sun were yawning with the pure pleasure of being there. The air smelt of lions and of fire and I breathed it as if it were the essence of friendliness which had, at last, included me. All the passers-by were preoccupied with each other, basking in the evening light. I remember thinking they were like the lions. And suddenly I was happy.'

'But in what way were you happy? Like someone resting? Like someone who is cool again after having been very hot? Or happy as other people are happy every day?'

'More than that I think. Probably because I was unused to happiness. A great surge of feeling overwhelmed me, and I did not know what to do with it.'

'A feeling which hurt?'

'Perhaps so, yes. It hurt because there seemed to be nothing which could ever appease it.'

'But that, I think, is hope.'

'Yes that is hope, I know that really is hope. And of what? Of nothing. Just the hope of hope.'

'You know if there were only people like you in the world, no one would get anywhere.'

'But listen. You could see the sea from the bottom of each avenue in that garden, every single one led to the sea. Actually the sea really plays very little part in my life, but in that garden they were all looking at the sea, even the people who were born there, even it seemed to me, the lions themselves. How can you avoid looking at what other people are looking at, even if normally it doesn't mean much to you.'

'The sea couldn't have been as blue as all that since you said the sun was setting?'

'When I left my hotel it was blue but after I had been in that garden a little while it became darker and calmer.'

'But you said a wind had come up: it couldn't have been as calm as all that?'

'But it was such a gentle wind, if you only knew, and it was probably only blowing on the heights: on the town and not on the plain. I don't remember exactly from which direction it came, but surely not from the open sea.'

'And then again, the setting sun couldn't have illuminated all the lions. Not unless all the cages faced the same way on the same side of the garden looking into the sun?'

'And yet I promise you it was like that. They were all in the same place and the setting sun lit up each lion without exception.'

'And so the sun did set first over the sea?'

'Yes, you're quite right. The city and the garden were still in sunshine although the sea was in shade. That was three years ago. That's why I remember it all so well and like talking about it.'

'I understand. One thinks one can get by without talking, but it's not possible. From time to time I find myself talking to strangers too, just as we are talking now.'

'When people need to talk it can be felt very strongly, and strangely enough people in general seem to resent it. It is only in Squares that it seems quite natural. Tell me again, you said there were eight rooms where you worked? Big rooms?'

'I couldn't really say since I don't suppose anyone else would see them in quite the same way as I do. Most of the time they seem big, but perhaps they're not as big as all that. It really depends. On some days they seem endless and on others I think I could stifle they seem so tiny. But why did you ask?'

'It was only out of curiosity. For no other reason.'

'I know that I must seem stupid to you, but I can't help it.'

'I would say you are a very ambitious person, if I have really understood you, someone who wants everything that everyone else has, but wants it so much that one could almost say your desire is heroic.'

'That word doesn't frighten me, although I had not thought of it in that way. You could almost say I have so little that I could have anything. After all I could want to die with the same violence as I want to live. And is there anything, any one little thing in my life to which I could sacrifice my courage? And who or what could weaken it? Anyone would do the same as I do: anyone I mean who wanted what I want as much as I do.'

'I expect so. Since everyone does what he has to do. Yes I expect there are cases where it is impossible to be anything else but heroic.'

'You see if just once I refused the work they give me, no matter what it was, it would mean that I had begun to manage things, to defend myself, to take an interest in what I was doing. It would start with one thing, go on to another, and could end anywhere. I would begin to defend my rights so well that I would take them seriously and end by thinking they existed. They would matter to me. I wouldn't be bored any more and so I would be lost.'

There was a silence between them. The sun, which had been hidden by the clouds, came out again. Then the girl started talking once more.

'Did you stay on in that town after being so happy in that garden?'

'I stayed for several days. Sometimes I do stay longer than usual in a place.'

'Tell me, do you think that anyone can experience the feelings you had in that garden?'

'There must be some people who never do. It's an almost unbearable idea but I suppose there are such people.'

'You don't know for certain do you?'

'No. I can easily be mistaken. The fact is I really don't know.'

'And yet you seem to know about these things.'

'No more than anyone else.'

'There's something else I want to ask you: as the sun sets very quickly in those countries, surely, even if it set first on the sea, the shade must have reached the town soon afterwards? The sunset must have been over very soon, perhaps ten minutes after it had begun.'

'You are quite right and yet I assure you it was just at that moment that I arrived: just at the moment when everything is alight.'

'Oh, I believe you.'

'It doesn't sound as though you do.'

'But I do, completely. And anyway you could have arrived at any other moment without changing all that followed, couldn't you?'

'Yes, but I did arrive then, even if that moment only lasts for a few minutes a day.'

'But that isn't really the point.'

'No, that isn't really the point.'

'And afterwards?'

'Afterwards the garden was the same, except that it became night. A coolness came up from the sea and people were happy for the day had been hot.'

'But even so, eventually you had to eat?'

'Suddenly I was no longer very hungry. I was thirsty. I didn't have dinner that evening. Perhaps I just forgot about it.'

'But that's why you had left your hotel, to eat I mean?'

'Yes, but then I forgot about it.'

'For me, you see, the days are like the night.'

'But that is a little because you want them to be like that. You would like to emerge from your present situation just as you were when you entered it, as one wakes up from a long sleep. I know, of course, what it is to want to create night all around one but it seems to me that however hard one tries the dangers of the day break through.'

'Only my night is not as dark as all that and I doubt if the day is really a threat to it. I'm twenty. Nothing has happened to me yet. I sleep well. But one day I must wake up and for ever. It must happen.'

'And so each day is the same for you, even though they may be different?'

'Tonight, like every Thursday night, there will be people for dinner. I will eat chicken all alone in the kitchen.'

'And the murmur of their conversation will reach you the same way? So very much the same that you could imagine that each Thursday they said exactly the same things.'

'Yes, and as usual, I won't understand anything they talk about.'

'And you will be all alone, there in the kitchen, surrounded by the remnants of food in a sort of drowsy lull. And then you will be called to take away the meat plates and serve the next course.'

'They will ring for me, but they won't waken me. I serve at table half-asleep.'

'Just as they waited on, in absolute ignorance of what you might be like. And so in a way you are quits: they can neither make you happy nor sad, and so you sleep.'

'Yes. And then the guests will leave and the house will be quiet till the morning.'

'When you will start ignoring them all over again, while trying to wait on them as well as possible.'

'I expect so. But I sleep well! If you only knew how well I sleep. There is nothing they can do to disturb my sleep. But why are we talking about these things?'

'I don't know, perhaps just to make you remember them.'

'Perhaps it is that. But you see one day, yes one day, I shall go into the drawing-room and I shall speak.'

'Yes, you must.'

'I shall say: "this evening I shall not be serving dinner." Madam will turn round in surprise. And I will say: "why should I serve dinner since as from this evening . . . as from this evening" . . . but no, I cannot even imagine how things of such importance are said.'

The man made no reply. He seemed only attentive to the softness of the wind, which once more, had risen. The girl seemed to expect no response to what she had just said.

'Soon it will be summer,' said the man and added with a groan, 'We really are the lowest of the low.'

'It's said that someone has to be.'

'Yes, indeed and that everything has its place.'

'And yet sometimes one wonders why this should be so.'

'Why us rather than others?'

'Yes. Although sometimes, in cases like ours, one wonders whether it's being us or someone else makes any difference. Sometimes one just wonders.'

'Yes and sometimes, in certain instances, that is a consoling thought.'

'Not for me. That could never be a consoling thought. I must believe that I myself am concerned rather than anyone else. Without that belief I am lost.'

'Who knows? Perhaps things will soon change for you. Soon and very suddenly: perhaps even this very summer you will go into that drawing-room and announce that, as from that moment, the world can manage without your services.'

'Who knows indeed? And you could call it pride, but when I say the world, I really mean the whole world. Do you understand?'

'Yes I do.'

'I will open the door of that drawing-room and then, suddenly, everything will be said and for ever.'

'And you will always remember that moment as I remember my journey. I have never been on so wonderful a journey since, nor one which made me so happy.'

'Why are you suddenly so sad? Do you see anything sad in the fact that one day I must open that door? On the contrary doesn't it seem the most desirable thing in the world?'

'It seems utterly desirable to me, and even more than that. No, if I felt a little sad when you talked of it—and I did feel a little sad—it was only because once you have opened that door it will have been opened for ever, and afterwards you will never be able to do it again. And then, sometimes, it seems so hard, so very hard to go back to a country which pleased me as well as that one did, that occasionally I wonder if it would not have been better never to have seen it at all.'

'I wish I could, but you must see I cannot understand what it is like to have seen that city and to want to go back to it, nor can I understand the sadness you seem to feel at the thought of waiting for that moment. You could try as hard as you liked to tell me there was something sad about it, I could never understand. I know nothing, or rather I know nothing except this: that one day I must open that door and speak to those people.'

'Of course, of course. You mustn't take any notice of what I say. Those thoughts simply came into my mind when you were talking, but I didn't want them to discourage you, In fact quite the opposite. I'd like to ask you more about that door. What special moment are you waiting for, to open it? For instance why couldn't you do it this evening?'

'Alone I could never do it.'

'You mean that being without money or education you could only begin in the same way all over again and that really there would no point to it?'

'I mean that and other things. I don't really know how to describe it, but being alone I feel as if I had no meaning. I can't change by myself. No. I will go on visiting that Dance Hall and one day a man will ask me to be his wife. Then I will open that door. I couldn't do it before that happened.'

'How do you know if it would turn out like that if you have never tried?'

'I have tried. And because of that I know that alone . . . I would be, as I said, somehow meaningless. I wouldn't know any more what it was to want to change. I would simply be there, doing nothing, telling myself that nothing was worth while.'

'I think I see what you mean: in fact I believe I understand it all.'

'One day someone must choose me. Then I will be able to change. I don't mean this is true for everyone. I am simply saying it is true for me. I have already tried and I know. I don't know all this just because I know what it is like to be hungry, no, but because when I was hungry I realized I didn't care. I hardly knew who it was in me who was hungry.'

'I see all that: I can see how one could feel like that: in fact I can guess it although personally I have never felt the need to be singled out as you want to be; or perhaps I really mean that if such a thought ever did cross my mind I never attached much importance to it.'

'You must understand: you must try to understand that I have never been wanted by anyone, ever, except of course for my capacity for housework; and that is not choosing me as a person but simply wanting something impersonal which makes me as anonymous as possible. And so I must be wanted by someone, just once, and even if only once. Otherwise I shall exist so little even to myself that I would be incapable of knowing how to want to choose anything. That is why, you see, I attach so much importance to marriage.'

'Yes I do see and I follow what you are saying, but in spite of all that, and with the best will in the world, I cannot really see how you hope to be chosen when you cannot make a choice for yourself?'

'I know it seems ridiculous but that is how it is. Because you see, left to myself, I would find any man suitable: any man in the world would seem suitable on the one condition that he wanted me just a little. A man who so much as noticed me would seem desirable just for that very reason, and so how on earth would I be capable of knowing who would suit me when anyone would, on the one condition that they wanted me? No, it's impossible. Someone else must decide for me, must guess what would be best. Alone I could never know.'

'Even a child knows what is best for him.'

'But I am not a child, and if I let myself go and behaved like a child and gave in to the first temptation I came across—after all I am perfectly aware that it is there at every street corner—why then I would follow the first person who came along, the first man who just wanted me. And I would follow him simply for the pleasure I would have in being with him, and then, why then I would be lost, completely lost. You could say that I could easily make another kind of life for myself, but as you can see I no longer have the courage even to think of it.'

'But have you never thought that if you leave this choice entirely to another person it need not necessarily be the right one and might make for unhappiness later?'

'Yes I have thought of that a little, but I cannot think now, before my life has really begun, of the harm I might possibly do later on. I just say one thing to myself and that is: if the very fact of being alive means that we can do harm, however much we don't want to, just by choosing or making mistakes, if that is an inevitable state of affairs, why then, I too will go through with it. If I have to, if everyone has to, I can live with harm.'

'Please don't get so excited: there will be someone one day who will discover that you exist both for him and for others, you must be sure of that. And yet you know one can almost manage to live with this lack of which you speak.'

'Which lack? Of never being chosen?'

'If you like, yes. As far as I am concerned I should be so surprised if anyone chose me, that I should simply laugh.'

'While I should be in no way surprised. I am afraid I would find it perfectly natural. It is just the contrary which astonishes me, and it astonishes me more each day. I cannot understand it and I never get used to it.'

'It will happen. I promise you.'

'Thank you for saying so. But are you saying that just to please me, or can people tell these things? Can you guess it already just from talking to me?'

'I expect such things can be guessed, yes. To tell you the truth I said that without thinking much, but not at all because I thought it would please you. It must have been because I could see it.'

'And you? How are you so sure the opposite is true of you?'

'Well I suppose it is because. . . . Yes, just because I am not surprised. I think it must be that. I am not at all surprised that no one has chosen me, while you are so amazed that you have not yet been singled out.'

'In your place you know I would force myself to want something, however hard it might be. I would not remain as you are.'

'But what can I do? Since I don't feel this same need it could only come to me. . . . Well, from the outside. How else could it be?'

'You know you almost make me wish I was dead.'

'Is it I in particular who has that effect, or were you just speaking in general?'

'Of course I was only speaking in general. In general about us both.'

'Because there is another thing I would not really like, and that is to have provoked in anyone, even if only once, a feeling as violent as that.'

'Oh I'm sorry.'

'It doesn't matter.'

'And I would like to thank you too.'

'But for what?'

'I don't really know. For your niceness.'

(Translated by Sonia Pitt-Rivers and Irina Morduch)

Moderato Cantabile (1958)

The salmon, chilled in its original form, is served on a silver platter that the wealth of three generations has helped to buy. Dressed in black, and with white gloves, a man carries it like a royal child, and offers it to each guest in the silence of the nascent dinner. It is proper not to talk about it.

At the northern end of the garden the scent of magnolias arises, drifting from dune to dune till it disappears. Tonight the wind is from the south. A man prowls along the Boulevard de la Mer. A woman knows he is there.

The salmon passes from guest to guest, following a ritual that nothing can disturb, except everyone's hidden fear that such perfection may suddenly be marred or sullied by some excessively obvious absurdity. Outside, in the garden, the magnolias' funereal flowering continues in the dark night of early spring.

The wind ebbs and flows like the surf, striking the urban obstacles, then moving on, wafting the scent to the man, then whisking it away again.

In the kitchen the women, their honour at stake, sweat to put the finishing touches to the next course, smothering a duck in its orange-shrouded coffin. Meanwhile the pink, succulent, deep-sea salmon, already disfigured by the brief moments just past, continues its ineluctable advance towards total annihilation, slowly dispelling the fear of an unsuccessful evening.

A man, facing a woman, looks at her as though he does not recognize her. Her breasts are again half exposed. She hastily adjusts her dress. A drooping flower lies between them. There are still flashes of lucidity in her wildly protruding eyes, enough for her to succeed in helping herself to some of their salmon when it comes her turn.

In the kitchen, now that the duck is ready and put into the oven to keep warm, they finally find a moment of peace to put their thoughts to words, saying that she is really going a bit too far. Tonight she arrived later than the night before, well after her guests had arrived.

Fifteen people had waited for her in the main living room on the ground floor. She had entered that glittering assembly without so much as the slightest apology. Someone apologized for her.

'Anne is late. Please forgive Anne.'

For ten years she has never been the subject of any gossip. If she is bothered by her incongruity, she is unaware of it. A fixed smile makes her face acceptable.

'Anne didn't hear what you said.'

She puts her fork down, looks around, tries to grasp the thread of conversation, fails.

'That's true,' she says.

They ask again. Her blonde hair is mussed, and she runs her fingers listlessly through it, as she had done a little while before in a different setting. Her lips are pale. Tonight she forgot to make herself up.

'I'm sorry,' she says, 'right now a sonatina by Diabelli.'

'A sonatina? Already?'

'That's right.'

Silence moves in again around the question, and the fixed smile returns to her face. She is a wild animal.

'He didn't know what moderato cantabile meant?'

'No, he didn't.'

Tonight the magnolias will be in full bloom. Except for the one she is wearing, the one she picked tonight on her way home from the port. Time moves monotonously past this forgotten flowering.

'Darling, how could he have guessed?'

'He couldn't.'

'He's sleeping, I suppose.'

'Yes, he's sleeping.'

Slowly the digestion of what was a salmon begins. The osmosis of the species that ate it was carried out like a perfect ritual. Nothing upset the solemnity of the process. The other waits, snug and warm, in its orange shroud. And now the moon rises on the sea, and on the man lying on the ground. Through the white curtains you now could barely distinguish the shapes and forms of night. Madame Desbaresdes contributes nothing to the conversation.

'Mademoiselle Giraud told me that story yesterday. She gives my little boy lessons also, you know.'

'Is that so?'

People laugh. A woman somewhere around the table. Little by little the chorus of conversation grows louder and, with considerable effort and ingenuity, some sort of society emerges. Landmarks are discovered, cracks open, allowing familiarities to slip in. And little by little a generally biased and individually noncommittal conversation builds up. It will be a successful party. The women bask in their own brilliance. The men have covered them with jewels according to their bankrolls. Tonight one of them suspects he may have made a mistake.

In the sequestered garden the birds sleep peacefully, for the weather is still fine. The same sort of sleep as the child's. The remains of the salmon are offered around again. The women will devour it to the last mouthful. Their bare shoulders have the gloss and solidity of a society founded and built on the certainty of its rights, and they were chosen to fit this society. Their strict education has taught them that they must temper their excesses in the interest of their position. They stuff themselves with mayonnaise, specially prepared for this dish, forget themselves, and lap it up. The men look at them and remember that therein lies their happiness.

Tonight one of them does not share the others' appetite. She comes from the other end of town, from beyond the breakwaters and oil depots at the other end of the Boulevard de la Mer, from beyond the limits imposed upon her ten years before, where a man had offered her more wine than she could handle. Full of this wine, an exception to the general rule, she could not bring herself to eat. Beyond the white blinds lay darkness, and in this darkness a man, with plenty of time to kill, stands looking now at the sea, now at the garden. Then at the sea, at the garden, at his hands. He doesn't eat. He cannot eat either, his body obsessed by another hunger. The capricious wind still bears the scent of magnolias to him, taking him by surprise, tormenting him as much as the scent of a single flower. A light in the second story was turned out a little while ago, and was not turned back on. They must have closed the windows on that side of the house, to shut out the oppressive odour of the flowers at night.

Anne Desbaresdes keeps on drinking. Tonight the champagne has the annihilating taste of the unknown lips of the man outside in the street.

The man has left the Boulevard de la Mer and circled the garden, keeping watch from the dunes which bound it on the north, then he has retraced his steps and descended the slope to the beach. And there he lay down again in the same place. He stretches, stares for a moment out to sea, then turns and looks again at the bay windows with their white blinds. Then he gets up, picks up a pebble, aims at the windows, turns back again, tosses the pebble into the sea, lies down, stretches again, and says a name out loud.

Two women, alternately and cooperatively, prepare the second course. The other victim is waiting.

'As you know, Anne is defenceless when it comes to her child.'

Her smile broadens. The remark is repeated. Again she runs her fingers through the blonde disorder of her hair. The circles under her eyes are deeper than before. Tonight she cried. By now the moon has risen above the town, and above the man lying on the beach.

'That's true,' she says.

Her hand falls from her hair, and pauses at the wilting magnolia at her breast.

'We're all alike really.'

'Yes,' Anne Desbaresdes says.

The petals of the magnolia are smooth. Her fingers crumple it, pierce the petals, then stop, paralyzed, lie on the table, wait, affecting an attitude of nonchalance, but in vain. For someone has noticed it. Anne Desbaresdes tries to smile apologetically, as if to imply that she couldn't help it, but she is drunk, and her expression shamelessly betrays it. He scowls, but remains impassive. He has already recovered from his surprise. He has always expected as much.

With half-closed eyes, Anne Desbaresdes drinks another glass of wine in one swallow. She has reached the point where she can't help it. She derives from drink a confirmation of what was till then her hidden desire, and a base consolation for that discovery.

Other women drink in turn, raising their bare arms, their enticing, irreproachable, matronly arms. The man on the beach is whistling a tune heard that afternoon in a café at the port.

The moon has risen, and as the night advances it begins to grow cold. Perhaps the man is cold.

They begin to serve the pressed duck. The women help themselves generously, fully capable of doing justice to the delicacy. They murmur softly in admiration as the golden duck is passed around. The sight of it makes one of them grow faint. Her mouth is desiccated by another hunger that nothing, except perhaps the wine, can satisfy. A song she cannot sing comes back to her, a song heard that afternoon in a café at the port. The man is still alone on the beach.

He has just spoken the name again, and his mouth is still half open.

'No thank you.'

The man's closed eyes are caressed by the wind, and, in powerful, impalpable waves, by the scent of the magnolias, as the wind ebbs and flows.

Anne Desbaresdes has just declined to take any of the duck. And yet the platter is still there before her, only for a brief moment, but long enough for everyone to notice. She raises her hand, as she has been taught to do, to emphasize her refusal. The platter is removed. Silence settles around the table.

'I just couldn't. I'm sorry.'

Again she raises her hand to her breast, to the dying flower whose scent slips beyond the garden and drifts to the sea.

'Perhaps it's that flower,' someone suggests, 'the scent is so strong.'

'No, I'm used to it. It's nothing really.'

The duck continues on its course. Someone opposite her looks on impassively. And again she tries to force a smile, but succeeds only in twisting her face into a desperate, licentious grimace of confession. Anne Desbaresdes is drunk.

Again she is asked if she is not ill. She is not ill.

'Perhaps that flower,' the voice insists, 'is making you nauseous without your knowing it.'

'No, I'm used to the scent of magnolias. I just don't happen to be hungry.'

They leave her alone, and begin to devour the duck. Its flesh will be digested in other bodies. A man in the street closes his eyes, his eyelids fluttering from such willful patience. His body is chilled to the bone, and nothing can warm him. Again his mouth has uttered a name.

In the kitchen they announce that she has refused the pressed duck, that she is ill, there is no other explanation for it. Here they are talking of other things. The meaningless shapes of the magnolias caress the eyes of the solitary man. Once again Anne Desbaresdes takes her glass, which has just been refilled, and drinks. Unlike the others, its warmth fires her witch's loins. Her breasts, heavy on either side of the heavy flower, suffer from its sudden collapse, and hurt her. Her mouth, filled with wine, encompasses a name she does not speak. All this is accomplished in painful silence.

The man has left the beach and approached the garden railings. He seizes them and grips them tightly. The lights are still on in the bay windows. How come it has not yet happened?

The pressed duck is passed around again. With the same gesture as before Anne Desbaresdes implores him not to serve her. She is passed by. She returns to the silent agony of her loins, to their burning pain, to her lair.

The man has let go of the garden railings. He looks at his empty hands, distorted by the strain. There, at arm's length, a destiny was decided.

The sea wind blows cooler through the town. Most people are already asleep. The second story windows are dark and closed, to keep the scent of the magnolias from disturbing the child's sleep. Red motorboats sail through his innocent dreams.

Some of the guests have taken a second helping of duck. The conversation flows more and more easily, increasing the distance of the night with every passing minute.

Bathed in the brilliant light of the chandeliers, Anne Desbaresdes continues to smile and say nothing.

The man has decided to leave the garden and walk to the edge of town. As he goes, the scent of the magnolias grows fainter, giving way to the smell of the sea.

Anne Desbaresdes will accept a little coffee ice cream, for the sake of appearances.

In spite of himself the man will retrace his steps. Again he sees the magnolias, the railings, the bay windows in the distance, still lighted, still lighted. On his lips, the song heard that afternoon, and the name that he will utter a little louder this time. He will come.

She knows it. The magnolia at her breast is completely wilted. In one hour it has lived through a whole summer. Sooner or later the man will pass by the garden. He has come. She keeps torturing the flower at her breast.

'Anne didn't hear what you said.'

She tries to smile more broadly, but it is useless. The words are repeated. One last time she runs her fingers through her blonde hair. The circles under her eyes are even darker than before. Tonight she cried. They repeat the words for her benefit alone, and wait.

'Yes,' she says, 'we're going on vacation. We're taking a house by the sea. It will be hot there. In a house off by itself at the seashore.'

'Darling,' someone says.

'Yes.'

While the guests pass from the dining room into the main living room, Anne Desbaresdes will go upstairs. From the big bay window of the long corridor of her life she will look at the boulevard below. The man will already have left. She will go into the child's room, and lie down on the floor at the foot of the bed, paying no attention to the magnolia crushed to pieces between her breasts. And to the inviolable rhythm of her child's breathing she will vomit forth the strange nourishment that had been forced upon her.

A shadow will appear in the doorway leading into the hall, deepening the shadow of the room. Anne Desbaresdes will run her hand through her disheveled hair. This time she will offer an apology.

The shadow will not reply.

(Translated by Richard Seaver)

CLAUDE MAURIAC

A leading film critic and journalist, Claude Mauriac (b. 1914) is the son of the famous novelist François Mauriac and the author of several novels himself. His novels, of increasing complexity as he fell under the influence of Nathalie Sarraute in particular, show a group of people in the parisian social-artistic set, where the principal characters of one novel may be the minor characters of the next. Thoughts, conversations, impressions, become jumbled together as if recorded by a random microphone capable of recording them all. This extract, from the beginning of *The Marquise Went Out at Five*, needs little other introduction than the text which Claude Mauriac himself chose to preface it:

> Monsieur Paul Valéry recently suggested anthologizing as many first sentences of novels as possible, from whose imbecility he expected a great deal. The most famous authors would be laid under contribution. Such a notion still honours Paul Valéry who not long since, apropos of novels, assured me that as far as he was concerned, he would never permit himself to write: *The Marquise Went Out at Five*.
>
> (André Breton, *First Surrealist Manifesto*)

So Mauriac decided to take up the challenge, and launched out as follows:

(J.F.)

The Marquise Went Out at Five (1961)

. . . THE MARQUISE WENT OUT AT FIVE. Rested. Dressed up. Decked out. Big as life. That part's not so good. I really have to do something about this belly. Otherwise, in form. Fit even. Bad luck to talk about it. *Chère Marquise*. Hanging around the streets, at her age. Convenient living in this neighbourhood. Near Saint-Germain-des-Prés (but it's still a little too early) you meet more young people than anywhere else. Except the Boulevard Saint-Michel, of course, which is almost as close. But as Jef says, too much is too much. In gangs they scare me. There's that nice Monsieur Desprez, the autograph salesman, smoking on his balcony. Over his apartment building, at the corner of the Rue Mazarine and the Rue Dauphine, an invisible plane draws a thin line of smoke across the sky . . .

. . . On the other side of the Carrefour, my neighbour from the Rue de l'Ancienne-Comédie is at his window too. We have the same cleaning woman. She often tells me about him. His name is apparently well known in literary circles. He's separated from his wife who occasionally brings his children to see him. Interrupting the writing of my next catalogue of historical works and documents to give myself this break at the window (but it's even hotter outside), under my eyes, in one and the same glance, I have five minutes and five centuries of the life of the Carrefour . . .

. . . On the sidewalk to my left, in front of the fireplug, a child in a green sweater is standing motionless. My wife and my little girl, who have just left, are slowly walking toward him. That pink dress of Rachel's is pretty. This balcony is dusty again. The ivy Pilou brought back from Valromé filthy now . . .

'Then Chiffonnette took the satchel and went off to school as fast as she could. When she got there, she ran so fast, poor Chiffonnette, that bang, crash! she fell on her fanny. She got up again and left for cachali . . .'

'For what?'

'Cachali. That means white sand. Bigoudis didn't want to leave and she said: What are you looking at through the door? Bigoudis didn't want to leave, because behind the door was the Devil playing a tune on a cordion.'

. . . Unusual mistake. So little, and always the right word. Or else she makes up something exact enough to express an idea which is probably not vague except to us. Just four. Already four, our Rachel.

Bertrand's idea, living in such a place. And even that wouldn't matter
if at least he had fresh air and quiet. He almost never goes out any
more, just thinks about his next novel, takes notes. From time to time
I bring our daughter, like this afternoon. And Jean-Paul, when I can.
He looks at them gently, then seems to forget them, to forget me. I
straighten up his place a little, and we leave. It's better that way . . .

. . . Relayed from window to window over the roar of the cars, that
pretty tune, *Petit vin blanc*. There should be a decompression valve.
Really, a big belly is impossible. It can't go on. It's gone on almost
twenty years. Do exercises. No drinking with meals. No more bread,
etc. It's because the Marquise is so greedy! If I let her have her way!
Where will she end up tonight? I give her until ten. Five good hours
ahead of me. And after, to bed. And before, I hope. Quick, knock on
wood. There, that vegetable and fruit stand. Perfect . . .

'By the way, Madame Frivole, is that the right time, on your . . . ? I
forgot my watch today.'

'It has its moods, but it's on time today. We've just reopened for the
afternoon. Did you see my melons? Nice, aren't they? Monsieur
Frivole wouldn't stand for a minute's . . . You know how he is:
always on the dot.'

'I know what you mean! I had a husband like that. Five o'clock! I
must have left my job a little too early. It's hot work cleaning in this
weather. Oh well. Monsieur doesn't notice.'

'Monsieur Desprez?'

'No: Monsieur Carnéjoux. Monsieur Desprez is in the morning.
Funny thing is, the two of them are just alike, although they don't
know each other. Easy-going. Pay no attention to the dust around
them as long as you don't bother their work.'

'That's what I always say: bachelors . . . But who takes care of their
meals?'

'Monsieur Desprez does everything for himself, he leaves the dishes
for me. Monsieur Carnéjoux always goes to some restaurant . . .'

. . . The Marquise has her little whims. These lines crossing the
asphalt every now and then, I make it a rule never to step on them for
some reason, I try instead—I take aim and then bang! missed—to
stick the tip of my umbrella into them. It's not always easy for my
poor legs either. There are even some sidewalks where the spaces are
so wide that you have to give up. What did I tell you? Too bad. It's not
a good sign . . .

. . . From window to window of the bus slowly passing in front of
us so that we can't cross, I face my own reflection, unknown, familiar,
standing on the curb near a red fireplug with my daughter too short
for her image to appear in the glass . . .

'. . . Be careful, Rachel, don't start until . . .'

'And then she made a *pâté*, and a château with the sand from the
square, that's what she did so she wouldn't come and bother her.'
'Who?'
'You know, the lady. Not Chiffonnette's and Bigoudis' mother.
Another lady.'

. . . Myself, mingled with the other reflections of the Carrefour:
white patches of sky, fragments of walls, electric sign on at this hour,
that's peculiar, people and things distorted. And the outlines of the
passengers so close, so far away, drowned, diluted, blurred behind
these windows only one of which, lowered halfway, cuts off my head
and reveals a commonplace reality, the inside of the bus. Breathing as
little as possible until I can leave this stinking Carrefour, I wonder
how Bertrand can live here. What's that child with the shaved head
waiting for, his back to the street? Two snags in his sweater. Careless
mother. The bus has gone by. The policeman has raised his stick. We
can cross . . .

'. . . Come on, Rachel, come on. Quick now!'

. . . Dragging her, my little girl in her pink dress, Pilou crosses the
Rue de l'Ancienne-Comédie, careful to keep inside the markers. How
hot it is! The blue of the sky is striped over the Rue Dauphine with a
narrow line left by some jet plane I neither saw nor heard. Pulsation
of the perfume shop's electric sign. Roars, sputters, chugs. Cars of all
kinds, single file, in the Rue Mazarine, in front of the fried-potato
vendor, maybe the smell would come up here if the air weren't so
contaminated with gasoline. Humble people. Each with his little
problems, his enormous vacuum. I alone escaping that emptiness, not
that I'm more intelligent than these toiling insects. Or even more
cultivated. But I'm aware of my own nothingness and of theirs too. I
dominate our ephemeral existences. Since I left wife, children,
newspaper and relative comfort to dedicate myself, not to my
pleasures but to the comprehension of what my pleasures meant . . .

. . . That child motionless, face tense, mechanically picking at his
green sweater. Not letting himself cry. I'll never know what his agony
is. A child's disappointment, or real misery? If only he didn't hold
back his tears. And Jean-Paul or Rachel could be like that, suffering
alone without my being able to do anything, even though I am their
mother . . .

. . . My five minutes' recreation, while I stand on my balcony and
smoke the last cigarette in my last pack before going down to get
more (no shopping for tonight, the left-overs from lunch will do).
And the five centuries, no, call it eight, that's closer: at least eight
centuries of Parisian life in this same spot . . .

   . . . *De la Grant rue Saint-Germain*

Et en la rue Saint-Andry
Des Ars, mon chemin s'estendi . . .

. . . Emotion at realizing I am probably the only man in France, in the world, who knows by heart this *Dit des rues de Paris* in its different versions, the oldest dating from around 1280. Its author is Guillot . . .

. . . *De la Grant rue Saint-Germain*
Des Prez, si fait rue Cauvain,
Et puis la rue Saint-Andri
Dehors mon chemin s'estendit . . .

. . . The text is endlessly suggestive. The Rue Cauvain or Gaugain was our Rue de l'Éperon. *Saint-Andri Dehors* is a mistake, of course: it should be Saint-André-des-Arts . . .

. . . This Rue Saint-André-des-Arts never ends. I'm only as far as the Rue de l'Éperon. I dreamed about Valérie all last night. Sweet things. Beautiful. I longed to see her in real life, tangible. Disappointment at the first glance, in the school courtyard, this morning. Valérie, I love you, I love you, but it just happens that in your presence you mean nothing to me. In math today I gave you a pen. It's the first time one of my ball-points will write equations correctly. Our ten o'clock snack. I throw bread crumbs at Valérie. She throws one at me with a smile. I throw it back. She does too. All this without a word, but with a look . . .

. . . It's not much farther: at the end of the Rue de Buci, the Carrefour, the Rue Saint-André-des-Arts, and then I'll be there. Just in time, I can't last much more. If she knew what I did today. Or rather what my desires were, my thoughts. How ashamed I'd be! She admires me so much. Why did I cut class? Whatever it was that lured me away was stronger than I was. The young man I've become had to struggle all afternoon against the irresistible lure of sex. I refused to yield to this obsession as long as I could. I neither abused myself nor did anything very bad. After a day's battle with the carnal demon, it could only score a few points. Master of my senses, I'm going there, I said I would, but I should have refused. It's the first time I've been invited to her, I mean to her parents' apartment in the Rue Séguier
. . .

'That's what I always say, dear Madame Frivole, I have my pride. I'm not afraid of the dirt, that's what I'm there for. But you know how it is, the more you clean . . . The thing is, I don't want another woman in the house, or else up and be done with it, goodbye for good. Monsieur Carnéjoux lives alone. His missis comes to see him every once in a while, but that doesn't have anything to do with my housecleaning.'

'Monsieur Desprez is always in his . . .'

'Now the dirt, there, I beg your pardon, it's not even worth trying. And those old chewed butts of his, he drops them just anywhere. He doesn't have customers very often, you know. Besides, who do you think would bother about that stuff? The thing is: he doesn't want to sell, not at all. He's too crotchety for that, you know. It would tear the heart out of that man to be separated from a single one of his old papers. My other one, he writes all day long. I tell you, they're a couple of odd ones, and the . . .'

'It takes all kinds to make . . .'

'I shouldn't stand here gossiping all day . . . Two kilos of potatoes, Madame Frivole. That's just what it . . . It's time I . . . My kittens will be furious with me. They make a lot of noise, those Siamese'.

'All right, Madame Prioux. Rose will take care of you . . .'

'Tell me, while I think of it. What happened to that old woman . . .'

'The newsstand lady? A wedding, of all things. She's at a wedding. That's someone she found to take her pl . . .'

'That's what I . . . Did you see how she's made up, that . . . Now, Rose, are you forgetting about me?'

. . . Take your old potatoes. Takes time. Never stop, love. Never. Never should. Still several hours before I'm with him again. They close so late, grocery stores. Funny man. And he says I'm funny. Never stop, love. There you are, all ready, day after day. Three days we know each other. Hasn't gone out much. Probably hasn't gone out at all. Sick he says. Fine. Love, never stop. Never. Guess I'm lucky, really. Don't have to worry about his cheating on me. Why is it always over so fast? What else are we made for, why . . .

'Hurry up, my dear, I should be home by now . . .'

. . . At your age, you shouldn't be in such a hurry. You'll get to the cemetery fast enough. Love one good long time, enough to kill you. But no, selling potatoes instead . . .

. . . She looks dazed, that girl. As if she were asleep on her feet. Day dreaming. And slow! . . .

. . . No listen, Rose, put them aside for me now. I'll pick them up when I get my bread. My cats don't like to be alone so long, poor darlings . . .'

'Do as you're told, Rose! What are you thinking about! Oh, Madame Prioux, these young people, you can't understand them . . .'

. . . There, she's already gone. Pretty spry for her age. Hot today. Forgot to mention it to Madame Prioux, too bad . . .

. . . My house is built on Philippe-Auguste's moat. When it was filled in they replaced it by two streets of my Carrefour: the Rue Mazarine and the extension of the Rue de l'Ancienne-Comédie, which used to be known as the Rue des Fossés-Saint-Germain-des-

Prés or the Rue de la Comédie. In this relatively obscure spot in Paris where I have my apartment and my office, in the prow of this tall, splendid eighteenth-century building at the corner of the Rue Mazarine and the Rue Dauphine, it's the host of the dead who seem most alive to me . . .

'Well, Madame Miron, how's that foot of yours?'

'I'm making progress every day, Monsieur Coquart. I've been to the doctor. He's very pleased.'

'Well, I'm glad to hear it, Madame Miron. What can I do for you . . .'

'A nice little chop, Monsieur Coquart. The kind I like.'

'You know what's best, Madame Miron, no one can say the . . .'

'With this warm weather we're having, I don't feel so numb, I can get around a little better.'

'Glad to hear it, Madame Miron, glad to hear it. There you are. Pay over there.'

'In the sunshine . . . And you know what they say, sunshine's still the cheapest, when there *is* any . . .'

'We're having our share today. Hot enough for me. Two francs for Madame Miron . . .'

'Two hundred francs, it can't be, it just can't . . .'

'What do you think, Madame Miron, a prime chop . . . You tell me where you can do better!'

'Two new francs, all the same . . .'

. . . If I'd known, I wouldn't have asked for the best. Red-haired, red-faced, his big hands on his hips, he keeps his nasty eyes on me as I leave with my little chop. You think they're nice, and then, at the first opportunity . . .

. . . Nasty expression, and she leaves mumbling something between her teeth. They're all the same. I almost told her off. For all a customer like her brings in . . .

. . . Pilou and Rachel, walking slowly, gradually disappear. They'll probably walk home to the Quai d'Orléans, if Martine had wanted to take the bus she'd have gone the other way to get the 63 on the Boulevard Saint-Germain. At the rate they're walking, they haven't got there yet. Since I abandoned my too-easy life in my too-beautiful apartment on the Ile Saint-Louis for these two modest rooms with their high ceilings and their venerable age, their three windows and their old balconies, I've finally felt the beginning of peace. To my left, at the end of the Rue Mazarine, the dome of the Institut de France; to my right, the only trees visible from here, unfortunately, are the skimpy ones on the boulevard. I'll have to go and spend a day at Valromé. With Jean-Paul maybe. I see him so seldom. Today he was at school. On free days he has other things to do . . .

. . . Good-looking boy. But the Marquise wouldn't dare let herself have a Negro, after all. Otherwise she'd end up having problems. It wouldn't be the first time, dear. Pull in my stomach, never forget to pull in my stomach, that's the first thing. No HOPE. Oh yes, oh yes, there's always hope. From one end of the sky to the other, you can see from here, over toward the Seine, the blurred line that a few seconds ago must have been the straight trail left by a plane . . .

(Translated by Richard Howard)

ROBERT PINGET

Robert Pinget was born in Geneva in 1920, studied law and practised briefly, but after deciding to turn to painting, he went to Paris in 1946 where he had his first exhibition. In 1951 he published his first book *Entre Fantoine et Agapa* (still untranslated), and this was followed by a number of novels which gave him a very considerable reputation in French literary circles and led to translation into other languages. A writer's writer, he nevertheless achieved popular success with *The Inquisitory* and *Someone* when the first became a runner-up for the *Prix Femina* and the second won it a year later. Pinget's work is characterized by delicate humour, poetic description and an oblique way of conveying what is happening in the mind or the viscera, that is not dissimilar from the technique of Marguerite Duras, although it is with Samuel Beckett that he is more often compared. Robert Pinget has written successfully for the stage and for radio and his later work shows an ever increasing refinement of style. John Updike in a major article in the *New Yorker* recently said of him:

> It is with some embarrassment that a reviewer recommends to readers a writer whom he scarcely understands, whose works are more than a little exasperating, and who furthermore writes with a high degree of colloquiality in a foreign language. Yet Robert Pinget, as glimpsed through translation and through the cloudy layers of his own obfuscations, does seem one of the more noble presences in world literature, a continuingly vital practitioner of what, a weary long quarter-century ago, was christened *le nouveau roman*. . . .
>
> [He] has advised a recent English translator, 'Don't bother too much about logic: everything in [my novel] is directed against it.' And a comment of several pages appended to another novel enunciates a principled surrealism inimical to logic and intelligible plot: 'It is not what can be said or *meant* that interests me, but the *way in which it is said*.' . . .
>
> Pinget strikes us as free of any basically distorting mannerism or aesthetic pose. His recourse remains to the real, without irony. In a France of smiling mandarins and chilly chic, he manifests the two essential passions of a maker: a love of his material and a belief in his method.

Mahu, first published in 1952, is the narrative of a man who unlike his brothers has no ambition and looks at the lives that other people lead with incomprehension, describing them so that they become incomprehensible to the reader as well. Rich in humour, often resembling Queneau, it is the best possible introduction to the work of an author who often provides considerable intellectual difficulties to readers. His next novel *Baga* appeared in 1958 (it is also dramatized as *Architruc*) and is the first person narrative of a king in a mythical country who allows his prime minister to usurp power, ruining the country, until he finally brings the king back from exile. Pinget uses the fable to poke fun at monarchy, government, the church and authority generally, while pointing out the advantages of the reflective life in comparison to the lust for power. In *No Answer* he conveys his love of the country and village life and this novel also has a dramatic version entitled *Dead Letter*. A father writes to his son who has left the village many years ago. Daily he goes to the post office hoping to find a reply, but it never comes. M. Levert, the father, writes to his son long descriptions of village life and local gossip, recreating a world to which he hopes his son will one day return. *The Inquisitory* provoked considerable discussion in France as many critics read special meanings into it, even suggesting that it obliquely suggested Sade's world of the *120 Days of Sodom*. This very long novel consists entirely of question and answer between the visitor to a large empty house and the caretaker he interrogates about what has happened there in the past. The interrogator appears to have some authority, but the answers are a mixture of truth and lies which become apparent as the contradictions build up. The interweaving of truth and falsehood is very elaborate and logical and the author has gone to great pains to ensure that there are no inconsistencies other than those intended. *The Inquisitory* is an epic achievement and mirrors one of the principal preoccupations of the *nouveau roman*, the delineation of truth as a subjective phenomenon with an underlining supposition that there is no real truth.

Robert Pinget's later novels are much shorter, but continue his preoccupation with mystery and detection that begins in *The Inquisitory*. In *Someone*, 1965, the principal character is again a dropout from conventional society whose monologue is a duel between his memory and the contradictions he finds in it. *The Libera me Domine* (1968) is a long monologue where a crime appears to have been committed and the narrative revolves around the nature of the crime, who committed it and the possibility that there has been no crime at all in a novel where the question remains unresolved as to who is mad and who is lying. His most recent novels *Recurrent Melody* and *Fable* continue to probe the catastrophic power of memory to distort and govern our view of the world we inhabit. The later plays were written for radio which is especially suitable to Pinget's style and pre-occupations. They revolve around the same recurring characters and the monologue of an observing narrator.

The three extracts that follow are from *Baga*, *The Inquisitory* and *Fable*. In the first we see the king prior to the disastrous and totally unnecessary war that his prime minister involves him in, and to his escape to the forest to become a hermit. In the second extract from *The Inquisitory* there are amusing references in the street names to Samuel Beckett and his wife, and to his French publisher (Jerome Lindon).

Fable contains more erotic and violent content than is found elsewhere in the work of this essentially gentle writer and the smoothness of style which he has refined to a very individual narrative technique contrasts dramatically with this content, which seems to predict a world returning to barbarism. The pages given here open the novel.

(J.C.)

Baga (1958)

This morning I woke up with a heart ache. Heart aches are lacerating dreams. They make us bleed inside, and in the morning the wound hasn't healed. One knows nothing of what's happened. The imagination overworks. Madness. Madness. Drive out the imagination.

So a laceration, and my royalty seems to me to be even more ridiculous than usual. I hardly have the courage to get up. Fortunately Baga arrives. He says:

'You have invited some ambassadors?'

'Me? Never.'

'They're coming nonetheless. Two express messengers are here already.'

'Where? When?'

'Right now. They're waiting in the parlour.'

'I've already told you not to call it a parlour, it makes it sound like a convent.'

'Parlour or not they're asking to see you.'

'What are they like?'

'Motorcyclists. The ambassadors will be here this evening.'

'Go and fetch them.'

'You're going to get dressed?'

'What's the point?'

Baga goes out. I feel nervous. One has to react and compose oneself. Water Ducky. I take my little watering can. I go and fill it in the bathroom. I notice myself in the mirror at the same time. I look like a corpse. I powder myself and brush my teeth. I pick up the watering can again and go to water Ducky. At that moment Baga comes in with the motorcyclists.

Nobody ever knocks on the king's door. It's a bourgeois gesture. The king must be ready to receive no matter what the circumstances. Of no account that I would have preferred to be on my pot than with a watering can in my hand.

'Good morning gentlemen. What can I do for you?'

'Sire, we come to announce the visit of ambassadors from Novocordia.'

'Very well, gentlemen. Sit down.'

Baga has them sit. I place my watering can on my bedside table and sit in my easy chair. I don't know quite what to say to these messengers.

'So gentlemen, what's new in Novocordia?'

'Sire, our ambassadors will answer you.'

'Oh, Oh, I see. Mum's the word?'

'Yes, Sire.'

'All right, gentlemen, too bad. May one offer you something? Baga, see if there's any pernod in the cupboard.'

Baga produces the pernod. It's very tempting. But as I've said, I'm forbidden to drink it before lunch. However, I ask Baga to let me have some just once.

'Just once, Baga!'

'All right, just once. We don't have messengers every day of the week.'

'Oh, lovely.'

I start to clap my hands. Baga looks at me sternly. He's afraid I might make a bad impression on the messengers. But the impression one makes on people has no importance. Even if I behaved regally, would that stop the neighbours from declaring war on me? Why do I think of war? These past days. . . .

'Your health, gentlemen.'

'Your health, Sire,'

Good. The messengers leave, telling me that the ambassadors will arrive this evening about seven-thirty. In fact, I'll have to invite them to dinner. People have no shame. They could have come for tea instead. I must discuss the menu with Baga.

'Baga, what shall we give them to stuff themselves with?'

'Not beef for the love of heaven.'

'What?'

'I said, since we have ambassadors for once, there'd be no harm in a change. Besides, suppose they don't like beef?'

'What then? Black pudding? Snails?'

'No good asking me. I gave up thinking about it long ago.'

'Call the cook.'

Baga rings for the cook. I'm quite agreeable to honouring the ambassadors with an unusual menu, but I don't much care for this 'for the love of heaven' of Baga's. I say to him:

'Really, are you so unfortunate to share my beef? It disgusts you as much as that?'

'It doesn't disgust me; it stupefies me. And when it comes to ambassadors it's essential to keep your mind clear. You must be able to argue, to act with finesse. We should eat something light and dainty.'

'Dainty!'

'Yes dainty. To make a better impression on them.'

'Oh, you annoy me with your impressions. Will it stop them from stabbing me in the back because I'm dainty?'

'Stab you in the back—who?'

'Them—the neighbours.'

'Who's talking about stabbing you in the back?'

'I don't know. I have a feeling that something's in the wind. I don't know what.'

'My poor dear fellow. Come in, Cook.'

'Cook, suggest a dainty menu for us this evening.'

'Pardon?'

'Yes, a delicate menu, a light menu.'

'Sire, I'll need time to reflect.'

'All right. Go and reflect in your kitchens and come back in half an hour, three-quarters of an hour.'

'And your lunch, Sire?'

'Put it off until afterwards, off you go.'

Baga goes off too and Corniflet arrives. I can't restrain myself from telling him the news. He doesn't seem very astonished—which astonishes me.

'Did you know something about it? Someone told you?'

'No Your Majesty. But, after all, we're a state like the rest and we certainly have the right to receive ambassadors from time to time.'

'What folly, Corniflet! What stupid vanity! What do ambassadors mean to you?'

'To me? I don't know Your Majesty.'

'I mean why do you find it normal that they should be received? Why are you flattered by their visit?'

'I'm not flattered Your Majesty. I'm a citizen of a state, I find. . . .'

'My dear Corniflet, what is a state?'

'It's a country with a king.'

'So?'

'So the king has a right to receive foreign ambassadors.'

'But why, Corniflet, why?'

'Because then we have official receptions and we all watch.'

'Watch what?'

'We watch our king greeting the ambassadors or accompanying them to exhibitions.'

'And you enjoy that?'

'Oh yes.'

'Corniflet, you are a good barber and I'll pay you for it. But you are a nit, my friend. Understand that the ambassadors are coming neither for an exhibition nor to shake my mitt. They're coming. . . .'

'Why, Your Majesty?'

'It's a state secret.'

'Oh, go on—tell me.'

'Swear you won't say anything to your wife.'

'I swear, Your Majesty.'

'All right, my friend, they're coming to prepare for war.'

'Holy Virgin!'

'They're coming to massacre your children, plunder your home, throw you in gaol.'

'My God, Your Majesty. We must drive them away, kill them.'

'Ah you see. You see, little idiot. And everybody will be crushed, hacked to pieces. No more state, no more king, nothing. Careful, or you'll cut me.'

'But Your Majesty, we must do something. We must arrest them, we must . . . I don't want to die.'

'Don't get excited. I'll attend to it all. Just understand that everything that comes from abroad is pernicious. And instead of rejoicing at this sort of news, close the shutters of your home and embrace your wife.'

'As you command, Your Majesty. Oh, she's a fine women. She's a fine, good woman, she's. . . .'

'Good. Now cut the cackle and finish your work.'

There. I'm shaved. Corniflet leaves. Baga comes back with the cook who reads us a menu full of soufflés and vol-au-vent. I am disappointed.

'My dear fellow, I find it inconsistent. If one doesn't eat anything how can one answer the ambassadors. Our arguments carry no weight. In any case I don't go along with the *alcoli volatile* nor the *esprit-de-vin*.'

'That's just for appearances, Sire. I've made provision for cognacs and marcs.'

'Can't you slip a little beef in somewhere?'

'Certainly. . . .'

'No,' Baga says. 'I say no! If we allow. . . .'

'Who gives the orders here?'

'Excuse me. But as you were saying, these ambassadors certainly have perfidious intent. If we stuff ourselves, we won't see through it.'

'Fair enough. Just for once. Let's get to the food. I'm starving.'

I'm really going to relish my beef this lunch-time. Nothing for this evening. Have to help ourselves beforehand. I remain in my dressing gown, which produces a certain stupefaction in the assembly when I arrive. I feel I should say a few words before I sit down.

'Gentlemen, ladies. You see me in this apparel because I haven't had time to dress.'

Baga whispers in my ear:

'Speak in the plural.'

I start again:

'We haven't had time to dress. We are going to receive some ambassadors this evening. We are advised to observe the greatest discretion. We see in the arrival of these persons a bad omen and I would have difficulty persuading us that these persons don't wish us any harm. . . .'

Baga whispers again:

'Say "I", it'll be simpler.'

I continue:

'I consider, in fact, that intrusions from abroad are pernicious, as I was saying to Corniflet. One never knows what can come of them. I advise you to stay at home this evening and not to talk about it. I'll make arrangements with your king so that he answers . . . so that I answer, suitably. . . . I've ordered a light menu to this purpose and I approve of it. I approve of myself. I think I am able to say to myself in fact. . . .'

Baga, again:

'Enough. That'll do.'

I sit down. I'm starving. The soup tastes burnt.

On consideration, I lack method. Should one narrate as if things were over or as if they were going on? Sometimes I imagine that I'm in the act of doing what I'm writing. An unexploited power there. It probably comes from divine right. What a beautiful ceremony my coronation was, when I think of it! Mama had completely prepared my attire the night before. I can still see the red robe and the ermine coat on my bed—I had slept on the divan that night. I was awakened at five the next morning as if we were going on a journey. I say to my father-confessor:

'Good heavens, it's as if we were going on a journey.'

'It is a great journey, Sire. God will be your pilot on this mystical boat, which is the whole of your subjects. You are going to navigate on the ocean of vicissitudes. . . .'

'What's that?'

'What, Sire?'

'Vicissitudes.'

'They are different stages through which the world passes in perpetual revolution.'

'Oh, I have a horror of revolutions.'

'It's up to you to avert them in your kingdom by wise government. God will help you.'

'How?'

'By showing you the direction to follow. God is the compass of the devout navigator.'

Obviously I had no answer to that. I was young. But even now I wouldn't have one. All these symbols leave me cold. I have papers to sign and ambassadors to receive. The connection with the compass escapes me. I don't understand this mania they have of comparing the concrete with the abstract. Perhaps that's what causes all the evil. People have their heads in the clouds and break their necks falling down potholes in the ground. Mama came to tell me to get a move on instead of talking. She was right. She helped me on with my robe and my coat. The crown was too big and they had to pad it with paper. When I looked at myself in the mirror, I died laughing. I said to Mama:

'What a nit I look!'

'Don't say that. Watch your language. You must set an example to your subjects.'

They had formed a procession and I was all atremble. It's true, these showy affairs put you in a blue funk. There were I don't know how many duchesses and archduchesses, not counting their husbands. We had to cross the garden to get to the chapel, which was next to the stables. To disguise the stables, they'd draped hazel branches and garlands across them, like on Corpus-Christi day. Mama had told me not to look at my feet while walking, but it wasn't easy. The robe was too long and I had to raise my shoulders. I was thinking of the boat and I narrowly missed taking a nose dive. We arrived at the chapel and the subjects were glued to the barriers. There were swarms of policemen. Baga, who was not yet Prime Minister, simply Queen's officer, said to me:

'May Your Majesty smile at the populace.'

I smiled. I saw the faces of these people and immediately I thought of the boat again. As long as I didn't drown them all. That priest was an imbecile to frighten me like that. Lifebuoys, life. . . .

Mama whispered to me:

'What did you say?'

'Nothing. I was thinking of the drowning people.'

We went in. Mademoiselle Chonchon, who is a schools' inspector and organist made a discord in the grand overture. Mama lifted her head towards the organ loft and gave her a really dirty look. But that evening I told her that Chonchon wasn't responsible for it. She was just panic-stricken and that's normal. She was paid her rupees, thanks to me.

The masses went on for quite a time. I had to stand up straight and look ahead. I got a bit giddy. I saw the bishop and the priests coming and going with the choir boys, who moved in and out. At one point I had a sort of vision. The bishop was on both sides of the altar at once and he swung back to the centre like an accordion. He unfolded again and they handed him some candles. I turned my head towards Mama,

who must have seen my anguished look for she smiled at me the way
one smiles at the sick. It was simply the lack of food making me see
double.

Afterwards, they gave me the royal unction. Chonchon played
some dreadfully sad music and the choir sang. I wanted to be sick, but
it was due to the fasting and the incense. I felt drops of sweat sliding
down my temples. I lost consciousness for a few minutes, but didn't
fall and I saw the boat with bats' wings and the confessor puffing out
his cheeks in order to sink it. Mama was saying: 'Hold yourself
straight; it will pass.' When I opened my eyes again, Mama had me by
the arm and we were preparing to leave. It was over. Chonchon was
playing louder and louder. One could hear the bellows of the organ
and I wanted to be sick again. I told Mama I didn't feel very well. She
said: 'Breathe deeply; it will pass.' I waited to get outside. It was
raining. Umbrellas everywhere. Mama quickly passed me a biscuit
she had taken from her bag. One of those ginger biscuits which burn
your mouth. It did me good and I smiled at the photographers. The
duchesses were annoyed because they had no umbrellas. Baga had to
ask the common people to lend theirs and, hey presto—fifty
umbrellas offered by out-stretched arms. I asked myself why these
people were helping us instead of stoning us. They fought amongst
themselves for the honour. The police knocked down one or two and
the crowd cried, 'long live the king.'

We returned through the garden, which was completely soaked. I
had my Swedish leather pumps—next to nothing—and we sank in up
to the ankles. The confessor had picked up a shovel; he was covered
with mud. A luncheon awaited us at the palace. Mama didn't like to
throw money away and had said that for the price of a coronation
lunch we could pay for lavatory pans. The lavatories were in the
Turkish style—five in the house altogether. They hadn't yet been
changed. During my reign I've fitted out only my bathroom. The
courtiers manage somehow. Between ourselves, I wouldn't say their
apartments are very hygienic. But nor are their morals.

We had cheesecake and gooseberry tart with sparkling wine. And
petits fours. I stayed in the Venus salon with Mama and her officers.
The minister at that time was a man named Mougre, who was Baron
of the Sippets. He had not been seen since the morning and he was
found under a table. Doctor Tronc diagnosed natural death. He was
pushed in a corner with a table cloth over him for the time being. My
nephews, who had come up from the country with their parents, were
making a lot of noise. They had some little trumpets, sold for the
benefit of the crown, so that one couldn't make them shut up without
ridicule. Besides, their mothers who had studied child psychology
said that children must be left to their instincts. Another reason why I

shouldn't have any. I would always be asking myself if it was a question of instinct or something else.

People came to kiss my hands. Mama was proud of me and rearranged my hair all the time. At that time I wore the parting in the middle. I was twenty but I looked forty due to my stoutness. I perspired a lot. Nonetheless it had been a good day. I hadn't found that I was any more stupid than the others. I was very much afraid of appearing in public, but after all, it's something to be done from time to time. One is able to assert oneself on various subjects. For example. Madame Bois Suspect asked me what I thought of the gooseberry tarts and I replied that they were too sugary. I added:

'It's true that it's not quite the season for them. The chef will have been afraid the fruit might be too acid.'

'And the cheesecake? It's our own cheese?'

'Yes Madam. During my lifetime only our national products will be eaten.'

'Ah? You are changing your politics?'

'It's my first day of politics, Madam.'

And there you are. She changed the conversation.

After the fête I found myself alone in my room again. I was suffering from stomach acidity. It would soon be time for dinner and I had to eat to please Mama. I rang for my valet. He told me he had nothing left in his medicine chest, but that Monsieur Baga was sure to have something. This officer ate and drank a lot. I had him called and he came with something that made me belch. My friendship for him dates from that moment. We chatted casually. At the end of the conversation I appointed him minister in place of Mougre. What a business with Mama! She didn't want to hear anything about it for three weeks and she no longer spoke to me. But what could she do? She'd lost her rights; I was the boss. It was painful for me to go against her wishes but I was sure I wasn't mistaken. I have a sixth sense. And the proof is that Baga is still my friend. Moreover, he's an excellent minister.

Here I am with the ambassadors on my neck. They are arriving in half an hour. I am in ceremonial dress and Baga is cutting my nails. I am calm.

'You might have put on your blue tunic, Baga. That one's a little shabby.'

'You think it's noticeable? The blue one's being dyed.'

'Remind me to buy you another. Two tunics isn't overdoing it. And you never go to the hairdresser's.'

'For these savages it's of no consequence.'

'What do you suspect them of plotting? Their agreement with Tranarcie frightens me.'

'But it's commercial, purely commercial. It's for the sale of their vine poles.'

'That's what they say, that's what they say. But who says the Transarcidoines need vine poles more than rifles? One or two can always be slipped into the bundles. . . .'

'What are you trying to read into it? . . . Pass me the other hand.'

I'm sticking to my idea. There's something fishy in it all. And come to negotiate what with us? We have nothing to export. They have political motives—that's for sure. A little kingdom like ours where everybody's quite content is no longer in season. Today you have to be oppressed, unbalanced or drunk with boredom. It's not that nobody's bored here, but my subjects have the mentality of first communicants, always hoping for a miracle. They are disarming. The hopes of one produce the despair of others. I am afraid of the reactions of our neighbours.

A valet comes to tell me the ambassadors are here. Baga goes to receive them. I wait ten minutes and then I send the chamberlain ahead of me. He opens the door of the Mercury salon. I enter. There are two ambassadors. I tell them that before hearing their business I wish them to dine with me. They protest politely and we go through to the dining room. All the candles are lit and the valets in state dress. I glance at the ambassadors out of the corner of my eye. They seem to be dazzled. In order to frighten them I tell them that the tiger skins are hunting trophies.

After the meal we have coffee in the Venus salon and the ambassadors beg leave to speak. Gentlemen, I am listening. One of them gets up and delivers this speech:

'Sire. You are not unaware that Novocordia, your neighbour, is a peaceloving and industrious nation. Our laws are good, our ideas healthy, our people disciplined. Now for some years a region close to our borders, which happens to belong to you—we mean to say Chancheze—has been an element of disturbance for our country. We have already drawn your attention to the fact that the rats which overrun this valley tend to infest our territory. After each of our requests you have declared that you have undertaken the deratisation of Chancheze. But the effects of your measures have not been apparent—quite the contrary. It is established that the number of rats transgressing the frontier is in the ascendant. Our government, six months ago, directed you to act with more efficacy. But in vain. Now, Sire, we come to tell you today that Novocordia has decided to occupy Chancheze. We will deratisize this region and keep it for ourselves in recompense for these services. You are not unaware, furthermore, that our country is overpopulated. This valley will shortly be colonised, cultivated and productive. The occupation will be carried out by our troops tomorrow between eleven o'clock and midday. That is all, Sire.'

Ah, the monsters! Well I knew it. I say to them:

'Get out! Get out immediately or I'll cut your balls off.'

They get out. I ask Baga:

'What are we going to do?'

'Sound the drums, assemble the people and leave at once. General mobilisation. We must defend Chancheze.'

'Do I understand you, Baga? You want war?'

'I am concerned only for your honour.'

So that's how we went to war, dear nephews. I was saying a few pages earlier that it wasn't my business. I swear I had nothing to do with it. The rats were a pretext on the part of our neighbours. As for honour, your uncle could well do without it.

We left around four in the morning. I was in Papa's old taxi. It was very good for making war. Baga was beside me with a machine gun, the poor fellow. We had tins of sardines in the boot for snacks and long-lasting military rusks. My ammunition pouches squeezed my belly; my clothes were unbuttoned. We had three motor cyclists clearing our path. Behind us followed the whole capital. My worthy subjects. I have changed my view. They responded as one man to the call and they equipped themselves like lightning. The arsenal was ransacked, all the cars requisitioned. It went very smoothly. The next day was a market day and the lorries from the country were on the spot. I didn't know our arsenal was so well stocked. Baga tells me in the taxi that the profits we derived from our exploitation of Chancheze had been appropriated over ten years for our provision in war material. I ask him what exploitation. He replies—the rats. What, we do something with them? Yes, musk with the musk rats, ivory black with the bones, mink with the furs. And which are our markets? His reply stuns me: our neighbours. So we, too, do business! Baga had assumed this responsibility, as they say. He knew that I would never have agreed. Thanks to him we had become the main suppliers of rats to the whole world. That's how we were a nation, that's how. . . .

'But Baga, is it really true the rats are overflowing into Nova-cordia?'

'It's inaccurate. I receive monthly reports from the gamekeepers. They exterminate the rats within a two-kilometre strip along the frontier.'

No kidding! To think that I had been playing an international role!

Main world supplier! I wanted to ask Baga for all the details, but it wasn't the right moment.

We were at the head of the convoy. The capital was following, as I've said, in lorries, cars, motor bikes, tricycles with sidecars, anything with an engine. Along the route we gathered in the contingents from the districts and the villages, which had been informed by telegraph. It was a black night, but when I turned, I could see the long, glittering ribbon of the convoy. At every crossroads a contingent was waiting, headlights blazing. What organisation! I say to Baga:

'How many people would you say in all? Two hundred? Three hundred?'

'Thirty thousand men, twenty thousand women.'

'My God, Baga! My God! Are there as many people as that in the country?'

I started to weep. It was out of gratitude for poor Baga who had done everything for ten years without seeming to. And there was I making him empty my chamber pot! All at once I tightened my ammunition pouches, I blew my nose and I told myself I would die to defend my people. I admired the way Baga had pretended to be amazed when I mentioned war to him. It was so as not to scare me. He knew we were ready.

There's only one route to Chancheze. The roads from the villages converge on it from the right and left in the pattern of a fish bone. We drove for three hours, pulling in fresh contingents all the time and we arrived at seven o'clock. We came to a halt at the entrance to the valley and got out of the taxi. The first car behind us was our headquarters. The general, rather ancient, and lieutenants Fouille, Vivi and Basset, who are young and healthy. Baga discussed the positioning of the troops, but his plan had been ready long before. There would be a formation at the entrance to the valley, one on either side of the valley on the heights—each of which would advance towards the frontier or fall back, according to circumstances—and another at the frontier to bear the brunt of the first attack. Novocordia had no aeroplanes, which simplified matters. I took a very deep breath and said: 'I want to lead the forward formation.'

That threw a spanner in the works. Baga turned quite pale. He told me I was not to think of it. I insisted. He suggested I take the general with me in case of emergency. I agreed. There was no time to vacillate. It was necessary to give orders to those waiting in the queue and the lieutenants took care of that. The flank formations started to climb and I set off with my troops, that's to say 15,000 men and the general. It was eight o'clock. We had one hour to cross the valley, two hours to take up our positions.

I am severely abridging everything because I don't know military language and because I don't understand how 50,000 men arriving at a valley in single file could get organised so rapidly. Probably throughout the country they were skilled in manoeuvres, learned them at school. God knows. I must ask Baga. In any case I'll decorate him with the Order of St. Honoré. He'll be my cousin. In short, the operation moved at an unbelievable speed. I drove on with my men behind. I had responsibilities and that made me feel quite strange. I wasn't afraid. I told myself it was destiny. I am even sure that to have demanded that command was my destiny. Obviously it wasn't a question of courage—I was no less of a coward than usual.

The rats were starting to come out of their holes. They watched us go by, or they fled. The more we advanced, the more there were. It was the noise of the convoy which was waking them by degrees. Soon they were everywhere and we began to crush them. Still more . . . and more. . . . We could no longer see the route. Some even sprang onto the mudguards, the bonnet, the roof. And in the fields great swellings of grey waves. The driver pushed through as much as he could. At one point I noticed factory chimneys on our right. The general told me they were mink manufacturers. They had a very important air. The workers couldn't have been alerted for the chimneys were smoking. I appreciated this mark of confidence in victory on the part of Baga.

We arrived at nine o'clock as anticipated. There were far fewer rats now. I decided to deploy my men in the two kilometres where the rats had been exterminated. I divided them into fifteen groups of a thousand and I appointed fifteen leaders. Each group had machine guns and cannons with an ammunition supply from the lorries spread all around. I told my men we would fight to the last bullet. Men and women yelled, long live the king. Then we placed ourselves at strategic points on both sides of the defile and lay in wait.

What an adventure, good God! Up to that point I hadn't realised I was a nationalist. I was in a group with the general. He was senile. He didn't understand the situation and he was laughing all the time. In the end, everyone was laughing. I found it very good for the morale.

At a quarter past eleven we heard the rumbling of the enemy's motorised column. I saw the first motor cyclists crouching at the entrance to the valley and the cannons being brought into position. They opened fire, but we didn't reply. I had given the order to wait until the Novocordian troops entered the valley. They came on, meeting no resistance. We opened fire on the last tank. Immediate riposte and start of the battle. The observers took some time to locate us, by which time we'd already done a lot of damage. My plan was to immobilise the vehicles, to destroy the motorised column first. It

worked well. But what I hadn't foreseen was a second motorised
column. We were too occupied with the first and things began to go
badly. Suddenly I had an idea. I would send a group behind them,
beyond the two-kilometre band, with orders to set fire to the brush.
The wind was blowing against us. At the same time I would order the
rest to climb the slopes, continuing to fire on the vehicles.

After an hour and a half of sputtering, we saw the smoke from the
fire sealing the valley. It advanced rapidly. And soon came the flames.
And the rats. The rats in droves of millions. The enemy was virtually
demotorised, though lively. The effect produced by the rats was as I
had anticipated. The creatures, terrified by the fire which pursued
them, rushed upon the Novocordians. Rather than be devoured alive,
the enemy flowed back to the defile. The rats pursued them and now
entered Novocordia. The fire petered out close to the frontier where
the brush disappeared. We were sheltered in the heights.

In the other sectors battles were raging. The enemy had attacked
along the lateral ridges and clashed with our formations. They had
been driven back. And so forth. . . .

It's painful. I wanted to go as far as possible. To play the game, as
they say. It was clear that I didn't believe in it, wasn't it? What to
believe in? From what point is everything false? The ambassadors?
No, I remember having talked to them. Our departure in the night?
My taking command? I no longer know, no longer know. . . . This
drowsiness, this desire for sleep which invades me.

To get back to my room. Water Ducky. Do away with the servants?
Do the housework, the cooking? That will come. I am not intended
for great purposes. To confine myself to my exterior. Talking of that,
this is my body. I have a fat, pimply head. Swellings, pustules. My
lashes droop in my eyes. I have a nose like a potato and cauliflower
ears. My hair is sand-coloured. So are my teeth. My neck is fat and
white, chest slack, held up under the arms by a yellow bush of hair. I
have three hairs on my sternum which I shave every Saturday. My
belly bulges from the stomach down. Once I could pull it in like
everyone else, but not now. I can only see my sex by bending over.
There's nothing crazy about the surprise packet. Hair a little less
yellow than under the arms. A stumpy rod and a slack scrotum. It
hangs low. By pulling up the skin as I straighten up, it's possible to
cover over all my lower belly with it. That's the game my women play.
My thighs are lank and my behind enormous. When I look at myself
in the mirror, I seem like a fat, white worm. From the knee my legs are
bloated, as I've said. They are varicose. I have two logs under the foot
of my bed. I mean the legs of the foot. For a better nocturnal
circulation. My toes are the best part of me. Not at all deformed,
thanks to the swansdown. I have my grandmother's hands except that

I don't wear rings. It appears that they're pretty, but they rather disgust me.

After the war, for the war took place, but not like I said, another one, slow, year after year, a war resembling leprosy, in which one could do nothing, one decomposed, I slept all the time, there were no more newspapers, the rats came right up to the town, the enemy finally gave up and there were barely 1,500 inhabitants left in the kingdom. . . . After this illness, Baga awakened me and I had become so thin. I should have. . . . I should have. . . . I don't know. I left. I have been in the forest. There, I am in the forest. I am sitting down. I am writing this. No, I have written. Or I was writing.

(Translated by John Stevenson)

The Inquisitory (1962)

What do you know about Pierre Hottelier

He often used to come too I told you during the day or to parties, he tried very hard to look well-bred but it stands out a mile that he's not I don't know his family they're from the West, Marthe says they must have been actors their son looks so much as if he's playing a part she doesn't like actors at all, there were several among my gentlemen's friends

How could you tell he had no education

Various little details always combing his hair or scratching at some spot on his trousers or too much of his handkerchief showing from his top pocket, or talking with his hand in front of his mouth or his way of walking or sitting down things like that

Why did you observe him in particular

I didn't say that

Who were these actors who were friendly with your employers

Douglas Hotcock Michael Donéant Ralf Morgione Sylvie Lacruseille Babette Saint-Foin and also young Jean Duval on one of his flying visits he's almost settled in Hollywood now he's one I almost saw come into the world you might say, his poor mother as good as died of grief when he got in with that cinema crowd she was sure he'd go to the bad

Was Jean Duval a pseudonym

Yes his real name is Martin Coulon the stockbroker's son, his mother was a Parazou Yolande Parazou she worried herself sick over him it's no exaggeration to say it killed her, my sister knew her well she was very pious and she went to Lourdes when Martin made his first film, she used to tell my sister she was praying for him to be cured as if the cinema was a disease my sister's sure that was it but it didn't work and I tell you she didn't last long after that, she used to come and see my sister every day to talk to her about Martin always in tears and three years later she died, my sister was sure she must have had something wrong with her chest grief alone could never have finished her off so quickly anyway she could never understand what poor Yolande found so awful about her son's career, he's never given rise to any scandal in any case not here with us on the contrary we always thought he was more like a shy little girl

Who is Douglas Hotcock

An American in the forties he speaks French badly but he says he only likes French films, he's been in one or two small ones I've seen him with Marthe two or three years ago now he acted with Florence Barclay in that one what was it called something like The Blood of the Roses or The Blood of the Flowers, he acted some chap who gambled at the casino and Florence Barclay was his mistress he deceived her with some other women from the casino it was at Monte Carlo I think, and in the end she kills him you see him lying on the floor beside a vase of flowers that's been knocked over yes they were roses she was always wanting him to buy her some it comes back to me now, she's the actress I've always liked best she never seems to grow any older I don't often go to the cinema it's not my strong point I've said that before I've seen perhaps twenty movies in all.

Who is Michel Donéant

He acts for the theatre never has any work he used to belong to a company The Amphitheatre or The Amphitryon they went touring in Morocco, he was sacked by the director I believe he took part in cabarets he had no right to or he'd signed a contract with another theatre, anyhow he must be about thirty the look-at-me type he tries to get by with radio work he says he's often on but Marthe never sees his name in the radio magazine, she knows he borrows from everyone and he does some filing too at his brother-in-law's who has an insurance office, all the time he's in trouble with the police I mean for his income tax and his tailor for example my gentlemen told him to go to Nantet they'd have paid but he doesn't want to, it seems he doesn't like Nantet's cut you can see the sort of bird he is

In trouble with the police you say

I don't mean the police but the authorities and the lawyers

Who is Ralf Morgione

A cinema actor too he's Italian but the only one that's rich, got a lovely Farina car at times there are eight of them in it he races up to the house and shoots the gravel all over the place and on to the lawns again and again his filthy wheels making ruts I had to even out or else the gardener and sow fresh grass, once I was there to open the car door he'd just ruined one of the lawns and they were all killing themselves with laughter, Morgione shouted *scusa scusa* into my ear but he didn't give a damn just like the American with his sorries he'd knock us down or run over our feet he couldn't care less just says sorry but it's as good as saying drop dead

Who came with Morgione in the car

Friends they weren't always the same, rushing about all the time and smashing glasses they got me down

Who is Sylvie Lacruseille

She's on television she's the friend of Mademoiselle Babette they always come together very nice both of them, Mademoiselle Sylvie always has a very strong scent which lingers on till the next day in the drawing-room, Marthe says it's called *Ton Coeur* and Mademoiselle Babette's always smoking cigars it's funny for a woman, they live in a flat in town Rue Gou the new block of flats on the eighth floor I know the concierge he doesn't like them, as if it was any business of his if they live together this tittle-tattle about people it's of no interest to me if they're pleasant they can live with whoever they like, they're very sweet they often used to bring me tobacco

What kind of tobacco

Dutch for my pipe you can't get it here, they often go to Holland for the television or to order tulips, they've got a little place at Rottard-Chizy they've shown me some snaps of their tulips there's a great flower-bed in front of the house with five

Babette Saint-Foin is she also on television

I think so yes

When they go there do they visit Rivière

They don't go to Amsterdam they go to Holland, Amsterdam is the Low Countries

What impression do they make physically

What do you mean

Describe what they look like

Mademoiselle Sylvie is fairly tall she's got rather short brown hair, she's a large hook nose as she says or as she used to say when I could still enjoy a little chat, she almost always wears trousers it's Nantet who makes them for her she has a large green ring and her scent as I said what else she's got a nervous tick lifting her shoulders as if she was hampered by her clothes and Mademoiselle Babette is blonde and small rather plumpish, she has black eyes and ear-rings at least a dozen different pairs last time I saw her she had some that hang down to the shoulders I don't think much of that, she's got very tiny feet and Italian shoes Marthe says she knows, she's very fond of a chat with these young ladies who always come to the kitchen they bring her chocolate and they've given her several recipes Mademoiselle Sylvie that is, for example let me see yes the Soufflé Baptiste with almonds and rum and a green sauce she's invented tarragon with a pinch of mint and several others, she took a cookery course she doesn't hold with pressure cookers just like Marthe but Mademoiselle Babette says they're both antediluted and you've got to be up-to-date pressure cookers save a lot of time

Describe Douglas Hotcock

He's on the tall side thin with wavy grey hair he must appeal to the women, always an impeccable shirt with a button-down collar and those little suits they have over there you know very fine cloth and tight all over, it's only his shoes that don't go my gentlemen make fun of him but he doesn't like modern shoes, it's true in town you get used to seeing young chaps with elegant shoes he won't have them although he says he's so fond of our fashions, he's got blue eyes I think and his mouth and nose well I can't remember

Why do you say he must appeal to the women

Because he's a handsome man with soft eyes and always well-dressed the best cocks as they say aren't always the fattest

Do you think he appeals to your young ladies

How should I know they all lark about together they've been good friends for a long time as for the rest I don't know

Describe the others

Morgione always well-dressed too quite tall but rather fat he perspires all the time he has a spare shirt in the boot of his car, he's got black eyes and hair too like all Italians and fat hairy hands and a diamond on his little finger that's said to be worth a couple of million, he's been getting a corporation over the last few years what can he be somewhere about thirty-five

Michael Donéant

Pale and weedy with long fair hair and terribly thin hands, the young ladies were very fond of him he never stops talking he has a sister who came a few times tall and affected never says a word

Is she a friend of the young ladies

I don't know I only know she was engaged to someone called Tolkovitch or Toklovitch who trafficked in drugs he committed suicide in her house they said something in the papers at the time, an article by that Lorpailleur woman I remember

Did your employers know this Lorpailleur woman

There was a time when they talked about her they'd gone to a cocktail party at her publishers for one of her novels they found her quite ridiculous with her blue stockings it seems, when you think what some people will do to be famous it really makes you wonder, it's like Morgione if he's the richest it's because he's the biggest show-off all that publicity about his so-called engagement in the illustrated papers even last week an article in the Agapa Echo just imagine, I'm sure it's my gentlemen who were responsible for that

What do you mean by so-called engagement

Nothing at all he's never been engaged the girl with him in the photos is a friend of that Odette or Yvette who needed some publicity too, she's gone off to Mexico or somewhere like that

Who is this Odette or Yvette

Donéant's sister

What do you mean by they all lark about together

I told you they drink like fishes all night they're lucky not to have any other neighbours but farmers and gardeners, even at that distance Clément used to say he couldn't sleep at times

Do you know when

When what

What times

You really make me wonder what you're after, how do you expect me to know

How do you know Morgione had a spare shirt in his car

Because they used to damn well tell me to go and fetch it and once even I found the boot full of photos all scattered about I had to gather them up before I could find the shirt underneath

What kind of photos

Just photos

Answer

Dirty photos

Describe them

Not on your life it's worse than animals

Was the boot left open

No he used to give me the key and that time with the photographs he must have forgotten about them till later, he told me he had a photographer friend who was doing some research and he laughed

Was Morgione in these photographs

You couldn't see the faces

Sylvie and Babette you say you know these young ladies' concierge

Yes that's Soulevart André an old army pal of Pompom's and his wife's a Juvy Marguerite Juvy, you can forgive them really for not being very agreeable they've had a lot of trouble that business with Nollet's bank they lost everything in that, they intended to retire to a lodge they had near Crachon but they had to sell up it wasn't worth much and they found this place in the new block of flats, they'll never get over it I mean to say first they found a two-roomed flatlet at 16 Rue Vieille but it was too dear for them and then this job, they're fairly comfortable mind they've two rooms there too and the fridge and not much to do for the staircase there's a woman who comes poor old Margot has aches and pains she can't do much now neither can he, he was quite a handy man once when they were still at Fantoine they had the grocer's next to the Migeotte laundry he used to knock up shelves in the shop and potter about the room at the back where they used to hang out in the end he'd made it quite habitable, he had his son to help him then Philippe young Pipo as they called him he was killed in the war, their daughter Agathe married Sinture the ex-postman's son she's settled in town now he's in an office some export business I think, she doesn't see her parents any more they quarrelled her husband's not baptised old Sinture's as hard as nails they're bringing their two children up without religion, it made old Margot

quite ill and they've never met since but now after all her disappointments she'd like to make it up with her daughter who's not too keen
because of her husband

Whereabouts is Rottard-Chizy

It lies to the west about a hundred and twenty-five miles there are
springs for the digestion and the liver a luxury hotel where the young
ladies go, my gentlemen have been there too two or three times but
they prefer Vichy, at Rottard there aren't many amusements apart
from walks through the valley, but a little while ago I saw in the paper
they'd made a golf course so perhaps that will bring some customers
back, the Mayor is related to Mademoiselle Babette that's what gave
them the idea of buying something there, a Monsieur Borra or Borro
where they get invited there's a swimming pool it seems with water
from the springs that cost him a packet specially as he had a long
drawn-out law suit but he won, the young ladies said that after the
verdict he threw a great banquet at home and a lady fell into the pool

Did your employers know this Borra or Borro

I don't know

Did Ralf Morgione bring his so-called fiancée to see your
employers

No I told you it was last week, once he brought a negress Marthe
was horrified she said that lot should stay where they were born they
called her Boubou she was very smart the Josephine Baker type and
not very dark, they'd organised a leopard hunt for her it was all so
stupid, the leopard was Gérard with cat's fur sewn all over his clothes
he hid in the garden and jumped around and they shot arrows at him
that I'd made up out of bamboo with a piece of cloth at the end so as
not to hurt him, for two hours they played about at this game
then they took the car out with the leopard at the wheel and they all
ended up at the Trois-Abeilles, there was a picture in the *Petit
Photographe*

What do you know about this Gérard

He's one of my gentlemen's friends I told you

Why do you say you don't put him in the same class as Monsieur de
Longuepie and the other gentlemen

Because it's true

What do you mean by that

He's a hooligan from the village I mean a loafer his parents never
knew what to make of him, he's twenty-four or five better if he'd
stayed in the colonies after his military service, his father is Vélac the
coal-merchant he tried to get him interested in commerce but the
boy's always junketing in town or at my gentlemen's place, they tried
too to get him in with Monnier the picture dealer but that didn't work
either when he got out of the army he married one of the Quinche girls

the Curé's cousins they're rich, Gérard managed to extract some money out of his wife which he put into the Hottencourt flour mills a good investment just before his divorce, the Quinche family wanted to take him to court for swindling but it was a gift from their daughter she'd signed a paper you can see he knew how to fiddle it, it was to be separate maintenance there was nothing they could do or else they just gave it up, so the dirty work goes on last year he nearly married an English widow he got to know in the coach on the trip to the ruins he often goes as guide in the summer, she stayed three months at Sirancy they put out they were engaged she gave him some money and then she had to go back home for someone who died, Gérard was rid of her but she chased him up it's Louisette who knows all about it, the English woman wrote to her they got to know each other at the bistro she must have been one for the bottle those English women you know, but Gérard dropped her he's on the track of someone else just now always thanks to the ruins where he picks up his foreign women, an old maid who doesn't know what to do with her millions Norwegian or Swedish staying at the same hotel as the English woman it's bound to end the same way, come to think of it these foreign women must all be potty you don't have to look at him twice to see his little game as my mother used to say when a girl wants to stray her wits fly away, all this I know through Marthe we still see each other in town at Gorin's she loves their *petits fours* but now she puts it all down on paper for me

Are you a hopeless case, have you seen a specialist

I saw one a couple of years ago and he prepared me for it so now, but you get used to it you're more observant you see everything that goes on around you at the café for example once upon a time I'd never even have noticed, now I tell myself it's a compensation if I've got a long time ahead of me perhaps I'll acquire an innane gift as they say for observation

Térence Monnier does he sell pictures or restore them

Both he has a studio for restoration and framing Rue Surtout where he has two experts at work and he sells pictures too at his gallery Rue de Biron, that's where they wanted Gérard to go he'd have been quite good at it he's got the gift of the gab

Why did you say your employers took their custom to the flour mills at Vériville

Because they do what else do you think they did with their crops, the farmer has a right to half he keeps what he needs for the chickens and the rest goes to the flour mills at Hottencourt, my gentlemen take their half to Vériville it's one of their arrangements to try and please everyone

Who was the flunkey

Fellow named Randon Eric he joined the household five years after me didn't know a thing I'm the one who showed him everything you'd think he'd never seen a bed or a bath, came straight from his backwoods Lozère and at once started pretending he knew it all one blunder after another and it didn't do to remind him of them later, sometimes Marthe would say to him when he annoyed her why don't you have another go at the parquet he'd washed the whole drawing-room floor with soapy water you can imagine, another time it was black coffee in the breakfast cups another time a whole dish of *quenelles* on the carpet of the large dining-room, another time the office curtains he got them so they wouldn't pull and we had to have the furnisher in, another time he handed Marthe a bottle of *marc* for a sauce instead of cognac she had to start it all over again at the last minute believing me she'd never ask him a favour again, not to speak of his waiting at table three weeks I spent on him nor his behaviour nor his way of opening doors or anything else, so to see my gentlemen make a joke of it got on my nerves they'd easily give a housemaid the sack in a week even less for some nonsense or other, but him they kept him he was cunning he used to flatter them or he'd make his excuses in all the right words but I'm sorry for his accent, Marthe told me he used to say *môchieu* for monsieur and cooberd for cupboard perhaps that's what used to amuse them it wasn't so funny, even Marthe at table though she didn't trust him she'd laugh and correct him she's had some education I told you, when she had her jewellers shop she used to see the right people and she reads books just to show you she writes down in an exercise book every day what interests her and things about people she calls it her diary and it's very well written, about the flunkey for example she'd heard quite a bit all in all from the village or the town amongst other things the time he'd spend in front of the men's clothing shops, he blew everything he earned togging himself up we wondered how he could have bought his suede jacket and his shirts from Jacquot's it's the most expensive shop in Agapa only for tourists, he must have worked some fiddle with someone from the shop and that reminds me his radio set fifty thousand he paid for that in his second month I'd stake my life he didn't have that when he arrived, his parents are muck-rakers in the back of beyond he must have borrowed from someone I don't know, then he got on well with Luisot they used to go out together and you can ask the boss of the Colibri that's the bar in the Rue des Albigeois which leads onto the Quai des Moulins, Servais his name is he only serves whiskies and vodka a thousand francs the glass again I ask you how could they both pay that price, Servais said they were good customers but I don't believe it worked some fiddle with him too probably, still it's a crying shame in our profession the kind of people

get handed on to us now a well-trained valet no-one knows what that
is any more they used to be classy in my day even the company they
kept

You said you used to meet him sometimes in town, who was he with

With Luisot or some of the others a rum lot of lads not even clean
about their person a bunch of drunkards and tarts like that redhead
she hangs round the Colibri too, girl called Viviane whose bit of
pavement is the corner of the Rue des Casse-Tonnelles and the Rue
Charles very central her hotel's in a cul-de-sac the Deux-Gros they
say she gets up to twenty clients on a good day, the market's not far
off plenty of people all through the evening it's a place for tourists I
told you

Who is this Jacquot

The posh shirt-maker in the Avenue Dominique-Lapoire next to
the Mouton Gras it's on the corner of the Rue Filière which at the far
end leads onto the Place des Maures if you understand, he started as a
draper quite a tiny shop in the Rue Octave-Serpent it's during the war
he made his pile now he's successful you can't even wish him good-
day, he's bought a villa on the outskirts too his wife's an old cat
always pushing him on one of the Pintonnat girls very ordinary
family, her parents both worked for Boche it was the grandmother I
knew best she was a washerwoman she slaved away for us all right my
mother never did the washing we weren't without means, when I see
Mother Jacquot it makes me think of old Ma Pintonnat and I have a
good laugh people forget they're not the only ones who have a good
memory

What do you mean by working some fiddle with someone from the
shop

How do I know an assistant or a saleswoman or the boss how can
you tell unless

Unless what

Unless Mother Jacquot but that's between ourselves it seems she's
not above a little slap and tickle as Renée says, she used to know her
well she still went in for it while she was engaged with a chap called
Sureau and she's meant to have gone on after the wedding

What do you mean by muck-rakers

Peasants clod-hoppers

What do you know about the boss of the Colibri

Servais oh him no need to worry he'll always fall on his feet you
know the kind of bar it's only your backside that counts forgive the
expression but it's true, Viviane isn't the only one who goes there
she's only there from time to time, there are three or four other tarts
and boys too it seems it's disgraceful it's never empty, they close at six
in the morning special licence no-one could ever find out why but I

suppose it's the Mayor who does it for the town an advertisement like anything else, Servais uses it as a hotel too on the quiet there are bedrooms on the upper floors the building belongs to him, if you like foreigners that's where you go you'd think it was only when they came to us that they let their hair down, men you'd take to be gentlemen and so-called society women you should see them rolling under the table, there are some old regulars women like the Princesse de Hem and the Duchess they've been laid by all the lads in the district and the negro type they know them too, talking about negroes there's often a fight there Servais has threatened to keep them out, you can say what you like about racialism there's a good side to it I'm like Marthe they haven't got our way of thinking, I don't mean their morals we're all tarred with the same brush I mean their sense of humour they're too offensible they don't understand and Bob's your uncle a brawl

Whereabouts is the Quai des Moulins

Along the river on the left bank on the west side of the town it continues to the north along the Quai des Tanneurs to the south along the Quai Henri-Vachon, it's one of the oldest districts after the centre round Les Oublies and the cathedral, that's where I most like to take a walk around Les Moulins there's one mill left on the corner of the Rue des Rats not been used for a hundred years now, all the houses round about are half-timbered going back to the Middle Ages there's an *estaminet* with an inn sign the Pou-qui-rote and a little cobbler who looks as old as his workshop, he wears a skull-cap winter and summer alike old Père Michel as he's called in memory of his wife old Mère Michel because she used to feed all the cats in the district, the roofs are dark brown tiles they use mass-produced tiles to repair them much redder they spoil them, good thing if the Mayor looked into it it's true for the visitors but there are still some who look at the old bits not only the baths and the ruins, not far off there's the Rue du Trou-de-Poil funny name the Curé from Sirancy says it's a deformation of the Latin I remember Marthe had noted it down in her book, it's *troncus* and *politus* that means polished trunk there must have been some cabinet-makers in these parts in Roman times it joins the Rue des Rats to the Rue des Albigeois, a bit further there's the Rue du Son because of the old mills where there's a potter who makes souvenir pots red or black with Agapa written on them, not very modern when you compare them with the shops on the main avenues but they sell all right to the English anyway there are other things in his shop but it's chiefly the pots that go well, I could stay for hours in those streets you can see the windows all crooked I mean the house-fronts all askew full of dents and bulges and tiny little balconies, most of them are being removed they're dangerous but they're restoring the ones at the Maison-Bertrand that belongs to the Archaeological Society the president is Monsieur Carré a friend of my gentlemen's as I said, I often sit on the embankment under the plane trees we have very beautiful plane trees

The name of the river

I was just going to say it's the Manu which runs from east to west but after the forest it bends to the south, then it winds back to the north and again to the west it makes a great curve round the Plateau as it's called, that starts behind my gentlemen's house rises slowly and then falls away again about nine miles further on down to the town so when you're on the embankment the river flows from north to south, in fact in the Rue Octave-Serpent past the Rue du Son there's the Plumet bookshop on the corner where they have an old map in the window you can see it all, not a map like nowadays the houses are all there and the trees too it's very practical, the Rue Octave-Serpent used to be called the Rue des Chaudrons this Serpent was a town councillor before the fourteen war there's a plaque I've forgotten the dates, the Rue de Broy finishes on the right one of the longest streets that goes on to the Avenue des Africains in front of the hospital, the whole of this area's full of little streets you can easily get muddled if you don't know and on top of that they change their names, for example the Rue du Nid after the Rue Serpent becomes the Rue des Trappes then it joins the Rue de Broy and as it bends round just at that point you might think it still went on the same but after that it's the Rue Chattemite et cetera, it's the history of these streets and houses that's so fascinating they'd do far better to run a regular column in the Echo or the Fantoniard instead of those articles by that Lorpailleur woman on the new novel as she calls it her theories don't interest anyone, yes the old streets in that part as far as Les Oublies there's a book mind at Plumet's but it's an old one not so easy to understand it's worth twenty-thousand francs just imagine that for a book

Where is the site of the old triumphal arch

I told you Les Oublies, from the embankment you can take the Rue Gou near the Rue des Rats you cross the Rue des Marquises and go straight on along the Rue Souper-Trombone you see the name changes, according to Plumet this one comes from *super* and *tropoum* Latin again because of the triumphal arch, so if you follow that road you come out just at the right spot there's a railing in the little square you go down into a kind of cellar and you can see the stones that are left, its like the baths you can find them on the right if you go on up the Rue Edouard-Flan you cross the Rue du Magnificat then Casse-Tonnelles and you're in the Rue Charles, twenty yards along on the left the cul-de-sac of Deux-Gros with the old baths almost opposite you go down as before, mind you when you leave the embankment it's shorter to go up the Rue des Albigeois, you cross Les Marquises turn to your left and the first on your right is the Rue du Cimetière which takes you straight there it bends round and comes into the Rue Charles, I tell you if I'd known I'd have studied when I was young to become a guide instead of spending my life in other people's houses

You mentioned the main avenues, which are they

Let's just say the avenues there's the Avenue Dominique-Lapoire that goes from Les Oublies to the Place de l'Hôtel-de-Ville, the Avenue Georges-Pompier which runs from the Quai Henri-Vachon and also ends up at the Hôtel-de-Ville, the Avenue Paul-Colonel which starts at the Quai des Tanneurs and leads to the crossroads at Les Oublies, the Avenue des Africains which comes from the Place de l'Hôpital and is continued on the north side by the Avenue Amélie-XXXIII and the Avenue de Douves which shoots off Dominique-Lapoire towards the station

From your Quai des Moulins how do you get to the cathedral

The easiest way is to follow in the direction of the Quai des Tanneurs, you pass the Rue Gou on your right and you take the next turning the Rue Surtout you follow that up to the Rue Croquette on your left go up that street then cross the Rue Bassinoire and straight on till you reach the Avenue Paul-Colonel, you go along there for a while on the right-hand side so you can cross at the crossing and then the Rue des Irlandais which is almost opposite, there's first the Rue Sam then the Rue Suzanne on the left the Rue du Coucou on the right and the narrow Rue du Triet you go straight on till you get to the Rue Jérôme, it's not really worth crossing though you could mind the Rue des Irlandais goes on as the Rue des Omelettes, that comes into the Rue Pisson and there you're quite near the square but you might just as well take the Rue Jérôme for a while on the right it's easier you run straight into the Rue de L'Enfant-Dieu which joins the Rue des Trouble-Fête to the Place Karl-Marx, that's the old cathedral square they've changed its name right in the middle there's a statue of the philosopher holding a dove it's by a sculptor called Surprend such a nice little square it spoils it, before there was a statue of Sainte Fiduce patron saint of the church they've sent that to the museum, in stone all crumbling away she wears a crown but not because she was queen it's the crown of the virgins and martyrs, she didn't want to sleep with some barbarian chieftain I ask you it was during the invasions they threw her in the river with a stone round her neck it's written down in the little guide-book they sell Rue Baga a few doors away, except they say marry instead of sleep with of course, they explain the construction of the cathedral too its length and width all that, and how the Bishop doesn't reside in Agapa as you know they have a Canon you'd have to look up the guide for the details anyway all this part is the oldest you can go for long walks there to Les Moulins for example, and on the other side of the square there's the Rue Saint-Violon which corresponds to the Rue Baga, they join up again in the Rue du Crève-Tombeau which crosses the Rue de la Chèvre and goes on till it reaches the Avenue Amélie-XXXIII passing in front of the castle, it's not bad with a big square keep in the middle and round the curtain wall the Tower Amélie-XXXI, the Jews' Tower on the corner of the Avenue and the Dualie Tower behind the corner of the Avenue and the Rue des Tatoués, the fourth one collapsed that was the Tower of Bois-Suspect the Dukes of Bois-Suspect were once the Lords of Agapa but the castle's belonged to the state for a long time now, you can visit it Wednesdays and Saturdays there's nothing inside everything of interest has gone to the museum, you can climb up the Dualie Tower and have a view of the Avenue with the shops and museum opposite, the Place des Maures on the right and the Rue de Biron which goes to the station the steps are very steep and frighten the ladies there's a notice up warning slippery steps, you cross the main courtyard you can't visit the keep that's where the caretaker lives with his daughter money for jam, all he does is take the visitors to the bottom of the steps he doesn't even go up any more and close the main door after the visit, in the building to the south there's the police-station on the Rue des Tatoués you can go back that way, cross the Rue Magnasse which forks off towards the cathedral leave the Rue des Singes behind on the left then take the Rue du Panier-à-Pain till you get to the Rue des Clous, cross it and take the narrow Rue du Docteur-Tronc which leads into Trouble-Fête, turn to the left and the first on the left is the Rue Duport with the house of Antoine Duport head of the Merchants' Guild the house is intact all carved with garlands and local worthies with its beams and tiny stained-glass windows they had then, there's a boundary stone in front which used to mark the end of the monastery estates I forgot to say that the monastery

Do you know if there are any surviving members of the Bois-Suspect family

Well in a way there's the Duchess Madam Sham we call her too, she's no more a Duchess than I am she's from the Balkans mind Rumanian or Bulgarian who knows, twenty years ago she married the old Duke Alphonse who still had a house near the Hospital he died soon after in narrow straits, this is where they first met she'd already been a bit of a rolling stone, married again straight after Alphonse died married a Greek shipowner chap called Patrocles Frimides then he died too and left her his millions, she insists on being called Duchesse de Bois-Suspect she must be nearly seventy, every year she stays at the Grand Hôtel I mean that before the Grand Hôtel the

Hôtel des Bains was the smartest and the Grand Hôtel was completely transformed ten years ago, every year she comes for the season with her friend old fat Hem they meet here for the waters so they say they're more often out than in

There are waters at Agapa you say

I should jolly well think so since Roman times the springs are still running for the circulation rheumatism all that, the old pump room still exists Rue Bitard opposite the ruins but no-one goes there much now it's not well kept up and there are no mud baths like in the new buildings, the local people some of them still go it makes a big difference in the price but visitors go to the new one the S.B.A. runs that too the Society for the Baths of Agapa comes under the Corporation, they don't want for luxury there marble everywhere by that I mean the stone's from Chanchèze and when it's polished it's like a kind of marble, there are little springs in every corridor birds that spit water because of the name of the pump room Les Oiseaux-Baigneurs, it's all fitted up in the latest fashion the mud comes from Malatraîne round that way it's Dumans who sees to the transport

Whereabouts is the new pump room

Not far from the old Rue des Bains as they call it now it used to be the old Rue du Goret-Sifflard between the Rue Charles and the Rue des Marquises, there's a swimming pool and private bathrooms and on the first floor the mud, they've a large staff two doctors masseurs and masseuses servants and waitresses, a bar on every floor where the whisky's as dear as at the Colibri but you should just see how they get through it, that sort of crowd don't need treatment any more than you or I do, behind the pump room they've knocked the old houses down to make a garden with a swimming pool too and an outdoor bar open to non-residents

Who is this Princesse de Hem

The Duchess's friend they go tippling together I told you she lives in Vienna in Austria, a plump blonde about fifty it seems her husband's been in the government she looks more like a housemaid in spite of her pearls and her Cadillac she gets her chauffeur to drive it here Petit-Louis nice fellow, the journey takes him three days you can't say he likes his mistress you know how it is but he's been working for her for fifteen years, he told us she'd made advances to him at the start even if something did happen for a while it's all over now she gets herself a new gigolo every year, last year it was one called Franz a fair boy who came to my gentlemen's with her and Madam Sham

Did he come from Vienna with her

Yes she's brought several with her like that or else she finds one on

the spot out of those who come for the season, Gérard's had his turn
too but that didn't last a fortnight later she'd found another called
Albert which caused a row at the Colibri with Gérard

Why if Gérard visits the Colibri does he chase after women at the
ruins

The questions you ask, I suppose he finds they're the real thing as
he says besides at the Colibri he's too well-known

The Duchess and this Princess did they often visit your employers

Yes during the season they generally arrive in June and stay a
month

What do you mean by the season

That's from May to September they tried one year to keep the baths
open in winter with a smaller staff, they only had four or five visitors
it wasn't worth the candle they didn't repeat the experiment

(Translated by Donald Watson)

Fable (1971)

Looking for somewhere to spend the night he stopped at an abandoned barn, went in, made a hole in the hay and fell asleep in it, his haversack under his head.

But someone had seen him in the moonlight, a belated traveller.

There are times of initial despair which alternate with others when the soul is liberated but little by little the alternation stops and that's when the head begins to rot.

Did he think about it before he fell asleep or did he only count the beams in the roof.

And that other belated person.

The town had evaporated as a result of a cataclysm, nothing was left but the dross.

The people were camping in little groups in the ruins or making their way into the fields.

This future to be dissolved.

A man called Miaille or whatever but the time isn't ripe.

Poppies in the morning were reddening in the oats.

So the night is over.

He goes off to the blazing meadow and he says poppies for the children, fading nosegays, far-away years, far-away and pleasant.

He takes some cheese out of his haversack and a bottle of wine.

Naked men with leather belts come out of the river and make their way towards the corpse lying on the bank. They carve it up with the knives hanging from their belts and start to devour it. Their leader has reserved the phallus for himself and he makes short work of it before starting on the groin.

Or those clusters of delphiniums when June starts yellowing in the fields.

A little kitchen garden full of aromatic herbs.

It seems he didn't go straight to sleep, but counted the beams in the roof, attaching the day's images to them, the poppies, the naked men, the ruins of the town.

The corpse on the river bank was that of a boy with white skin and blue hair, as beautiful as ivory and ultramarine.

But the men attacked it again, carved it up again, devoured it all but its head which they hung from the leader's saddle. They went off at a gallop.

And he saw the people coming up behind and all the golden

landscape, his beard was covered with poppies, his eyes were open.

It was the images of the night that made his head heavy now, all the pleasant years, far-away and pleasant, like a ton of vomited sugar or a stinking defaecation.

The past to be dissolved likewise.

Little by little the alternation stops.

Very little landscape, some yellow on the plain, a few trees, the time is still not ripe.

This present which made him speak, not to know any more what it's composed of.

I can see that rotting, bleeding head attached to the saddle.

And always the groups of exiles picnicking, tins of food, greasy papers, pallid faces, they go off then stop then go off again.

The town still smoking.

A house that was ours he said and here I am among the exiles eating dry bread and weeping endlessly from one stop to another, from one night to another, until the day when this possession will be no more than a photo in my pocket between my passport and a postcard.

And no longer see.

And only just hear.

Just a muffled, inarticulate lament, perceive it piecemeal then lose it then pick up its harmonics again on the threadbare old string of the instrument eviscerated by the barbarians.

Lament, lament again, the poppies are fading and the photo is yellowing in his pocket, it was put there yesterday, centuries of avalanches, of clashes, of mortal wounds.

This Miaille or whatever his name is who found himself alone in the barn which he later recognized, he found his way back there by instinct, he weeps until morning and then until the following night, he can't bring himself to leave the place, an old conformist, time has done its work, made into the past what even yesterday was still the unique present.

He went the rounds of the barn again, and the stable and the farm buildings, still carrying his haversack for fear that the other man, the moonlight observer, might come and take it from him.

It contains neither wine nor cheese but letters, letters, diary notes, laundry bills, eating-house bills, notes written in haste, goes the rounds of the farm buildings, pulls up a nettle here, replaces a stone there, mortal wound, the merciless sun dissolves all that remained of a tenderness in which no one recognizes himself any more.

A little kitchen garden full of aromatic herbs.

When June starts yellowing in the fields, the delphiniums, unless they are his tears, turn blue, the sky is reflected in them.

When June brought the table back under the arbour, the midday and evening aperitif, old conformist, yesterday's old tenderness in which neither furtive kisses nor hours spent by the fireside recognize themselves any more.

And why is it that that town, those ruins, why is it that those exiles in the fields who speak another tongue, only perceive it piecemeal— never spoken that language—why is it that they come back like someone else's obsession, that of the man in the moonlight or of the person who is absent.

There were absences in my life which were a comfort he said, then there was a presence that ruined me.

Still going the rounds of the farm buildings, he pulls up a nettle here, replaces a stone there, when all of a sudden everything crumbles and the voice comes to him out of the ruins, he recognizes its timbre and its harmonics on that threadbare old string of the eviscerated instrument, he runs, it was a mirage, the sun was setting just as he was waking out of a nightmare, step by step going the rounds of the kitchen garden, the aromatic herbs of death, there is no possible time any more.

A blue cluster in which the phallus flowered, a white and pink rod, balls the colour of virginia tobacco.

One single mouthful the leader made of it before starting on the groin where the flesh is so tender, blood was dripping down his hairy chest and down his stomach.

These sorts of public images.

To get a taste of other secrets as bitter as gall in the shadow of the years to be dissolved, this death accompanied by the aromatic herbs of the little garden overrun and invaded by the image and then by its own shadow and then by the never-ending darkness, the delphiniums and the corpse merge into a single faded sheaf that you can only just make out in the moonlight.

Then he lay down in the grass, he tried to go to sleep but the oppressively hot sun made him get up again and sit down under the nearby elm-tree, he could see two people dressed in white robes walking along the road, one had his arm round the other's shoulder, he believed he could hear them composing a difficult letter, first learning it by heart, the one correcting the other, the other inspiring the one, and with a common voice repeating the phrase dragged up out of the fathomless depths of their consciousnesses, they disappeared into the wood.

Where the only thing that might happen would be an attack by savages but an attack so thoroughly confused with the agonies of the nightmare that the recipient, the reader purified by the lost years, would grasp nothing of it but a vague grief transcribed in puerile terms, no symbols and even fewer reminiscences.

From his haversack he once again extracts the so-called fatal letter and in re-reading it discovers nothing but an adventure transcribed in the wretched, vulgar wording of a popular almanac, some charlatan must have dictated it, some rupture in time must have appropriated it and concealed it in the depths of its crevice like a secret that has no connection with the intangible peace that is his own and was such in his immemorial future.

Likewise to be dissolved.

To be dissolved and sown in the surrounding fields like the ashes of a Narcissus in one of those naïve prints, a caricature for the use of concierges, those females who guard nothing but the imaginary.

The voice in the ruins, then, was double, dictating the letter that was in love with itself, reverberating over and beyond the herb garden on to the road like the steps of the people walking along it which simulate a language, such effrontery, but what's impossible about it in the circumstances in which only the person weeping in the grass turns over in his memory the poisoned phrase.

Two figures in white robes, their long hair plaited with oats and cornflowers, they went into the wood for their evening copulation, long ecstasy repeated until morning when their genitals separated in the dew.

Come out of the wood as the sun is crossing the clearing and shake themselves in the poppies and then lick each other, their morning ablutions, then from the hollow of a tree pull out some honeycomb, their first meal.

But another atmosphere, that of a tormented conscience which only accepts controlled images, distorted in the direction of possible salvation, an old chimera when candour used to triumph on Easter mornings, the initiate finds himself back in the age of passions and lacking any sense of discrimination.

This obscure navigation between senses and reason which so far as we are concerned is no more than unadmitted duty, a rigidity that is even more unpractised than it is sterile.

A blackbird whistled three notes.

There would be no more elm-trees or farm buildings, there would be nothing but a room in the town smoking under its ruins, spared by a miracle in reverse, a deceptive refuge, a charnel-house, death had been there from the first day and had gone unnoticed thanks to the neighbouring premises not yet affected by the cataclysm, a sort of routine that aped life had become established.

It has to be accepted as it is, now, death in the midst of the ruins, going the fantastic rounds of a cemetery in which the only things that move are chimeras, the picnickers are sitting on the graves having their snacks before moving on to the next cemetery, that's the way they go about in the country that was once theirs, leaving behind them here and there those who can no longer follow, they get put under a slab with a flower in their hands, they've earned their rest.

The confused mass of possibilities before he yielded to what had to emerge, but what it was he didn't know, even though he had a presentiment of something serious he could no more than barely calculate its weight, tons of tears and vomit, maybe some connection with the destruction of the town and the hastily-erected cemeteries as if from the very first day, that of its foundation, this city had not been menaced, madness to have built it within reach of the lava but the good weather had caused irresponsibility to triumph, years of sun and unruly and somewhat affected joy, they'd got the better of reason.

Looking for somewhere to spend the night he stopped at an abandoned barn, went in and suddenly in spite of the darkness recognized a certain lay-out, unchanged proportions which made him rediscover the echo of his steps on the mud floor then in the hay where he made a hole not to sleep in, sleep forsakes unhappiness, but to think about those lost years.

As for the belated traveller he was none other than that Miaille of bygone years, with blue eyes and blond beard, years of waiting, years of nothingness.

Watched himself stumbling in the darkness, soul adrift, hole in the hay like the lowest stable lad, he recognizes the echo of his footsteps on the mud floor.

As for the belated traveller he was none other than a foreigner, they'd commented on his accent at the bistro, from then on kept out of the way and prowled about at night in the moonlight.

That hope to be dissolved.

His eyes were still blue but his gaze was no longer the same, a sort of terror or vague humility, flight or renunciation, as for the emaciated face, the deteriorated dentition, the stooping carcass . . .

Time which is the petty, spasmodic malady, joy that forsakes, consciousness of all vanity, the carcass steers itself compassless towards its last resting place as if the theme of survival were henceforth obsolete.

Was thinking about that hotchpotch transformed by the magic of successive revelations, they were pretty precarious.

Unless they were only alive in so far as despair might have uprooted them.

Suddenly as the memory of this thought comes back to him he sees the foreigner of former days looking at him, he wants to go up to him and give him his hand, but the other vanishes.

The sleep that has forsaken me is playing tricks on me, he says, but the other man's face was so innocent of all malice that he goes on looking for him in the dark and then gets up, goes out of the barn and walks over towards the road where earlier the white figures had been chatting.

But someone had seen him in the moonlight and was following him at a distance, not a ghost, a man of flesh and blood who is walking naked with a bunch of delphiniums in his hands, he can be seen approaching the kitchen garden where the aromatic herbs grow, he puts down his bunch of flowers and it comes back to life and stands up in the flower bed, it has never been picked, all its flowerets drinking the night air, the blue is very attenuated, attenuated.

Archangel's couplings. That sort of public image.

To taste other secrets as bitter as gall, so that it should no longer be a question of either beauty or of a comforter, will gradually resume the frightful solitude that breeds monsters and leads the dreamer to his destruction, that slab in the cemetery that he lifts up in order to slide underneath it and hear no more, is it true that death is deaf, that it's blind, that it no longer has the heart for the things that belong here below.

Unless they were only alive, these beliefs in survival, in so far as despair may have uprooted them, what fathomless depths to reach, no more question of the dreary frivolities of sex, no more question of revolt backed up with a plentiful supply of blasphemies, just the pure and simple horror of an attack of vertigo, one has to know.

A boy with white skin and blue hair, he had sat down on the bank, he was looking up at the sky, he stretched himself in the summer sun, he got up and ran into the splashing water, he laughed like a child, no one in this deserted place, he swam a few breast strokes then came out still laughing, he lay down on the sand.

And the person observing him thinks this: that the victim is less to be pitied than the torturer.

That slab in the cemetery, maybe the observer is already underneath it, a little thought for him.

Or the Saviour disfigured by torture, his face looms up on all sides in the mortal hours, or his circumcised sex organ.

There will be no necessity to separate what since childhood has been united, Sacred Heart and sacred arse, that hotchpotch in which no one recognizes himself until his last breath but it would be useless to add any further comment.

That shadow keeping watch on him, disappearing and then reappearing in the darkness or is it already daybreak, a bird was trying out a tune, the frogs had stopped croaking, a sort of calm reigned all around, not a breath, preceding the dawn, what has it in store for us, the drama to brood over all the day that is about to follow or a respite, a truce, the sleep, finally, that a sick, exhausted conscience doubts whether it deserves.

The town smoking under its ruins.

The boy with the delphiniums.

A shattered, rampant passion that adopts a multiple form to retrieve its scattered fragments, Proteus of despair.

Or from the opposite point of view a legend full of sentimental allegories, images profoundly rooted in the night of the soul which were seeing the light in this childish, picturesque and saccharin form but which none the less remained mortal for anyone who might take it upon himself to reverse its meaning, mortal since nothing that has anything to do with life, a word that has no meaning, remains innocuous for longer than a day, the time for a sunrise and a sunset, even time for love.

Or the sleep that forsakes unhappiness.

But an angel comes and tells him fear no more, wherever you are, there I shall be whatever happens, or let us rather say that I have become your dream, no part of it from now on will ever be irretrievably lost, but alive and as necessary as any tiny little mechanical part is to a meticulous watchmaker, these will be the images that will animate your thoughts, whatever happens, whatever it costs me.

Now the angel was naked and crowned with poppies.

Then a second then a third joined him and together they performed the gestures of love and went into raptures in the morning grass.

A house that was ours he said and here I am among the exiles eating dry bread and weeping endlessly from one stop to another, but the angel said what do you know about destiny, a word that has no meaning, your dwelling-place is still the same, occupied by a breath that is also still the same, unchanged in spite of appearances, and do you know any more about appearances, perhaps yourself reflected in the eyes of anyone who looks at you, perhaps yourself.

There were absences in my life which were a comfort, then there was a presence that ruined me.

Endless sadness of all this tedious repetition, I want a new fable he said which would muster my energies for the last time, it would be the best of me but he went on lying in the hay, he heard the angel guffaw and the blackbird whistled Rise, take up thy bed.

He must have got up, then, gone the rounds of the farm buildings once again, the new fable would only emerge from ruins and deserted places, there would be no tedious repetition but rather a fervent will to say everything anew in order to renew everything.

Prolegomena.

A man called Miaille a stranger to the parts he lived in was one evening approached by a traveller who plants himself in the doorway and says let me unpack my suitcase here, I have chosen your dwelling-place, I'll be the maid and the gardener and the caretaker, I have finally come to the end of my afflictions, I saw this house from afar and hastened to it to find you, don't despise my services, I shall have others for your pleasure. The sedentary man opens his eyes wide and lets the traveller in.

Lived thus in oblivion, their gazes penetrating each other all day long, their thoughts the mirror one of the other, peace disseminated from the landscape over their minds and in their bodies, from their breaths over the landscape, an uninterrupted embrace prolonged even into their dreams, you had to call that happiness, now what is a gaze that penetrates another, what is a mirror, what is a dream, but the question was only asked after the mystery had been solved.

The one was reluctant to see it solved as anyone might be reluctant to cut a flower or to squash an insect, the other didn't give it any thought.

He was reluctant he said to see it solved, it was better to go no further than the premises but how to make them last *ad vitam*, the conclusion imposes itself with the force of a battering-ram or of a shoot propelling itself out of a seed.

He heard the angel guffaw.

Their gazes not penetrating each other.

It's funny said the traveller, your eyes are like needles trying to pierce mine, you frighten me. And the sedentary man encouraged by this remark resorted to what he believed to be his power. Now that of the traveller did not reside in his eyes, they were only blank windows.

To say everything anew in order to renew everything.

But the angel disappeared leaving the dreamer in the hay, why get up it's barely dawn, this malady killing him won't go away by magic.

It was at the midday hour that he retraced the erstwhile path, going through the wood in which the white figures were loving each other, then through the fields along the road where the naked men were riding, with that blood-covered head attached to the saddle. To go beyond grief. A day will come when the new fable will emerge.

To go beyond grief.

From that room like a watch-tower.

That photo in my pocket he said between the passport and the postcard, the haversack under my head full of sighing words. Nothing. There has never yet been any night that could put the head back on the truncated neck.

Or the business of the contents of the haversack, bills from eating-houses or whatever which just as fast as they were compiled would reveal that vanished happiness.

Whiff of some old filth.

Reticule of a dead woman.

They find her lying on her kitchen floor with the gas pipe in her mouth, they all knew her in the neighbourhood, a madwoman who passed herself off as a poetess, she knew a lot about that Miaille or whatever his name was, she'd frequented him all her life.

Modestly collect odd straws in the wind.

Crossroads of possible directions.

The madwoman's reticule.

He remembered having seen her go by along the road holding her handbag against her stomach like a muff, dressed in woollies in the middle of the summer, red and sweating, telling her chaplet of doggerel the way a she-goat strings out her droppings, she went and sat down at the edge of the wood and took out of her reticule a diary in which she scribbled a poem, an old barcarolle, an old elegy which was unravelling itself in her brain and which she was trying to remember, suddenly gripped by enthusiasm and then sinking back into melancholy, then going into gales of laughter which made her stand up, walk round a tree then sit down again with a sob that dissolved into hiccups, doggerel, hiccups, she stood up again only in order to sit down again, started scribbling again, hiccuped once more, a quivering pythoness, a priestess of the pauperism into which her lonely, distorted soul had sunk.

He remembered having seen her in the company of white figures in the moonlight, lifting up her skirt and showing her behind to the devil whom she smelt out in the ditch or behind a little wall, exorcism, all three of them went into the wood, they could hear other people whispering and the old woman sat down on a tree-trunk and watched the frolics and couplings as if she were at a strange Mass, here and there accepting in her mouth whichever stiff member approached her, they could hear her choking and spluttering, the vicious, depraved old harpy, she kept on versifying, mixing the names of Christ and Mary with her obscene remarks to the hilarity of her companions.

He remembered having seen her riding pillion behind one of the horde of horsemen, she was tickling the blood-stained head dangling from the man's belt, she herself was shaking all over with her madwoman's laugh, the troop climbed hills and mountains and arrived at a corner of the firmament beyond the clouds where it scattered leaving the old woman between heaven and earth like a snowflake falling slowly, gently, down on to the grass where it melted at dawn, they found her shawl, her pince-nez that a lad went and returned to her in her kitchen, she's dozing in a chair, she starts, mumbles and versifies more than ever, producing a nursery rhyme that the child brings back either home or to school in mint condition.

These sorts of abandon.

Or the boy with the white skin who joined the others in the thicket and took part in their frolics.

These sorts of public images.

To taste other such secrets.

The alternation must take place, don't doubt it any longer, certainly redemptive, or rather giving way to a palpable serenity, installed in what should no longer be called either the heart or the brain but the soul perhaps representing the framework of all this disintegrating hotchpotch, the certainty of remaining alive, compact and without fissure in aeternum.

This present that makes him talk, not to know any more what it is composed of.

I can still see him bending over his notebook scribbling the poem he was trying so hard to remember, saying it over and over during his walk only to forget it again that evening, he takes up his pencil once more, scribbles again and versifies late into the night, the angel took possession of his sleep which he strewed with gulfs and mountains, intolerable awakening, had he slept, he was brooding over the old, long-vanished sadness, obsessed by time seen as a sequence of days, a precarious vision, everything must finally give way to . . .

I have chosen your dwelling-place.

It was one morning, the man called Miaille was barely emerging from sleep, was looking out of the window at the hens scratching about in the yard, coffee cup in hand, when the stranger comes and plants himself down in the doorway and offers his wares, wicker baskets, here, have this one it isn't dear, the Lord will reward you. A gypsy with coal-black eyes and a whore's smile, hair curling against the back of his neck, wide shoulders, thin hips in the trousers wrinkling over his feet.

Offers his wares.

Opens his pants.

The Lord will reward you.

Brings out the Blessed Sacrament.

Show us the fruit of thy loins.

That the devil and all his works must have extracted from his sleep, he was versifying at a poem that he was doing his utmost to remember, getting up early, scribbling all day, amazed at the sumptuousness of the Word, like a child at a peacock in his pride, I can still see him at his table which he called his desk then at noon heating up the previous day's stew then snoozing before his walk, versifying, hiccuping, versifying, then once again scribbling by the fireside with a blanket over his knees and the wound in his heart that never heals.

Eyes of anthracite, a whore's smile.

He planted himself down in the doorway.

That the devil and all his works.

But prayer, he said, is only a way of landing on the banks of Eros, a whole conventional hotchpotch, the bleating of a frustrated old nanny-goat, it moves along unknown paths and ends up in the skin quivering under the partner's caress, the gardener of the enclosure hidden from prying eyes, where a lilac is in blossom, and wallflowers, and daffodils, the scents of aromatic herbs, we shall knock down these enclosing walls so that everyone can enjoy them, he's talking nonsense the neighbours said, how can you expose yourself like that, someone will end up telling the police.

Then the gendarme came and he scratches his head, doesn't know what to say to the gentleman who offers him a drink, sit down, gendarme, what brings you here. The fellow stammers the sergeant sent me but don't go thinking, just gossip that's for sure, the law is the law, that someone says he saw a person walking around with all due respect in the neighbourhood dressed in nothing but dark glasses, have you by any chance seen him, the sergeant you know, or the neighbours, they get ideas into their heads, it wouldn't surprise me, you know their daughter's mad, the one that calls herself a poetess, he pronounced it poytess. Miaille gave him a sideways look and laughed up his sleeve or even bursts out laughing, he says they certainly do have bees in their bonnets over at the neighbour's but rules are rules, it's all right it's not your fault.

Or that in fact he might have seen someone at nightfall down by the river, was it a man or a woman, he only had a back view, who did seem not to have much on but what with the heat and given the isolation of the place really that wasn't anything to get excited about, in any case as I said night was falling and my eyes are so bad, have another drink.

The white figures.

The rider with the bleeding head.

The poetess pulling up her skirts.

Or the Saviour disfigured by torture.

His circumcised sex organ.

But the town was still smoking under its ruins, the old nightmare would reawaken, with the grinding of teeth, this past to be dissolved as it was no longer part of the system, roots plunging into nothingness, the future likewise.

The blackbird whistled Rise.

He rose, went back to the little road that leads nowhere, saying I shall be the strongest, chafing at the bit, restraining his tears, I have always been an exile, we shall make a virtue of it, only absences comfort you.

But someone had seen him in the moonlight.

It was the gypsy of that morning who hadn't found anywhere to sleep, his baskets on his arms, he is whistling between his teeth so as not to frighten him, goodness says the other, still in the district, did you have a good day. The Romany replies no but we're used to it, he was looking for a barn to spend the night in, Miaille indicates his own within a stone's throw, there's some nice fresh hay you'll sleep well there and tomorrow morning a cup of coffee. The man thanks him without servility and he adds you wouldn't have a drop of soup left would you, I haven't had anything to eat today. So it was in company that the sedentary man retraced his steps, they go into the kitchen, they heat up the stew and while he's eating the basket maker tells him about his wife and child, he's left them with some friends not far away, a few kilometres, to make it easier for him to get rid of his baskets here, he's giving himself one more day and then he'll join his family and they'll go south, the horse too needed rest. But Miaille wasn't listening to him, he was concentrating on something else, perhaps his tone of voice which recalled other similar ones, those destinies you know by heart and which are recounted in the same way, gently, without bitterness, lying words perhaps but what does that matter, they come from the same desert and go back to it in the same way, a former Eden still perceptible but only at long intervals, it has disappeared from people's memories, it only now and then manifests itself in a voice, an inflection, an accent, a second breath, a semi-silence and then nothing, nothing, go back into your wife and into your desert, the Lord will reward you.

That voice under the ruins.

He adds that he had had dealings with the gendarme, the swine said he'd seen me naked in broad daylight, he wanted to take me to the police station, I got your neighbours to intervene, they had to admit that at the time he was talking about I had fallen asleep under the walnut-tree in their field within a stone's throw of here and that they had seen me later going off to the hamlet with my baskets, cops are all the same, always setting traps for you but I know them, I don't fall into them any more.

But Miaille wasn't listening to him, he was concentrating on something else, a bizarre image that was taking shape somewhere beyond his interlocutor, it was growing, it reached the top of the walnut-tree and then went on up to the clouds which it transgressed, and was now installed in the corner of the firmament where the troop of horsemen was scattering, but it was unclear, troubled, weak, Proteus of despair.

(Translated by Barbara Wright)

ALAIN ROBBE-GRILLET

Alain Robbe-Grillet was born in Brest in 1922, trained as an agricultural engineer, worked first at the Institut Nationale de la Statistique and until 1951 on research projects in tropical countries. His first novel *Les Gommes* (*The Erasers*) was published by Les Editions de Minuit in 1953 and attracted intense interest in literary circles. It is a retelling of the Oedipus legend in modern terms, although it was some time before this was realized by critics and academics, in spite of many hints: there is for instance, a rubber eraser with *Oedipe* printed on it which plays a key role, and a telling of the riddle of the sphynx also occurs in the narrative. In the novel, a murder which has been committed before the beginning appears to recur again at the end, but either it is the activity of the detective, Wallas, who is investigating the crime, that leads him to commit it, or else the crime that is committed in his mind is his own preparation for it. The deliberate flatness of the description and dialogue gives no hint as to which observed gesture, described object, or words overheard have particular significance: the reader must make his own judgements, sifting words, thoughts and descriptions and deciding for himself the proper time and sequence of events. It becomes increasingly obvious that much of the action and observation is taking place in the mind of Wallas (the Oedipus), and that the description of the murder must also be imaginary becomes evident as well. But aside from the puzzles and the distorted (in terms of the traditional novel, not necessarily of real life) importance given to the different things that are observed, it is also a detective story with a menace that grows throughout the book.

In *The Voyeur* (1955), Mathias, a travelling salesman, returns after many years to the island of his birth. While he is there, a young girl is brutally raped and murdered. The events and a variety of tiny details in connection with them build up in his mind into an obsession. The reader may conclude that Mathias has committed the crime himself, that he has only imagined a non-existent crime, or simply that he is obsessed with a real one. *Jealousy* (1957), his shortest novel, is probably the best-known and much of the description of a tropical banana plantation in it is obviously based on his experience as a researcher in such places. The ground plan of a house opens the novel, showing the exact situation of the veranda and the four chairs arranged on it, the living rooms, bedrooms and other locations. The geography of the house is very important, because the observer makes his jealous deductions from the way that chairs are arranged or that part of the body can be seen through a certain window at a certain angle. The detailed description of objects and of the two characters, A ... and Franck, one the wife of the unnamed and unseen narrator and the other his neighbour, are obsessively detailed and may be a combination of memory, actual observation and imagination. Although the time of the novel is early evening, the imagined events of the day impinge constantly and the time is always the present, but certain events, such as the squashing of a centipede on the wall, act as an anchor and bring us back to the obsessive mind of the narrator, himself never described or seen, although his presence is made clear by the implications given by the author, the presence of three glasses on the table, for example.

Robbe-Grillet's novels, like those of Raymond Roussel, can start from anywhere and are total works of imagination sometimes emerging from the first sentence, which may describe the pattern of the wallpaper. The starting point of *In the Labyrinth* is an engraving showing the aftermath of a military defeat, apparently visible from the author's work table. From this situation he creates a novel of quest, in which a soldier, after a military defeat, crosses a town with a parcel to deliver, but is killed before he can do so, although it is not clear whether it is this particular soldier who is dead, or what the parcel contains, or whether it could not have been as easily posted. The novel ends with the author, his ashtray full of cigarette butts, mistily following in his mind's eye a figure moving through the rain outside, seeing at the same time the patterns in the wallpaper and the marks of his slippers in the dust.

His fifth novel *The House of Assignation* (1965), set in a Hong Kong brothel, starts with random thoughts on a favourite subject, female flesh, and it gives free rein to his erotic imagination, creating in an imaginary Eastern port the kind of intellectual fantasy so frequently found in French literature where money, power, sexual bondage and libertine exploration are fused into narrative. The author has parodied the erotic novel as a *jeu d'esprit*, but at the same time has used his superb technique to free the reader from any sense of reality or identification with character or locale. Similarly in *Project for a Revolution in New York* (1970), he is not writing about a revolution or about New York, but about the imaginary events that can be spun from the simple action of turning a key in the door and entering his own apartment in Paris.

In the work of Robbe-Grillet, content emerges from form. His early work was based in each case on a pre-conceived theme, a legend, a theory about the way the mind works or an obsession, but ever since writing *In the Labyrinth*, random factors and free imagination have played a greater role in his novels, and the reader can assume that the author no more knows where his imagination will take him when starting the novel than does the reader. In spite of this, the later novels are easier to read as entertainment, because superficially they resemble the traditional novel in their narrative technique.

But Robbe-Grillet is also a distinguished film-maker and the strong visual element in his novels has successfully been translated to the screen, most notably perhaps in his first ciné-novel *Last Year at Marienbad*, which takes place at a luxurious resort hotel, where a woman is told by a man she meets that he already knows her, that they knew each other at Marienbad the year before and had a love affair. As he describes the previous summer to her, images form in her mind (and on the screen) and she sees herself with him at Marienbad, until with a flash she realizes that the place she sees in her mind as he describes it is the place where she is at present. It is up to the audience to decide where the truth lies. *Marienbad* was directed by Alain Resnais, but thereafter Robbe-Grillet decided to direct his own films, and with *The Immortal One, Trans-Europe Express, L'Homme qui ment* and *Glissements progressifs du plaisir*, the last three still untranslated, he has developed increasing technical confidence. Unfortunately the increasing erotic content of his later films has tended to their becoming misclassified in many instances.

Robbe-Grillet's seventh novel *Topology for a Phantom City* is a form of literary crossroad where sex, blood, the free interflow of time, space and imagination combine into a narrative with a science fiction plot, but with constant interest to the reader in its description of situation and use of words. And his more recent work shows an awareness of his acceptance as a modern author much taught in universities, as he sets exercises for language and interpretation inside the context of his novels.

The selections from Robbe-Grillet's work that follow show different facets of his writing technique. *The Dressmaker's Dummy* is the first of the *instantanés* or 'snapshots' demonstrating his very precise description and ability to humanize objects. The human present is felt through the coffee pot from which the pleasant smell of hot coffee is coming, signifying a presence in the room, but no coffee cup is on the table. The reader can add to the picture presented his own interpretation of the significance of the scene, taking into account the angle from which it is observed and the clues given by the objects described.

(J.C.)

The Dressmaker's Dummy

The coffee-pot is on the table.

It is a round, four-legged table, covered by a piece of red and grey checked oilcloth. The background to the checks is neutral, a yellowish white which might once have been ivory—or white. In the middle is a tile, being used as a table-mat; its design is entirely obscured, or at least made unrecognisable, by the coffee-pot standing on it.

The coffee-pot is made of brown china. Its shape is that of a sphere, with a superimposed cylindrical filter equipped with a mushroom-shaped lid. The spout is an S with attenuated curves, with a slight bulge at the base. The handle might be said to be shaped like an ear, or rather the outer rim of an ear; but it would be an ungainly ear, too rounded and with no lobe, which would thus be shaped like a 'pot handle'. The spout, the handle, and the knob of the lid are cream-coloured. All the rest is a very even light brown, and shiny.

There is nothing else on the table; only the oilcloth, the tile and the coffee-pot.

On the right, in front of the window, is the dummy.

Behind the table, supported by the mantelpiece, is a large, rectangular pier-glass in whose mirror can be seen half the window (the right half) and, on the left (that is, on the right side of the window), the reflection of the wardrobe. The window can be seen again in the mirror in the wardrobe, this time in its entirety, and the right way round (that is, the right-hand section of the window on the right, and the left on the left side).

There are thus, over the fireplace, three halves of the window, which succeed one another almost without a break, and which are respectively (from left to right): one left half the right way round, one right half the right way round, and one right half the wrong way round. As the wardrobe is right in the corner of the room and extends to the very edge of the window, the two right halves of the latter are only separated by the narrow upright of the wardrobe, which could be the wood dividing the two sections of the window (the right-hand upright of the left section joined to the left-hand upright of the right section). The leafless trees in the garden can be seen, over the short curtain, in the three divisions of the window.

In this way the window takes up the whole surface of the mirror, with the exception of the upper part in which a stretch of the ceiling and the top of the wardrobe can be seen.

Two other dummies can also be seen in the mirror over the fireplace; one in front of the first section of the window, the narrowest one, on the extreme left, and the other in front of the third (the one which is the furthest to the right). Neither the one nor the other is full face; the one on the right is showing its right side; the one on the left, which is very slightly smaller, its left side. But it is difficult to be certain about this at first sight, for the two reflections are facing in the same direction and so both seem to be showing the same side—the left, probably.

The three dummies are in a row. The one in the middle, which is located on the right side of the mirror and whose size is in between that of the two others, is exactly in the same direction as the coffee-pot standing on the table.

A distorted reflection of the window is shining on the spherical part of the coffee-pot, a sort of quadrilateral with sides like the arcs of a circle. The line made by the wooden uprights, between the two sections of the window, suddenly widens towards the bottom into a rather imprecise blur. It is probably the shadow of the dummy again.

The room is very light, for the window is exceptionally wide, even though it has only two sections.

A pleasant smell of hot coffee is coming from the coffee-pot which is on the table.

The dummy is not in its proper place; usually it is put away in the corner by the window, on the side opposite the wardrobe. The wardrobe has been put there because it is convenient for fittings.

The design on the tile represents an owl, with two big, somewhat terrifying eyes. But, for the moment, this cannot be seen, because of the coffee-pot.

(Translated by Barbara Wright)

Jealousy (1957)

In the pantry the boy is already taking the ice cubes out of their trays.
A pitcher full of water, set on the floor, has been used to heat the
backs of the metal trays. He looks up and smiles broadly.

He would scarcely have had time to go take A . . .'s orders on the
veranda and return here (outside the house) with the necessary
objects.

'Misses, she has said to bring the ice,' he announces in the sing-song
voice of the Negroes, which detaches certain syllables by emphasizing
them too much, sometimes in the middle of words.

To a vague question as to when he received this order, he answers:
'Now,' which furnishes no satisfactory indication. She might have
asked him when she went to get the tray.

Only the boy could confirm this. But he sees in the awkwardly put
question only a request to hurry.

'Right away I bring,' he says.

He speaks well enough, but he does not always understand what is
wanted of him. A . . ., however, manages to make herself understood
without any difficulty.

From the pantry door, the dining-room wall seems to have no spot
on it. No sound of conversation can be heard from the veranda at the
other end of the hallway.

To the left the office door has remained wide open this time. But the
slats of the blind are too sharply slanted to permit what is outside to
be seen from the doorway.

It is only at a distance of less than a yard that the elements of a
discontinuous landscape appear in the successive intervals, parallel
chinks separated by the wider slats of grey wood: the turned wood
balusters, the empty chair, the low table where a full glass is standing
beside the tray holding the two bottles, and then the top part of the
head of black hair, which at this moment turns towards the right,
where above the table shows a bare forearm, dark brown in colour,
and its paler hand holding the ice bucket. A . . .'s voice thanks the
boy. The brown hand disappears. The shiny metal bucket, immediately frosted over, remains where it has been set on the tray beside the
two bottles.

The knot of A . . .'s hair, seen at such close range from behind,
seems to be extremely complicated. It is difficult to follow the

convolutions of different strands: several solutions seem possible at some places, and in others, none.

Instead of serving the ice, A . . . continues to look out over the valley. Of the garden earth, cut up into vertical slices by the balustrade, and into horizontal strips by the blinds, there remains only a series of little squares representing a very small part of the total surface—perhaps a ninth.

The knot of A . . .'s hair is at least as confusing when it appears in profile. She is sitting to Franck's left. (It is always that way: on Franck's right for coffee or cocktails, on his left during the meals in the dining-room.) She still keeps her back to the windows, but it is now from these windows that the daylight comes. These windows are conventional ones, with panes of glass: facing north, they never receive direct sunlight.

The windows are closed. No sound penetrates inside when a silhouette passes in front of one of them, walking alongside the house from the kitchen towards the sheds. Cut off below the knee, it was a Negro wearing shorts, undershirt, and an old soft hat, walking with a quick, loose gait, probably barefoot. His felt hat, shapeless and faded, is unforgettable and should make him immediately recognizable among all the workers on the plantation. He is not, however.

The second window is located farther back, in relation to the table; to see it requires a pivoting of the upper part of the body. But no one is outlined against it, either because the man in the hat has already passed it, or because he has just stopped, or has suddenly changed his direction. His disappearance is hardly astonishing, it merely makes his first appearance curious.

'It's all mental, things like that,' Franck says.

The African novel again provides the subject of their conversation.

'People say it's the climate, but that doesn't mean anything.'

'Malarial attacks . . .'

'There's quinine.'

'And your head buzzing all day long.'

The moment has come to inquire after Christiane's health. Franck replies by a gesture of the hand: a rise followed by a slower fall that becomes quite vague, while the fingers close over a piece of bread set down beside his plate. At the same time his lower lip is projected and the chin quickly turned towards A . . ., who must have asked the same question a little earlier.

The boy comes in through the open pantry door, holding a large, shallow bowl in both hands.

A . . . has not made the remarks which Franck's gesture was

supposed to introduce. There remains one remedy: to ask after the child. The same gesture—or virtually the same—is made, which again concludes with A . . .'s silence.

'Still the same,' Franck says.

Going in the opposite direction behind the panes, the felt hat passes by again. The quick, loose gait has not changed. But the opposite orientation of the face conceals the latter altogether.

Behind the thick glass, which is perfectly clean, there is only the gravel courtyard, then, rising towards the road and the edge of the plateau, the green mass of the banana trees. The flaws in the glass produce shifting circles in their unvarying foliage.

The light itself has a somewhat greenish cast as it falls on the dining-room, the black hair with the improbable convolutions, the cloth on the table, and the bare partition where a dark stain, just opposite A . . ., stands out on the pale, dull, even paint.

The details of this stain have to be seen from quite close range, turning towards the pantry door, if its origin is to be distinguished. The image of the squashed centipede then appears not as a whole, but composed of fragments distinct enough to leave no doubt. Several pieces of the body or its appendages are outlined without any blurring, and remain reproduced with the fidelity of an anatomical drawing: one of the antennae, two curved mandibles, the head and the first joint, half of the second, three large legs. Then come the other parts, less precise: sections of legs and the partial form of a body convulsed into a question mark.

It is at this hour that the lighting in the dining-room is the most favourable. From the other side of the square table where the places have not yet been set, one of the french windows, whose panes are darkened by no dust at all, is open on the courtyard which is also reflected in the glass.

The pantry door is closed. Between it and the doorway to the hall is the centipede. It is enormous: one of the largest to be found in this climate. With its long antennae and its huge legs spread on each side of its body, it covers the area of an ordinary dinner plate. The shadow of various appendages doubles their already considerable number on the light-coloured paint.

The body is curved toward the bottom: its anterior part is twisted toward the baseboard, while the last joints keep their original orientation—that of a straight line cutting diagonally across the panel from the hall doorway to the corner of the ceiling above the closed pantry door.

The creature is motionless, alert, as if sensing danger. Only its antennae are alternately raised and lowered in a swaying movement, slow but continuous.

Suddenly the front part of the body begins moving, executing a rotation which turns the creature towards the bottom of the wall. And immediately, without having a chance to go any farther, the centipede falls on the tiles, half twisted and curling its long legs one after the other while its mandibles rapidly open and close in a reflex quiver. . . . It is possible for an ear close enough to hear the faint crackling they produce.

The sound is that of the comb in the long hair. The tortoise-shell teeth pass again and again from top to bottom of the thick black mass with its reddish highlights, electrifying the tips and making the soft, freshly washed hair crackle during the entire descent of the delicate hand—the delicate hand with tapering fingers that gradually closes on the strands of hair.

The two long antennae accelerate their alternating swaying. The creature has stopped in the centre of the wall, at eye level. The considerable development of the posterior legs identifies it unmistakably as the Scutigera or 'spider-centipede'. In the silence, from time to time, the characteristic buzzing can be heard, probably made by the buccal appendages.

Franck, without saying a word, stands up, wads his napkin into a ball as he cautiously approaches, and squashes the creature against the wall. Then, with his foot, he squashes it against the bedroom floor.

Then he comes back toward the bed and in passing hangs the towel on its metal rack near the washbowl.

The hand with the tapering fingers has clenched into a fist on the white sheet. The five widespread fingers have closed over the palm with such force that they have drawn the cloth with them: the latter shows five convergent creases. . . . But the mosquito-netting falls back all around the bed, interposing the opaque veil of its innumerable meshes where rectangular patches reinforce the torn places.

(Translated by Richard Howard)

Project for a Revolution in New York (1970)

The short bald man, realizing that he is now alone, closes the library door more calmly behind him, while staring, under the double cone of harsh light from the spotlights, at the young brown-skinned woman who is struggling hard in her bonds; and having come closer, he now understands what keeps her from raising her head or the upper part of her body: the cords which tie her torso and arms together, sinking deep into the flesh where it is tenderest and fastening the wrists up under the shoulder blades, are furthermore attached on the left and the right to the heavy cast-iron bases of the two spotlights. The unfortunate Sarah, who cannot beg for mercy or assistance, because of the gag lacerating her mouth, nor release her bruised hands, nor even move her shoulders, any more than she can close her thighs an inch, has seen the hairy animal, with which the doctor was preparing to continue his lunatic experiments, leap upon her, run zigzag over her bare flesh in tiny, rapid jerks broken by sudden halts, from the sweat-beaded armpit to the delicate neck, then toward the exposed belly and down to the hollow of the thighs, then back up the right side of the anus and the hip to the breast crushed by two rough cords which cross just under the nipple, finally over to the other breast, the left one, remaining somewhat freer between two twists of hemp whose proximity to one another nonetheless squeezes the delicate hemisphere, forcing the elastic tissue to bulge into a smooth, tight globe of pain, which seems ready to burst at the least prick. Yet it is this spot that the giant spider seems to have selected, wandering more slowly over these few square centimeters of hypersensitive skin, where its eight hairy legs produce the unendurable sensation of an endless electric discharge.

The locksmith voyeur, leaning over the scene because of his extreme shortsightedness, cannot tear his eyes away from this batlike body covered with a black fur with violet highlights, waving like tentacles an alarming number of long hooked appendices, if not from the harmonious lines of the victim exposed to its bites, rendered still more interesting by the fetters which bind her, squeeze her flesh, oblige her to remain in a cruel position, expose her utterly to the view of the onlookers. The most recent of these notices, in this regard, a curious detail: the equilateral triangle of fur, clearly outlined and of modest proportions, which embellishes the pubic area, has a splendid jet-black color like that of the animal itself.

The animal, having doubtless found, at last, the best place to bite its victim, has come to a halt at the edge of the swelling aureole, painted a bright sepia. Here, the chelicerae of the mouthparts, surrounded by continually moving maxillary palps, approach the coppery skin several times, then draw back as if they were licking or savoring in tiny mouthfuls a delicate food, finally attaching themselves to a point of the slightly grainy surface, speckled with lighter papillae, and slowly thrust in, pinching the flesh together, like the iron pliers with their sharp red-hot hooks, which are torturing another blessed virgin with the name of some iridescent stone, in a public square, in Catania.

The girl is then seized by violent, periodic spasms, producing a kind of shifting, rhythmical contraction which extends from the inner surface of her thighs to the navel, whose precise folds form, in intaglio, a miniature rose just beneath one of the excessively tight strands of the cord, which narrows the waist still more, making a deep curve above the hips and belly. Then the lovely head, the only part of her body she can move at all, flings itself convulsively to the right and the left, once, twice, three times, four, five, and finally falls back lifeless, while the whole body suddenly seems to go slack. Then, the girl remains motionless and slack, like one of those Japanese slave-dolls sold in the souvenir shops of Chinatown, abandoned to every whim, the mouth permanently silent, the eyes fixed.

The spider has loosened its jaws, withdrawn its venom fangs; its task completed, it climbs down to the floor, wavering slightly, makes another slow, broken line and suddenly, at a speed so great that it seems more like a shadow, leaps toward a corner of the room, climbs from shelf to shelf up the empty bookcases to the top, whence it had come, and where it once again disappears.

After a moment's thought, the short bald man extends a timid forefinger toward the coppery temple. The slender artery is no longer throbbing. The girl is certainly dead. Then, with gentle, meticulous gestures, he decides to set his toolbox down on the floor, having shifted it to his left shoulder after working the latch and kept it there since, during his comings and goings in the corridor. Then he kneels between the cast-iron weights, lies down carefully on the amber-colored body, whose still burning vagina he deflowers with a well-aimed thrust of the hips.

After some time, busy violating the warm and docile corpse, the short man straightens up, restores order to his clothes, runs his hands over his face, as if the upper part of his neck were itching. He scratches a long time on both sides; then, unable to stand it any longer, he pulls off the mask of the bald locksmith which covered his head and face, gradually ripping off the layer of plastic material and gradually revealing in its stead the features of the real Ben-Saïd.

But suddenly, just as he has completely removed the mask, whose limp skin is now hanging from his right hand, he wonders anxiously who it was that screamed, just now, when he was looking out at the street through the still-open door. It could not have been the dazzling half-caste terrorized by the spider, since the thick gag prevented any sound from passing her lips. Was there another woman in the house? Stricken with an irrational fear, Ben-Saïd opens the door to the vestibule and cocks his ears. Everything seems still in the huge building. He pushes the door farther open. Opposite him he sees his own face in the mirror, above the table. A little too quickly, without taking the requisite pains, he pastes on the conscientious artisan's mask again, checking his gestures as well as he can in the mirror; but the skin, poorly fitted, produces folds under the jawbone, and a kind of nervous tic twitches across the cheek several times, as though trying to put things back in place, to no avail of course.

There is no time to lose. At random, although no longer knowing exactly where he is and what he is doing, Ben-Saïd, by sheer force of habit, leaves a calling card between the bruised breasts of the corpse, after having written on it in clumsy capitals with his felt marker, using the marble table top as a desk, these words which seem to him appropriate to the situation: 'So die the blue-eyed black girls the night of the Revolution.' Glancing at an unopened letter which is lying there, he is once again seized by a series of tics running from the base of his ear to the corner of his lips.

Finally, having glanced around the entire scene, to make sure everything is in order, he replaces the leather strap of his tool kit on his shoulder. A last movement of his head toward the mirror, several still undecided steps to the windowpane where the over-complicated cast-iron pattern makes it difficult to see clearly what is outside, and he makes up his mind to face the street: with quick, abrupt little gestures, he works the inside latch, slides through the opening once it is wide enough, crosses the threshold, walks down the three steps, and walks away along the wall, taking hurried little steps until he is out of sight. It is only then, while the muffled click of the latch and the long vibration of the heavy oak door are still echoing in his ear, having been pulled shut by the doorknob in the shape of a hand, that the short bald man remembers having forgotten on the marble table top, between the brass candlestick and the envelope probably delivered in the morning mail, the skeleton key with which he had worked the latch and opened the door.

On the opposite sidewalk, in the recess of the wall, the man in the black raincoat and the soft felt hat pulled down over his eyes again pulls out his notebook from his pocket, takes off his leather gloves, glances at his watch, and writes down this event after all the rest.

Laura, meanwhile, who has heard the door slam shut, and observed through the window at the end of the corridor, at the top of the fire escape, the reassuring presence of her guardian, begins climbing down from floor to floor in order to inspect all the rooms one after the other, opening the doors one after the other, gently turning the ceramic knob, then pushing shut the door . . . This time she is certain she heard suspicious noises, but coming from the lower floors . . . It is, in fact, only at the last door, all the way downstairs, that she discovers the lifeless body of the young half-caste with whom she had been playing all afternoon . . . yesterday afternoon, probably . . . She approaches, without showing any surprise at the sight of the apparatus of cords, cast-iron weights and spot-lights, to which her previous investigations have accustomed her, more astonished at seeing so little blood, even more astonished by the calling card whose text she reads over several times, without managing to grasp its meaning: 'So die the blue-eyed black girls . . .'

The young girl, as a matter of fact, cannot guess the similar mistake made at the same moment by the false locksmith and a little earlier by Doctor Morgan. The latter, as has already been reported, has managed to make his way into the narrator's house at a time when he believes him to be detained far away by Joan's execution, she having been sentenced by the secret tribunal when her triple adherence to the Irish race, the Catholic religion, and the New York police was discovered. To get into the building is easy, thanks to the fire escape: it is enough to break a windowpane, thrust a hand inside, work the latch, etc.

The surgeon, guided by a kind of muffled moaning which comes from the lower floors, then climbs down the main staircase to the ground floor, where he discovers a young girl bound fast, which scarcely surprises him: this is doubtless the best way of keeping the little imprisoned ward from committing some foolishness or even from running away. As for the coppery color of her skin, entirely exposed, and as for the inky hair, they are also easily explained, although they scarcely correspond to the descriptions provided Frank by the spy on duty, describing N. G. Brown's secret companion on the contrary as blond, pale pink, and more or less pre-pubescent. This must doubtless be a disguise intended to deceive possible visitors, for Brown is not naïve enough to be unaware that he remains at the mercy of a check instituted, unknown to himself, by the organization. And in that case, isn't a dark skin the best guarantee of all? A black-girl's mask, a wig, the plastic film covering the whole of the body, including a few additional charms, is the sort of thing to be found in any store. The subterfuge is obvious, and betrayed immediately, moreover, by the captive's blue eyes.

Without proceeding to a more thorough search of the house, Morgan, who is convinced he is dealing with Laura herself, does not even take the trouble to check the artificial character of her epidermis. He is eager to pursue upon this new patient, before eliminating her according to his orders, the experiments he has begun some months ago concerning the poison of various tropical animals: yellow scorpion, black widow spider, tarantula, centipede, and horned viper. His intention—as is well known—is to perfect a vesicant product which, applied to certain specific regions of the external genitals of a woman, would be capable of setting off a series of increasingly powerful and prolonged sexual spasms, rapidly becoming extraordinarily painful, ending after several hours with the death of the subjects in the combined convulsions of the most intense pleasure and the most hideous suffering. Such a preparation would of course be in great demand during the great celebrations marking the triumph of the revolution, which must include, according to the programme drawn up, in order to avoid a general massacre of the whites, a fair number of human sacrifices which would be particularly spectacular: collective rapes available to all passers-by on trestles set up at intersections and offering the city's loveliest creatures tied to special racks in various postures, theatrical performances in which certain chosen victims would be tortured in unheard-of ways, circus games revived from antiquity, public competitions for torture devices, tested before a jury of specialists, the most successful then being preserved—in the future society—as a legal means of execution, as was the case of the French guillotine, but in a much more refined class.

Unfortunately, Doctor Morgan has just lost at the same time one of his precious inmates (a fine white-ringed black widow from Mexico) and several of the most interesting pages of the memorandum he has been devoting to his researches. And now he is rushing like a madman through the endless corridors of the subway. And it is in pursuit of him that I myself am occupied. Yet I have long since lost all trace of him, and I continue walking, at a rapid, confident, regular gait, in the labyrinth of stairs and corridors, like someone who knows where he is going. Cut.

The trumpet player at 'Old Joe's' then begins raising toward his lips the mouthpiece of his shiny brass instrument, suspended about six inches in mid-air beneath his brown lips still tense with the effort of a soloist in the middle of a fortissimo. In the huge smoky hall, all heads turn back toward him. Laura's hand, already curved around an imaginary sphere, takes hold of the white ceramic doorknob. On the tape, the scene resumes its course. Cut.

But I have been wondering for some time if Laura is not staying in this house on specific orders from Frank himself, who has assigned her the mission of keeping an eye on the narrator even in the most intimate hiding places of his own residence, even in his inadmissible gestures, his old habits, his secret thoughts. She is, in this espionage work, in constant liaison with the false Ben-Saïd, who is keeping watch on the sidewalk across the street. They signal each other through the windows. And from time to time, he slips her a book in code through the broken pane on the sixth floor, a book whose stains, tears, and missing pages represent the most important messages of their correspondence; which explains the state of my library, as well as the sudden appearance of new detective stories, as frequent and unforeseeable as their sudden disappearance. Cut.

The trumpet player at 'Old Joe's' must be the same character, among others, as the man with the steel-grey face who has followed Brown to the fake psychotherapeutic clinic. Having heard, on the other side of the ground glass, the passwords exchanged by N with the nurse, he could easily have repeated them and thus managed to get himself into the heart of the story. Unfortunately, it is not known what became of him afterward. Cut.

I have also lost all trace of young Mark-Anthony, the boy wearing a stolen jacket with a letter embroidered over the breast pocket which might be the initial of the name 'William.' The leg of his trousers was torn on the occasion of the theft of the white car from a newlywed couple, a car which he must have later abandoned in an empty lot. Cut.

In pursuit of the criminal surgeon in the labyrinth of the subway shops under the Spanish district of Brooklyn, I once again pass in front of the big store dealing in religious items, which offers its customers imaginative clothes for communicants. In the window, the passer-by can admire twelve identical little girls, between thirteen and fourteen, pretty and shapely, more or less dressed in the successive items of the most expensive costume suggested for the great day, the first child in the row wearing only openwork black stockings with the chain and gold cross around her right thigh instead of a garter, the second having also pulled on the tight panties of bright red lace, all the way to the last entirely decked out in all her still immaculate veils. A few accessories of mortification hang among them, such as chains, cords, and whips. Inside, in order to give the children a taste for forgiveness and for sin, there are waxwork scenes, life-size, like the kind to be seen in police museums, but which here represent young saints at the most decorative moment of their martyrdom. Cut.

A problem arises. Who are the blonde nurses, mentioned at varying intervals in the body of the text? What are they doing in the service of the psychoanalyst who employs them? What is their precise role in the narrative? Why have I written, in their regard, 'false nurse'? And why are their white uniforms spattered with tiny red stains? Cut.

Retake. When Laura closes the library door behind her and turns around toward the big mirror, she notices on the black marble table top the skeleton key Ben-Saïd has forgotten. A remote smile passes like a shadow across her motionless face. With the slow movements of a sleepwalker, but without hesitations or breaks in continuity, she picks up the key, opens the door of her prison, neglecting to close it behind her, and walks down the straight street toward the subway station. Then it was certainly Laura whom I glimpsed from behind, pressed against the little rectangular window of the connecting door at the very end of the empty car I got into at the stop where I changed from the local to the express. A little later, as has been seen, she was captured by our agents who surrounded her on all sides: Ben-Saïd whose role consisted precisely in noting her flight and immediately warning the others, young W who is one of the three hoodlums encountered here and there in the narrative, Doctor Morgan himself, and M, The Subway Vampire. Cut.

Still later, Laura, who has been, during her entire interrogation, raped at great length and several times over by the two men, in various bizarre and uncomfortable postures which she has been forced to assume, which she has found very exciting after the nervous tension of her escape and the ambiguous pleasure caused by her own capture, is now imprisoned in the iron cage of the little underground room lined with white tiles. She has said disingenuous things to the surgeon on several occasions for the pleasure of lying, especially during the actual rapes. She recalls in particular the last confidences made at teatime by her brief companion Sarah Goldstücker, who seemed so eager to tell someone (whose mind she doubtless thought was shaky, which encouraged her to further outpourings, as she might have spoken to a deaf person or to a cat) the story of her dramatic youth: her eventful childhood, her difficulties during adolescence, the role of the sexually obsessed family doctor (whose name is not Müller, but Juard), etc. Cut.

Have I already indicated that even before the revolution, the entire city of New York, and in particular Manhattan Island, had been in ruins for a long time? I am speaking of course of the surface constructions, those in what is called the open air. One of the last houses still standing, the narrator's, located in the West Village, is now in the hands of a team of dynamiters. Having invoked the plan to construct soon, in its place, something higher and more modern, these four men with severe faces, dressed in dark grey sweatshirts, are skillfully and diligently planting all through the building their

Bickford fuses and explosive charges, with a view to an explosion which cannot be long in coming now. Cut.

You have asked me what her ravishers did with the young bride. I can answer you in a few words. She figured for several days among the white slaves who are obliged to submit to services of all kinds—generally humiliating ones—at the will of members of the organization, in the conquered sections of the underground city. Then she was executed, on the pretext of some minor fault she committed during a ritual ceremony. They initially amused themselves by burning her with their cigars at the most sensitive and secret points of her body. They also forced her (at the same time and subsequently) to perform certain services of an intimate nature which the doomed girl was obliged to carry out to the best of her ability, despite her lack of experience. Finally they attached her arms and legs to the floor and wall of a cellar provided with huge rings set into the stone. When the body was stretched out in the shape of an X, arms and legs drawn wide apart by the chains fastened to her ankles and wrists, they stuck long needles into her flesh, especially through the breasts, in the buttocks, the thighs and the belly, in every direction and all the way through, from waist to knees, and they let her die that way. Cut.

I still had left to describe, in the same order of ideas, the fourth act of the torture of Joan, the pretty milky-skinned whore. But time is short. Soon it will be day. And now there has just appeared a 'cat' somewhere in the sentence, apropos of Sarah the half-caste: a deaf man and a cat. The deaf man, I'm convinced, is the trumpet player at 'Old Joe's.' But the cat has not yet played any part here, to my knowledge; so that can only be a mistake . . . Apropos of the blonde nurses and their incomprehensible presence in the organization, I should have found out, above all, what had become of the nicest one, that tall girl with the big dark glasses and the strong perfume, who kept brushing up against me . . . But it is too late. In the grey light of dawn, the hammering tread of the patrol is already echoing outside, at the very end of the long straight street where they advance, right down the middle of the pavement, with their calm, regular gait . . . And Claudia . . . Who was Claudia? Why was she executed? . . . Yes, that's it, I was saying: with their calm, regular gait. The two militiamen are wearing navy-blue tunics and leather shoulder straps, with holsters over their hips; they are the same height, rather tall; they have faces that look alike—frozen, attentive, absent—under the flat-topped caps with very high front brims and the city emblem under it and a wide shiny visor which almost hides their eyes . . . And also: who is tapping in the blind room on the last floor, up at the very top of the big house? You're not going to try and make me believe it's old

King Boris? . . . It sounds like pointed nails tapping against a door, or against a cast-iron radiator, as if someone were trying to send a message to other prisoners, especially women prisoners . . . And in that regard, just how did the second meeting go between JR and the mad old uncle who was not yet known as Goldstücker at the time? In any case I've already described—it will be remembered—how that exceptional girl had been recruited by means of a want ad, not one of the ones regularly published in *The New York Times* by so-called sophisticated couples who belong to the establishment, something like this: 'Modern couple looking for weekend partners to play hearts. Photographs returned,' which moreover we always answer systematically, sending the undressed picture of a handsome black man grinning with all his teeth and holding in his arms a delicate white-skinned creature, which has always obtained excellent results, but on the contrary by means of a text written this time by us, in order to encourage a more timid, not yet specialized clientele. A certain Jean Robertson, whom we subsequently renamed Joan, had answered the ad immediately, on the assumption she was dealing with some naïve businessman, someone easy to lure into a complicated affair, soon inextricably mixed up with stories of defective heroin and more or less consenting minors, which is to say rather less than more. From our first experiments, the call girl's remarkable gifts, in the various realms which interested the organization, had then saved her life (and this all the more easily in that she had claimed to be one of our own people, exhibiting a family passbook which was probably forged), until the day at least when N. G. Brown had discovered that the girl had just sold out to the local police. It remains possible of course that Brown lied in the report he turned over to Frank, and that he invented this betrayal out of whole cloth, having chosen the surest method of ridding himself for good of an inconvenient witness who might have given away his personal secrets: the presence in his house of the little captive removed from Doctor Morgan's menagerie, or even his own double game as an informer. Still, the fact is that the suspect had been sentenced to death without further trial . . . But, now that I think of it, one thing is certain: if the pink-and-blonde complexion of the young nurses is not an artifice, they too must belong to the constantly renewed harem of war captives reduced to slavery. The little red stains, particularly numerous on the breast and from the hips to mid-thigh, would then be explained by the Pravaz needles which Doctor Morgan injects deep into their bodies through the white uniform (under which the reprieved victims generally wear nothing at all) in order to punish them for their daily delinquencies, the long hollow needles then having to remain planted in their flesh until the end of their night duty, even—or especially—if they make certain postures, certain attitudes, certain positions, or certain gestures extremely painful, which must in no case alter the professional smile enforced upon these creatures. (It has been shown, in particular, that the psychoanalyst prostitutes them to his paying customers whose sexual behavior he then studies by the direct experimental method.) The blood which trickles drop by drop through each slender steel channel . . . The cadenced sound of boots comes closer, and the regular rubbing of the holster against the leather belts, and the two black figures reflected in a gleaming double on the asphalt drenched by the recent shower . . . Faster, please, faster! And now, for the last act, Joan's splendid bloodstained body is lying on its back, head down, on the altar steps of an abandoned church in the depths of Harlem which has been used for a long time for expiatory ceremonies, but the blind organist keeps coming to play every day, so that the victims' screams can be drowned out by the uproar of the liturgical cadences. Moreover it is not impossible that the musician is also deaf, and that he is the one who plays the trumpet every night at 'Old Joe's.' The church in question has preserved all its old splendors: elaborate ornaments on every confessional and over each side chapel, huge black draperies which seem to smother the worshiper in the smoke of incense burners, gigantic carved motifs imitating the baroque where, among the arabesques, the billows, the scallops, the volutes, the scrolls, the garlands, appear the god of wrath, the god of the lightning, the god of tempests, each brandishing his attributes, the herald angels sounding their long trumpets, the mutilated corpses rising from their graves. Only the paving in the nave and the six steps of the high altar are of plain white marble. Here, surrounding the victim lying head down, legs wide apart, her feet attached to two giant candelabra which illuminate the scene with their countless tapers, the twelve still-virginal communicants in all their finery are kneeling, six on each side, on the marble steps, each one holding a lit black candle between hands fettered by a rosary instead of a chain. For an hour they have heard nothing but the religious music whose rolling waves break from the top of the vaults, occasionally resembling cries of mystic fervour; and they see nothing of the spectacle which is taking place ten feet away from them, because of the black bandages over their eyes, so that they still believe they are attending the high mass of their initiation, which remains true, in a sense. But in front of the twelve columns of the nave are already standing the twelve crosses to which the little girls are ultimately doomed: three crosses in the shape of an X, three in the shape of a T, three in the shape of a Y, three in the shape of an inverted Y. And beneath their blind gaze, the victim of the sacrifice lies in a pool of blood, the breasts torn off as well as all the flesh in the pubic area and the upper part of the thighs. Her delicate hands, carefully washed and very white, seem to caress these lacerations, in the hollow of the dark red wound which replaces the genitals; but these hands with their tapering fingers are like alien hands which are no longer attached to the body, for the arms too have been torn off and the blood which has gushed from the armpits has collected all around the head with its ecstatic smile resting on the slabs, the mouth and the eyes wide open, coagulating in the auburn hair spread out in cunning disarray, extending the curling locks in a flaming sun, like a scarlet octopus. But this time, I no longer have a minute to lose. I must return to that delicate girl who is still languishing in her cage, for M, The Vampire, and Doctor Morgan are now returning to the little white room in order to continue the interrogation, after having gone out for a sandwich to the drugstore in the nearby station. They remain standing, the two of them, in the room. They seem uncertain, exhausted. M pulls off his mask for a moment, with a mechanical gesture, trying to rub away, with the back of his hand, the wrinkles of his own face underneath; and Morgan, who then looks up from the papers accumulated on the table, recognizes with amazement the narrator's features. Without hesitating, realizing I have been discovered . . . Cut.

And suddenly the action resumes, without warning, and it is the same scene which proceeds all over again, very fast, always just as it was before. I have wrapped the girl in a blanket, as though to save her from the flames, climbing down the zigzag fire escape attached to a dizzyingly high building, where already the fire is roaring from roof to cellar. In the iron cage, padlocked once again, I have left in her place the slender skeleton of the other girl—the one the German television company did not want—whose bones are so neatly nibbled, so clean, so white, so varnished, that they seem to be made out of some plastic substance. And now I am closing the door behind me, after having set my precious burden down on the vestibule floor, while the police patrol stops to speak to the sentry on duty, in the recess of the house across the street, and now I am closing the door behind me, a heavy wooden door with a tiny narrow rectangular window in the top part, its pane protected by a . . . Cut. It is at this moment that I heard again the faint taps of a light hand, at the very top of the huge staircase of the enormous empty building, on a shaft of the central heating system. Laura has immediately raised her head, ears cocked, eyes fixed, lips pursed, as has already been said.

(Translated by Richard Howard)

Last Year at Marienbad (1962)

Throughout the film a man X, and a woman A, both staying at the same hotel, having apparently just met, walk around the corridors, public rooms and gardens together. The woman appears to be with another man who may or may not be her husband, but he seldom appears. X tells her, insistently, that they had met the previous year at Marienbad and had loved passionately. In the following scene she identifies, for the first time, the place where she is with the place described.

x: *If you say so.*

A silence. After a few steps, X continues, still in the same calm and impassioned voice.

x: *But I remember that bedroom very well . . . and that white lace spread you were lying on, on the double bed.*

A: (with a kind of terror) *No! Be still. Please. You're completely mad.* (A short silence.)

x: *No, no, please . . . I hear your voice the way it sounded then. You were afraid. You were already afraid.*

A silence. They walk down the hall as if A were fleeing X, who is in pursuit.

x: *You've always been afraid. But I loved your fear that evening.* (Without losing its sweetness, his tone gradually becomes more excited.) *I watched you, letting you struggle a little . . . I loved you. There was something in your eyes, you were alive . . . finally . . . I took you, half by force.*

A has just reached the threshold of a last passageway, no doubt a rather monumental one. She has turned toward X, who is behind her still in the hall, and she takes her last steps backward, terrified by his wild tone. X, who had stopped, walks toward her again, on the words *by force*; she turns around to run away, takes one step toward the door, while he, motionless again, speaks the last words in an almost relieved tone of voice:

x: *. . . at the beginning . . . remember . . .* (A pause.) *Oh no . . . Probably it wasn't by force . . .* (The end of the phrase may be heard offscreen.) *But you're the only one who knows that.*

The camera, which has pivoted to follow the fugitive, suddenly reveals the whole garden—the garden *à la française*, which has been seen in imagination since the beginning—at the same time that A herself discovers it.

X, who has remained behind, is now outside the field of vision. A, shown from behind, advances slowly along the terrace, toward the balustrade, the statues, the regular lawns and geometric shrubs. Brilliant sunshine would be preferable here. As though dazzled by this sun, A raises one hand to her eyes, then continues walking slowly to the balustrade. She is still seen from behind. She rests her hand on the stone balustrade, assuming precisely the pose in which the camera showed her, in this same spot, the first time. Then she turns her head, as then, but continues the movement, including the garden in a panoramic gaze.

The twelve-tone music already heard throughout the scene (notably in the concert scenes) now resumes, but imperceptibly: very low at first, a few scattered notes, then gradually acquiring volume, but without achieving its earlier violence. Slightly troubled music, but nonetheless indicating—by its arbitrary and atonal character, its sudden shrill notes, its abrupt jumps—the shock that the discovery of the garden represents: a kind of expected and therefore soothing shock. This music continues into the following shot.

Slow panorama of the garden, as it has already been seen throughout the film. A is no longer in the field of vision. The entire garden is empty, without a guest or a servant in it. Alone, down one path, a gardener bent over his rake, in the distance no doubt.

The camera movement stops on A still leaning on the balustrade, full face this time. She passes her hand in front of her eyes again. Behind her is the hotel: it is the façade already shown in a print, and is a shot of the garden (A walking down the long, straight path).

A in the same position, but at closer range, in the foreground. Behind her, X walks forward across the gravel. He joins her beside the balustrade and turns toward her as she shelters her eyes. They exchange a few lines, the words faint, spoken almost in an undertone, without tension; hoarse, almost broken voices. The music continues, mingled with the sound of footsteps and the words.

X: *What is it?*

A: *Nothing . . .*

X: *Are you tired?*

A: *A little . . . Yes . . . I think so . . .*

X: *It's a . . .*

A: (interrupting him) *The sun . . . all of a sudden . . .*

X: *Would you like to go in?*
A: *If you would.*

They turn around and walk toward the hotel, which is quite near. They are shown from behind, at a certain distance from each other, X slightly behind A. In a rather fast though unhurried scene, A twists her right ankle and stops. X approaches her and offers her his arm. She leans on it to take off her shoe and remains with her right foot resting on its toe, as in her first appearance in the bedroom. She is examining the broken shoe. Neither one speaks. Then X turns around toward the camera and the shot changes.

Shot of the statue already described and shown several times in the film. Stationary shot, taken at a distance, as if it was what X saw when he turned around. The music becomes more violent.

Card players in a hotel salon at night. There are seven or eight men sitting around a table, and each has several cards (face down on the table) in front of him. X and M are among the players. No one moves. The game they are playing is not specified. Fixed faces.

New shot of X and A dancing the waltz, among other couples. Attitude still as correct, but their faces, A's particularly, are clearly more dramatic, although also fixed.

The same twelve-tone music, very violent now, maintaining its choppy, discontinuous character, full of sudden silences. Consequently the dancers' movements have no relation to the rhythms heard.

A wanders, alone, through several salons of the hotel, with people in groups here and there; she seems a little forlorn, but her expression is still impassive, agreeable.

Another card table (without X): M is dealing cards, one by one, to a circle of five or six players. Fixed faces. M's rapid gestures are mechanically repeated throughout the entire shot.

Abrupt cut to X and A in a *tête-à-tête* in a corner of the garden. But no doubt there is no sunshine.

(Translated by Richard Howard)

MICHEL BUTOR

Michel Butor (b. 1926) has the rare distinction of being both an original novelist and a first-class critic. His essays and lectures on specific authors and on the craft of fiction today have been gathered into the two volumes entitled *Répertoire* (1960 and 1964). Perhaps the most interesting essay of the many he has written is the investigation entitled *Le Livre comme objet*. Here he tries to look dispassionately at the book as we know it: the fact that it has been of incalculable utility in the past does not imply, he argues, that it is irreplaceable; our civilization based on the printed word might well give way to a civilization founded on the tape-recording. 'That is why,' he says, 'every honest writer finds himself today faced with the problem of the book.' He goes on to argue that a book has one advantage over all other methods of preserving speech, and that is the ability to be opened at any page: the reader can skip, or turn back as much as he likes, since a book exists in space, whereas a recording exists only in time, and time cannot be reversed. Butor then makes certain recommendations, based on devices employed by Rabelais, Sterne and Mallarmé, to extend the range and the possibilities of the book, such as the use of different type-faces, the exploitation of margins, and so on. He himself has used many of these devices in his most recent books with such success that one is tempted to apply to him the praise he bestows on Sterne ('he is up till now the greatest artist that I know of in the organization of a volume').

Butor's beginnings as a novelist were, however, more traditional. *Passage de Milan* (1954)—the title is both the imaginary name of a Paris street and the flight of a kite—reveals an interest in the question of simultaneity, just as *L'Emploi du temps* shows an interest in place (the setting is Manchester, here called 'Bleston'), and more especially in imposing buildings, such as cathedrals. In *La Modification*, published a year after *L'Emploi du temps* in 1957, a man decides that he only loves his mistress because she personifies Rome for him, and so he abandons his project of bringing her to Paris to be near him: to do so, he realizes, would be to break the spell. *Degrés* gives a vivid picture of life in a Paris *lycée* and at the same time presents a book-within-a-book: Pierre Vernier, the hero, is himself writing a book not unlike *Degrés*. Similarly, the protagonist decides to write a book in *La Modification*, presumably in order to explain his 'change of mind' to himself and the world, and in *L'Emploi du temps* the narrator finds that a Penguin crime novel fictitiously entitled 'The Bleston Murder' helps him to come to grips with the alien, hated city.

Two years after *Degrés*, Butor published his first radically experimental book, *Mobile, étude pour une représentation des Etats-Unis* (1962). Its way had been prepared in 1958 by the collection of essays, entitled *Le Génie du lieu*, which attempts to render the essential quality of several southern places, such as Istanbul. (Butor is, incidentally, one of the few truly internationally-minded French intellectuals, and his culture is as wide as his travels have been extensive). *Mobile* takes us through all the states of the Union, not in alphabetical order or in the chronological order of their respective foundation, but by the association of place-names: from Concord on the west coast we switch to Concord on the east coast, then to Concord, Georgia and Concord, Florida, to take but one example. Comments on the time in each place and other details in roman characters intertwine with other matter in italics, such as the verbatim report of the notorious Salem witchcraft trial on which Arthur Miller based *The Crucible*, later adapted by Sartre for the cinema under the title *Les Sorcières de Salem*. Beside variations in type-face Butor uses three different indents from the margin according to the material he is using. Since the chain is continuous, the book can be begun anywhere—the reader is free to plan his own tour of the United States and, with Butor's guidance, will gain an impression of that country which is at once startling and accurate, as critics of his work who live there acknowledge.

From a huge, new country Butor turned to one of the most venerable monuments in Europe, St. Mark's Cathedral in Venice: the *Description de San Marco* (1963) intersperses an impressionistic description of the monument with the talk of tourists visiting it, and uses the full resources of the compositor's art to a greater extent even than *Mobile*. Perhaps fearing he might have exhausted the type-setter's patience as well as that of most of his readers, Butor dedicated *Illustrations* (1964) 'au compositeur'. This work consists of commentaries on various paintings, etchings and photographs which are not reproduced (gaps are left instead). The tone of the commentary ranges from the colloquial to the poetic and to the very literary (with quotations in the original language from Marlowe and Goethe); the whole work is thus an attempt to render in writing the essence of visual experiences in art.

One of the authors quoted in *Illustrations* is Chateaubriand, whose description of the Niagara Falls in 1791 forms the basis of *6810000 litres d'eau par seconde* (translated by Rayner Heppenstall for the BBC Third Programme as '1½ Million Gallons of Water a Second'), which appeared in 1965. Organized on much the same lines as Butor's other experimental books, this radiophonic poem covers the months of the year from April to March and ingeniously conveys the hopes, fears and disappointments of married people (the Falls are a favourite honeymooners' resort) and the impact of a great natural phenomenon on different sorts of men and women.

It is clear that Butor is a restless author, not easily satisfied by earlier successes, and always willing to try something quite new, whether it be radio drama like *Réseau aérien* (1962) which presents the reactions of two couples flying out to New Caledonia by opposite routes, or the 1961 essay on a dream of Baudelaire, *Histoire extraordinaire*, or even the opera *Votre Faust* (with Henri Pousseur— Butor is interested in and knowledgeable about the latest developments in music, and has written on Boulez) of which several possible versions exist. He has long since abandoned the novel form as it is usually understood, and, true to his original vocation as a poet, is seeking to write poetry in other media than verse. If he seems less gifted imaginatively than Robbe-Grillet, less sure of his path than Nathalie Sarraute, and less profound than Claude Simon, there can be no doubt that his fertile mind and his outstanding intellect make him a force to be reckoned with in contemporary writing, and mark him out as the least inhibited of experimenters active today. If it is reasonable to wonder how many of his innovations will prove more than simply interesting, one can readily accept that the book of the future, about which he has thought so much, will inevitably bear some trace of his experiments.

(J.F.)

Second Thoughts (1957)

Despite its experimental manner—exemplified by the now famous use of the second-person narrative form—*La Modification* is a classic love story, probably the most popular and readily accessible of Butor's novels. This extract is taken from the end of the book and describes the consummation of the hero's 'change of mind', when he decides that he can never live with his Italian mistress and will redepart from Rome on this trip without attempting to see her or even let her know he is in town. But like other *nouveaux romans*, the story also constitutes an account of its own composition, as the last paragraph but one of the novel makes clear.

The rain on the Stazione Termini made almost as much noise as the train had done, drumming in great waves on the transparent roof of the main hall, while standing in the bar you rapidly drank your cups of *café latte*, and on the square there were great puddles from which taxis sent showers of splashes flying; sudden squalls blew under the big penthouse where you were waiting together, motionless and silent, muffled in your coat-collars, in the black night where nothing save the bustle of trolley-buses indicated the approach of day.

You took Cécile's cases up to her landing in the Via Monte della Farina, then you left her quickly without kissing her, only whispering, as though to salve your conscience: 'I'll be seeing you tonight,' then you heard her turn the key in the lock and slam the door.

At the Albergo Quirinale, in a small room with a balcony, on the top floor, you set down your suitcases on the table and took out Volume I of the *Aeneid* in the Budé edition; you opened the shutters; daylight began to creep through the lashing downpour, then a bright rift in the cloudburst showed above the roofs of the Via Nazionale.

That evening, after an exhausting and tedious discussion at Scabelli's which went on far later than expected, long after the time for your rendezvous with Cécile on the Piazza Farnese, you walked slowly, pausing in front of shop-windows, roaming frequently from one pavement to another, making a detour through the Piazza del Pantheon just for amusement, in the cool and still dampish air, while dusk still lingered in the sky,

as though you wanted to avoid going to the Piazza Farnese (but your feet kept carrying you thither, and you felt a sort of inward fury against this stupid compulsion), hoping that she would not be there, that she'd have tired of waiting, especially after travelling all night and going back to work all day,

saying to yourself: she won't have waited for me, it's nearly seven, she must have gone home to make herself a sandwich and go to bed early;

but on the contrary there she was, at her usual place, looking through a fashion magazine and showing no signs of impatience.

You wanted to ask her how she'd got on in Paris, as if the words with which you'd introduced her to Henriette had corresponded to the truth, as if she really was a lady with whom you'd had dealings in Rome and who had always been very obliging to you.

She told you: 'I'm starving, I saw this morning that there's a new restaurant on the Largo Argentina, we might try it; after that I'll go home to sleep.'

That time you didn't even go upstairs with her or fix a meeting for the next day. She waved good night to you, with a yawn. You buttoned up your coat and walked back through the cold to the Albergo Quirinale, where you read Virgil till nearly midnight.

The far wall was tumbling down in great patches and the central figure took on a bluish tinge and seemed to dissolve in the opaque light, forming a sort of clot in the middle of the urban landscape which was gradually revealed in the night.

The vast figures bending over you were muttering as their fingers turned the pages of their enormous books.

You thought about her, saying to yourself; it's been merely an adventure, I shall see her again later on, we'll always be good friends; but next evening, under a rather misty sky, you couldn't bear it any longer, and when you came out of Scabelli's you hurried, almost running, towards the Palazzo Farnese.

You didn't show yourself at first; you followed her into the Roman night as she hurried off, with an air of nervous excitement, not in the direction of the Via Monte della Farina; you wondered, as you caught up with her: is she going to meet another man? then you drew level with her and walked beside her for a little while, your head turned towards her, unable to take your eyes from her; at last she saw you, she stopped, uttered a cry, dropped her bag and without even stopping to pick it up she flung herself into your arms.

You kissed her on the lips; you said to her: 'I can't do without you.'

'If I'd known I should meet you I'd have prepared dinner at home.'

All the memories of that trip to Paris, all the after-taste of it died away. You became young again; you had regained her at last; you had reached Rome.

After your meal in a little restaurant overlooking the island in the Tiber you went as far as the round Temple of Vesta, you passed through the Arch of Janus, skirted the Palatinum and the Park of Caelius, pressed close to one another, embracing frequently, uttering no word until you reached the ruins of Nero's Golden House (the Colosseum Square was still busy with motors and Vespas) and read the inscription saying that it could only be visited on Thursdays.

'That's why I've never been inside it yet.'

'I'll go and see it for you tomorrow.'

Now the moonlight is falling on the head of the old Italian woman and on the glass over the photograph of Carcassonne which you can see gleaming above her, a slender vertical rectangle of brightness. The handle you were holding in your hand begins to move; the door opens; a man looks in, then shuts it again.

The blind, its fastenings undone, began to rise in tiny jerks, leaving a slit of window which grew brighter and broader and gradually disclosed a strip of the Roman Campagna that changed colour from early-morning grey to green, then to yellow; then above the fields and vineyards, in the crook of the hills, there were triangles of bright sky.

Then somebody uncovered the window completely, and at a bend in the line the sun thrust its brazen pincers in and covered the cheeks and brows of the sleeping travellers with a plating of hot luminous metal.

A whole flight of rocks rose up over a farm, and beyond the corridor there were the waves of the sea, painted in sharp detail. 'Are we there already?' asked Henriette, opening her eyes. 'We're just coming into Civitavecchia.'

The town had not yet been destroyed. It was before the last war. There were black-shirted children on the platform.

You told her to go and tidy her hair and freshen her face with eau-de-Cologne, but she stayed there beside you, leaning her hand on your shoulder, blinking as she stared at the sun rising and scattering the baroque clouds behind pines and villas.

Outside the old Termini station, that heavy nineteenth-century building, there were no Vespas nor trolley-buses then, only horse-drawn carriages, and you drove off in one of these after breakfasting in the gloomy, closed-in buffet of those days.

Your knowledge of Italian was purely bookish then, you had not yet joined Scabelli's. Everything seemed marvellous to you, uniforms and *viva il Duce* notwithstanding.

You asked her if she wanted to rest in your room at the Hotel Croce di Malta in the Via Borgognone, near the Piazza d'Espagna, but she refused, she only wanted to walk about and see things, and you set off together through the hot streets to explore the famous hills.

The vast prophets and sibyls close their books; the folds of their cloaks, their veils, their tunics begin to stir, to stretch out, turn into great tapering black feathers; now there's only a huge flight of black feathers above your head, parting to reveal the hazy depths of the night sky.

You feel yourself sinking; you're touching grass. Looking to right and left, you see broken shafts of grey columns and bushes set out in orderly rows, at the far end of which stands a great half-ruined niche built of large bricks.

And now there come floating through the air, a few inches above your eyes, minute bronze figurines decorated with iron ornaments.

'I am Vaticanus, god of crying children.'

'Cunina, goddess of their cradles.'

'Seia, goddess of the grain of wheat sown in the earth.'

'Of the first shoots.'

'Of the nodes in their stalks.'

'Of the unfolding leaves.'

'Of the young ear.'

'Of its beard.'

'Of its blossom while yet green.'

'Of its whitening blossom.'

'Of the ripened ear.'

'We are the meticulous little gods of ancient Italy, gods of the minute dissection of hours and actions, from whose ashes rose Roman Law.'

'Jugatinus, who joins the hand of a man to that of a woman.'

'Domiducus, who leads the young bride to her new home.'

'Domitius, who maintains her in that home.'

'Manturna, who preserves her for her husband.'

'Virginensis, who unfastens her girdle.'

'Partunda.'

'Priapus.'

'Venus,'

who grows taller as she moves away, and whose body glows bright and golden as she stands, a vast figure, in the great niche, turning towards you and holding all her companions in the palm of her hands.

Above her head three great statues rise, one of bronze, one of iron, and the third, much more dimly seen, of black clay: Jupiter, Mars and Quirinus.

Then from all sides foregather men in togas, in armour or in purple mantles, increasingly laden with gold ornaments, crowns, gems and heavy embroidery on their cloaks. One by one you recognize them: all the emperors in succession.

You walked along the streets together, exploring the famous hills, holding your Blue Guide which was new then.

In the afternoon you visited the Forum and the Palatinum; in the evening, when they were shutting the gates, you climbed up to the Temple of Venus and Rome.

'Over there in that corner,' you explained to her, 'on the other side of the Colosseum, there are the ruins of Nero's Golden House, down there on the right Constantine's Triumphal Arch, and further off you can just see through the trees the foundations of the Temple of Claudius, for the emperors were considered as gods.'

There was a great deal of traffic all round the amphitheatre, but these cars were very slow-moving compared to last year's or today's. The Via dei Fori Imperiali had just been completed and opened, and this garden had been laid out in the ruins of the temple.

Suddenly, sitting on the bench, in the heady evening air, she asked you: 'Why Venus and Rome? What's the connection between the two?'

You're leaning right back now so that you can see the gleam of the glass rectangle over the photograph of the Arc de Triomphe above your seat. The lights of a station go by; it must be Tarquinia.

You say to yourself: I've got to keep still, I've at least got to keep still, this restlessness is absolutely useless; isn't the rocking of the coach enough to set all your convictions shaking and jarring against each other, like the parts of a machine that's been too roughly handled?

But you can't help it, that arm has simply got to relax. As if you were bending a bow and had suddenly let go of the string, your hand drops, your fingers spread out; you brush against somebody's cheek with the back of your fingers, which you draw back sharply as if you'd burnt them—against the cheek of that woman by your side, who sits up suddenly, and at whose face, whose now wide-open eyes you stare.

You had laid your right hand on the door-handle again, and you feel it move once more; the slit of orange light opens; a foot is thrust through, then a knee; this time they belong to Pierre, who hasn't been to shave since he's holding nothing in his hands, who edges his way in, his chin where it catches the light looking as dirty as though he were swimming through ink, groping with his hands, leaning forward and twisting one way and another, lifting his feet very high and very slowly, one after the other, finally turning over on himself before he settles down on the seat.

You see half of Agnés's dress, then her raised leg describing an uncertain arc, the tip wavering like the needle of a galvanometer, above your crossed knees, and the piece of pleated skirt, reflecting the light from the corridor, unfolds just at the level of your eyes like a great pheasant's wing; she rests her hand on your shoulder, then on the back of the seat beside you. She turns round, pivoting on the heel she's managed to insert, the edge of her skirt spread out over your trousers, your knees gripped between hers, a brief grimace puckering her features, which are now almost entirely veiled by the blue darkness; then the other pheasant's wing folds up and she turns round once more, leans both hands on Pierre's shoulders and swivels round into her seat, where she sits bolt upright, only her head slightly bent forward, watching the blue-black landscape go past with a few lamps splashing a few walls.

She hasn't attempted to close the door behind her; the old Italian puts out his hand as far as the handle, keeps it there for a few moments and then withdraws it; your knees are in the orange light and so are those of the woman by your side.

'Emperors and gods of Rome, have I not tried to study you? Have I not succeeded, at times, in making you appear to me at street corners and among ruins?'

And now a host of faces draw near, huge and hostile as though you were some sprawling insect, faces streaked with lightning, the skin falling away in patches.

Your body is sinking into the damp earth. The sky above you is streaked with lightning now, and great patches of mud fall down and cover you.

Your wrist is in the orange light. Sliding your hand along your thigh, you push your watch from under your shirt-cuff; it's five o'clock. These streets in which a few windows are beginning to light up must be those of Civitavecchia. You lift the blind on your right, and then the face of the Roman woman beside you is revealed, pale against the shadows and her black hair.

You won't sleep any longer now. You've got to get up, take your case and lay it on the seat, open it, take out your toilet things, then close the lid.

You've got to get that door open completely, though your legs will hardly bear you up.

You've got to go out.

Inside there, in the close warm air and the unfriendly smell, holding in your hand, in their cool, damp wrapping of red and white striped nylon, the shaving-brush, razor, soap, blades, the bottle of eau-de-Cologne, the toothbrush in its case, the half-empty tube of toothpaste, the comb, all the things you had spread out on the shelf beside the little washbasin without a plug and with a tap that yields water only in driblets, you rub your forefinger over your chin, which is almost smooth, your neck which is still rough and has a scratch on it, you look at the tiny drop of blood drying on the tip of your finger, then you lift the lid of your case and slip in the toilet things, you close both of its two thin brass locks, wondering whether to put it back on the rack or to stay in the corridor watching for the outskirts of Rome; on second thoughts, no, for you've still got nearly half an hour, you look at your watch, twenty-five minutes exactly.

So you hoist it up again. Thrust deep into the cleft at the back of the seat is the book you bought on leaving, which you haven't read, but have kept throughout the journey as a token of yourself, which you'd forgotten when you left the compartment just now, which you'd let slip while you were asleep and which had gradually slid under your body.

You take it in your hand, saying to yourself: I ought to write a book; that would be the way to fill this hollow emptiness within me, now that I've lost all other sort of freedom, now that I'm being carried along by this train all the way to the station, wholly bound, forced to follow these rails.

And so I shall go on with that unreal, soul-destroying work at Scabelli's for the sake of the children, for Henriette's sake, for my own sake, I shall go on living at 15 Place du Panthéon; and above all, on subsequent visits, I know, I shan't be able to resist going back to see Cécile.

At first I shall tell her nothing, I shan't speak to her about this journey. She won't understand why there'll be so much sadness about my embraces. She'll gradually come to feel what in fact she had always felt, that our love is not a road leading anywhere but is destined to lose itself in desert sands, as we both grow older.

Magliana station has gone by. Beyond the corridor, there are the suburbs of Rome already.

In a few moments you'll be arriving at that transparent station at which it's so wonderful to arrive at sunrise, as you can by this train at another time of year.

It will still be pitch-dark, and through the enormous windows you'll see the gleam of street lamps and the blue sparks of trams.

You won't go down to the Albergo Diurno, only as far as the bar where you'll ask for a *caffè latte*, reading the newspaper which you'll have bought, while daylight appears and gradually gains strength, richness and warmth.

You'll be carrying your suitcase when you leave the station at dawn (the sky is perfectly clear, the moon has set, it's going to be a marvellous autumn day), and the city appears in all its deep redness, and as you'll be able to go neither to Via Monte della Farina nor to the Albergo Quirinale, you'll hail a taxi and ask to be taken to the Hotel Croce di Malta, Via Borgognone, near the Piazza d'Espagna.

You will not keep watch over Cécile's windows; you will not see her go out; she will not catch sight of you.

You won't go and wait for her outside the Palazzo Farnese; you'll eat your lunch alone; throughout the whole of these few days you'll eat all your meals alone.

You'll walk about Rome quite alone, avoiding the district where she lives, and in the evening you'll go back alone to your hotel, where you'll go to sleep alone.

Then in that hotel room, alone, you'll begin writing a book, to fill the emptiness of those days in Rome deprived of Cécile, debarred from going near her.

Then on Monday night, you'll go back to the station, at the time you had intended, to take the train you had intended to take,

without having seen her.

Beyond the corridor the big petrol refinery goes past with its flame and the electric lights decking its tall aluminium towers like a Christmas tree.

You're still standing there, facing your seat and that photograph of the Arc de Triomphe in Paris, still holding the book in your hands, when somebody taps you on the shoulder, the young husband whom you call Pierre, and you sit down to let him go out, but that's not what he wants; he stretches out his arm and turns on the light.

All the passengers open startled eyes and show flustered faces.

He reaches up over his young wife's head, takes down one of the cases and lays it on the seat, opens it and looks for their toilet things.

You say to yourself: if there hadn't been these people, if there hadn't been these objects, these images on to which my thoughts fastened, so that, during a journey unlike my other journeys, cut off from the habitual sequence of my days and actions, a kind of mental machine was set up, making the various regions of my being go sliding one over the other, tearing me apart,

if there hadn't been this set of circumstances, if the cards had not been dealt this way, perhaps this yawning fissure in my being would not have appeared during the course of this night, perhaps my illusions might have held for a little longer,

but now that it has occurred I can no longer hope for it to heal or to be forgotten, for it opens on to a cavern which is the cause of it, which has been there within me for a long time, and which I cannot attempt to block up, since it is connected with an immense rift in the sphere of history.

I cannot hope to save myself by myself. All the blood of my being, all the sand of my days would run out in vain in my effort to achieve integration.

So then, the only possible way for me to enjoy at least the reflected gleam—itself so wonderful, so thrilling—of that future liberty which is out of our reach, would be to prepare the way for that liberty, to enable it, in however minute a measure, to take shape and substance, by means of a book for instance, although there could be no question of giving an answer to that riddle which the name of Rome suggests to our conscious or unconscious minds, of giving even a crude account of that prime source of marvels and of mysteries.

The station of Roma Trastevere goes by. Outside the window the first trams, their lights ablaze, cross one another in the streets.

It was pitch dark already and the headlights of cars were reflected on the wet asphalt in the Place du Panthéon. Sitting by the window, you were taking the *Letters of Julian the Apostate* from your bookcase when Henriette came in to ask if you'd be there for dinner.

'You know I prefer dining in the restaurant-car.'

'Your suitcase is ready on our bed. I'm going back to the kitchen.'

'Good-bye. I'll be seeing you on Monday.'

'We'll expect you; your place will be laid. Good-bye.'

The rain had stopped and the moon was showing between clouds above the Boulevard Saint-Michel, with its lively crowd of students of all colours forgathering at the beginning of term; in your haste to get away from that flat you took a taxi, which turned round the corner of the ruined palace attributed to the Parisian emperor.

At the Gare de Lyon, you bought cigarettes and reserved, on the platform, your seat for the second dinner; you got into a first-class carriage, you settled down in a compartment where there was already a stout gentleman of your own age, smoking small cigars, you deposited on the rack your suitcase and the brief-case of light-coloured leather full of files and documents, from which you extracted the orange folder dealing with the affairs of the Rheims branch.

It was only the start of an ordinary journey and yet already, almost casually, you had made enquiries in Paris about the possibility of a job that might suit Cécile; nothing had as yet rent the texture of your well-regulated life, and yet already your relations with these two women were drawing toward the crisis of which this exceptional journey, now nearing its end, marks the conclusion.

When the train left, you went into the corridor to look out through the window at the moon in its first crescent over suburban roofs and gasometers.

Outside the window, the full moon has gone, but in front of Aurelian's ramparts the Vespas are more numerous, and many lights are already shining in every floor of the new blocks of flats.

The man you called Pierre comes back into the compartment, looking fresher about the face, more wideawake, smiling; the woman you called Agnès goes out next, carrying her big handbag; the woman beside you, with the Roman face, gets up, straightens her coat and tidies her hair, and takes down her little suitcase.

You say to yourself: what has happened since that Wednesday night, that last time I set off for Rome in the usual way? How can everything be so utterly changed, how can I have reached this point?

The forces that had been accumulating for a long time already exploded at last when you decided to make this journey, but the fire thus started had far-reaching effects, for while carrying out the plan you had dreamed of so long, you were compelled to realize that your love for Cécile was dominated by Rome as though by some enormous star, and that if you longed to bring her to Paris it was in the hope that through her, Rome would be with you all the time; but you find instead that when Cécile comes to the scene of your ordinary life she loses her mediatory power and becomes just a woman like any other, a second Henriette with whom, in that sort of substitute marriage which you had intended to set up, the same sort of difficulties would occur, only worse, because you'd be perpetually reminded of the absence of that city which you had hoped she would bring nearer to you.

Now it is no fault of Cécile's if the radiance of Rome which is reflected and concentrated in her fades as soon as she comes to Paris; it's the fault of the myth of Rome itself, which, as soon as you try to embody it in any definite way, however timid your attempt may be, reveals its ambiguities, and you stand condemned. You were trying to counterbalance your dissatisfaction with Paris by a secret belief in a return to the *pax romana*, a world empire organized round a capital city which might perhaps not be Rome but, for example, Paris. You justified all your acts of cowardice by reference to your hope that these two themes might be fused.

Another women than Cécile would have lost her power, too; another town than Paris would have deprived her of it.

And thus you are aware that one of the great epochs of history has come to an end, that in which the world had a centre, which was not the earth set amidst the spheres, in the Ptolemaic system, but was Rome in the centre of the earth, a centre which shifted about, after the collapse of Rome tried to fix itself in Byzantium and then, much later, in imperial Paris, the black network of railways over France being a sort of shadow of the Roman roads.

The memory of the Empire, which dominated all the dreams of Europe for so many centuries, is now no longer an adequate image to represent the future of the world, which for each one of us has become far vaster and quite differently organized.

And that was why, when you tried to make closer contact with it on your own account, the image fell to pieces; that is why when Cécile comes to Paris she becomes like any other woman, and the sky that had shone on her is clouded.

You say to yourself; this book should show the part Rome can play in the life of a man in Paris; the two cities might be imagined one above the other, one of them lying underground below the other, with communicating trapdoors which only a few would know, while surely nobody could know them all, so that to go from one place to another there might be certain short cuts or unexpected detours, so that the distance from one point to another, the way from one point to another would vary according to one's knowledge, the degree of one's familiarity with that other city, so that every man's consciousness of place would be twofold, and Rome would distort Paris to a greater or less degree for each individual, suggesting authentic or misleading parallels.

The old Italian opposite you gets up, laboriously takes down his big black case and leaves the compartment, beckoning his wife to follow him.

A number of passengers, carrying their luggage, are already passing along the corridor and lining up beside the door.

The station of Roma Ostiense goes by, with the white tip of Cestius's pyramid showing faintly against the blackness, and, beneath you, the first suburban trains are arriving at the Roma-Lido station. On the iron floor-heater with its diamond pattern like an idealized graph of railway traffic, you gaze at the dust and minute scraps of filth that have accumulated and become encrusted there during the past day and night.

The following morning, Thursday, you went to see Nero's golden House, for Cécile's benefit; you had taken her home about midnight the night before, to 56 Via Monte della Farina, and she had answered your pleading look by saying that you couldn't possibly go upstairs with her then, because the da Pontes would not have gone to bed yet, and on Thursday evening you dined with her in her room, surrounded by those four photographs of Paris which you tried not to see and which prevented you from speaking.

You only felt able to tell her about your visit when you were both lying on the bed together with the lamp turned out, the room lit only by moonbeams that came in through the window with a slight waft of wind, the lights from neighbouring houses, and the headlamps of Vespas as they swerved noisily round the corner down below, sending orange gleams on to the ceiling.

You left her soon after midnight as usual; you went back to the Albergo Quirinale; the broken threads were joining up again; the wound had healed over very lightly; the slightest indiscretion would have torn it open again; that was why you never uttered a word to her about that time in Paris, and why, next day, Friday, despite all your fears, she never uttered a word to you about it, while you were lunching together in a restaurant near the Baths of Diocletian, nor while she was saying good-bye to you on the station platform, gazing at you and waving as the train moved out.

You had won her back; everything seemed forgotten. You never spoke of it again, and it's because of that silence that now the wound is incurable, it's because of that false, premature healing-over that gangrene has set in, in that inward sore that is festering so dreadfully now that the circumstances of this journey, the jars and jolts and the discomfort of it have torn off the scab.

'Good-bye,' you called out to her as she ran, looking so lovely with her head held high and her hair forming a crown of black flames round it, smiling and breathless. You thought then: I nearly lost her, I've regained her; I've been skirting a precipice, I must never speak of it again; now I shall know how to keep her, I've got her safe.

You stare at your shoes, streaked all over with grey creases, against the iron floor-heater.

And now that 'good-bye, Cécile' rings out in your head, and your eyes fill with tears of disappontment; you wonder, how can I ever make her understand and forgive me for the lie that our love has been, except perhaps by means of this book in which she would appear in her full beauty, adorned with the glory of Rome which is so perfectly reflected in her.

Would it not be better to maintain the distance between these two cities, all these stations and landscapes that divide them? But in addition to the normal routes by which one could move from one to another at will, there would be a certain number of points of contact, of immediate passages which would open at certain moments determined by laws which would only gradually become known to one.

Thus the principal character, walking in the neighbourhood of the Parisian Panthéon might one day, as he turned the corner of a familiar house, find himself all at once in a quite different street from the one he expected, under a very different light, with inscriptions in another language which he would recognize as Italian,

reminding him of a street he had already been through, which he would presently identify as one of those streets in the neighbourhood of the Roman Panthéon, and meeting a certain woman there he would realize that to find her again he only had to go to Rome like any one else who has the leisure and the money to spare, by taking a train for instance, by giving up a certain amount of time and passing through all the intermediate stations;

and in the same way this Roman woman would from time to time visit Paris; having travelled far to find her he would discover that, no doubt involuntarily, she had come to the very place he had just left, he might for instance get a letter from a friend describing her,

so that all the episodes of their love affair would be conditioned not only by the laws of these relations between Rome and Paris, laws which might differ slightly for each of them, but also by their degree of familiarity with these cities.

The young woman you called Agnès, about whom you know nothing, not even her name, nothing but her face and her destination, Syracuse, comes back into the compartment, sits down beside her husband, watches the Vespas interlacing in front of the gloomy wall of Aurelian, which moves off into the distance, hidden by embankments and the buildings around the Piazza Zama.

The train dives between walls and under the bridge of the Via Appia Nuova.

The station of Roma Tuscolana goes by. A man thrusts his head through the doorway and looks about as if to make sure that he hasn't forgotten something (perhaps he's the man who, for a few hours last night, sat in that empty seat opposite you and whose face you never even saw, since he was enshrouded in darkness while you were sunk deep in your uneasy sleep, in the agonizing flow of your bad dreams, and those questions that torture you now were slowly and painfully taking shape and germinating within you, and a dizzy terror seized you at the abyss that was opening up before you, that rift which widens and deepens as you come nearer your journey's end—and your arrival in a few moments is the only certain fact, the only solid ground that's left you—that rift in which everything you had built up was gradually being engulfed).

Everything was fresh to you on that spring night in Rome, as you walked back towards the Hotel Croce di Malta.

There was no Metropolitana yet, there were no trolley-buses, no scooters, there were only trams and upright taxis and a few horse-carriages.

Henriette laughed like yourself at the troops of priests, young and old, in their coloured sashes, rambling through the streets.

Clutching your Blue Guide, which was still brand-new, which has grown increasingly inaccurate ever since, which you used to bring with you on every journey until you started seeing Cécile and making use of hers, that guidebook which you've left in your little Roman bookcase near the window at 15 Place du Panthéon,

both of you tireless (in your room in the morning, while you shaved and she did her hair, you repeated phrases from the Assimil),

you visited the Vatican next day, wandering all round the walls of the City, laughing at the pious frippery in the shop windows, hurrying through the galleries full of inferior antique statues and gifts from modern sovereigns,

you gazed lovingly at people, streets and monuments, both of you convinced that this was only a first contact.

Then after a few all-too-brief days of this delicious sauntering, both with one accord abusing under your breath the countless uniforms you met at every turn, you had to make your way back once more to the old Stazione Termini, a shabby, grimy building in those days and quite unworthy of Rome, and as the train moved out you whispered to her: 'As soon as we possibly can, we'll come back.'

Another man thrusts his head through the doorway and looks around (perhaps he's the one who spent a few hours on the seat next to the newly-married young man).

You say: I promise you, Henriette, as soon as we can, we'll come back to Rome together, as soon as the waves of this perturbation have died down, as soon as you've forgiven me; we shan't be so very old.

The train has stopped; you are in Rome, at the new Stazione Termini. The night is still pitch dark.

You are alone in the compartment, with the young couple, who aren't getting off here, who are going on as far as Syracuse.

You hear the shouts of porters, the shrilling of whistles, the puffing and creaking sounds of other trains.

You stand up, put on your coat, take your case and pick up your book.

The best thing, surely, would be to preserve the actual geographical relationship between these two cities,

and to try and bring to life in the form of literature this crucial episode in your experience, the movement that went on in your mind while your body was being transferred from one station to another through all the intermediate landscapes, towards this book, this future, necessary book of which you're holding in your hand the outward form.

The corridor is empty. You look at the crowd of people on the platform. You go out of the compartment.

(Translated by Jean Stewart)

Mobile: Study for a Representation of the United States (1962)

This is Butor's imaginary—and imaginative—guidebook to the States. Since it is something of a seamless garment, it can be excerpted more or less at random. This passage is taken in fact from about a third of the way through the book.

WELCOME TO INDIANA

five o'clock in
LEBANON, across the eastern state line.

Smile!

The big Pigeon Creek that flows into the Ohio, the Kentucky border, 'Hello, Harry!'

LEBANON.

Around the beginning of the Christian era, the Adena Indians appeared in the Ohio valley and left in the state that now bears the name of this river over five thousand mounds, fortifications, and ruins of villages. They made ornaments of hammered copper, carved stone pipes and cut hands and other figures out of mica.

'Hello, Mrs. Auburn!'—The Miami River that flows into the Ohio, the Kentucky border.

LEBANON.

*Treaty of William Penn, founder of Pennsylvania, with the Delaware Indians in 1682:
"The Great God who is the power and wisdom that made you and me, incline your hearts to Righteousness,*

*Love and Peace. This I send to assure you of my Love,
and to desire your Love to my friends . . ."*

'Information to Those Who Would Remove to
America':
'Many Persons in Europe, having directly or by
Letters, express'd to the Writer of This, who is well-
acquainted with North America, their Desire of
transporting and establishing themselves in that
Country; but who appear to have formed, thro'
Ignorance, mistaken Ideas and Expectations of what
is to be obtained there; he thinks it may be useful, and
prevent inconvenient, expensive, and fruitless Removals
and Voyages of improper Persons, if he gives some
clearer and truer Notions of that part of the World,
than appear to have hitherto prevailed . . .'
                                   Benjamin Franklin.

Raccoon Creek that flows into the Ohio.

LEBANON.

Orchard orioles,
red-shouldered hawks,
redwings,
cliff swallows,
downy woodpeckers.

The sea,
waves,
sand,

waves,
slipways,
waves.

The Pequest River, tributary of the
Delaware, the Pennsylvania border.—telephone ringing.

AURORA, on the Ohio, Dearborn County.

Smile!

'Hello, I want Lebanon, Illinois,'—on the highway a tomato-coloured Chevrolet (speed limit 65 miles), 'get gas,'—Little Pigeon Creek and the Anderson River that flow into the Ohio.

AURORA, Portage County.

The Adena Indians were followed by the Hopewell Indians, who constructed funeral mounds and considerable fortifications.

A shiny tomato-coloured Chrysler driven by an old white man (60 miles), "two more hours,"—the Little Miami River and Owl Creek that flow into the Ohio.

CAMBRIDGE CITY, Wayne County, INDIANA, a livestock state.

Keep smiling!

Sunoco, 'we took the wrong road, we have to go back,'—the Little Blue River and the Big Blue River and Deer Creek that flow into the Ohio.

CAMBRIDGE, county seat of Guernsey County, OHIO, the most densely populated state after New York, California, Pennsylvania and Illinois.

After the Hopewell civilization, some four centuries before the Europeans arrived, the Woodland civilization.

B.P.,—Raccoon Creek and the Muskingum and Scioto Rivers that flow into the Ohio,—through Mongomery Ward, you can obtain a solitaire diamond with the new 'Glo' setting that makes the diamond look bigger than it is: 'Look at the difference our new setting makes! How much bigger the diamond looks! Four little reflector diamonds, slipped under the central stone, increase its sparkling beauty, its brilliance,—make it look almost twice as big as it really is.'

HANOVER, in the zinnia state.

Keep smiling!

Perch Lake,—Silver Creek and Laughery Creek that flow into the Ohio,—through Sears, Roebuck & Co., the 'Automobile Repair

Manual,' 1,120 pages, 'covers 1,967 models, from 1952 to 1959;
2,850 explanatory illustrations to make things ultra-simple; 225,000
repair problems, with 219 rapid reference tables, covering more than
30,000 essential specifications and dimensions. . . . All pointers on
maintenance, repair and emergency service for these 24 makes:
—Buick,

> HANOVER, scarlet-carnation state.

—Cadillac,

> *Indians of an unknown period and civilization constructed*
> *large mounds in the shape of eagles, quadrupeds or serpents;*
> *the greatest of the latter measures 411 yards, has a spiral tail,*
> *twists its body into seven deep curves and holds a kind of huge*
> *egg in its open mouth.*

—Chevrolet,

> The Maumee River that flows into Lake Erie,—Polson
> Creek that flows into the Ohio,—or an engagement ring,
> page 440 in the catalogue, 'eleven sparkling diamonds,
> totaling almost a carat, in the new "Glo" setting described
> above. Four chatoyants around them. Adjustable wedding
> band with six large brilliants. Standard quality.'

—Chrysler,

> HANOVER, York County, PENNSYLVANIA,—
> the Cornplanter Indian Reservation.

—Clipper,

> '. . . He finds it is imagined by Numbers, that the
> Inhabitants of North America are rich, capable of
> rewarding, and dispos'd to reward, all sorts of
> Ingenuity; that they are at the same time ignorant of
> all the Sciences, and, consequently, that Strangers,
> possessing Talents in the Belles-Lettres, fine arts,
> &c., must be highly esteemed, and so well paid, as to
> become easily rich themselves; that there are also
> abundance of profitable Offices to be disposed of,
> which the Natives are not qualified to fill . . .'
>
> *Benjamin Franklin.*

—Continental,

> "*. . . and when the Great God brings me among you, I*
> *intend to order all things in such manner that we may*
> *all live in Love and Peace one with another, which I*

hope the Great God will incline both me and you to
do. . . ."
Treaty of William Penn with the Delaware Indians.

—De Soto,

A chocolate Frazer driven by an old Negro (50
miles),—the Beaver and Allegheny Rivers that flow
into the Ohio.

—Dodge,

                    HANOVER, NEW JERSEY, smallest
                         state after Rhode Island, Delaware,
                    Connecticut and Hawaii.

—Edsel,
                    The sea,

—Ford,
            sand,

—Hudson,
                    trunks,

Imperial,
            sand,

—Jeep,
                    shorts,

—Lincoln
            sand,

—Mercury,
                    Bluebirds,

—Nash,
            Carolina kinglets,

—Oldsmobile,
        swallow-tailed flycatchers,

—Packard,
            rose-breasted grosbeaks,

—Plymouth,
                    wood peewees.

—Pontiac,
                    A chocolate Kaiser driven by a young
                    Negro (50 miles),—the Musconetcong and
                    Assunpink Rivers, tributaries of the Dela-
                    ware,—telephone ringing.

A black-throated blue warbler on a spray of Canadian columbine; on
another plate, two females on a viburnum.

WASHINGTON COURT HOUSE, county seat of Fayette County, OHIO, a livestock state.

—Rambler,

In 1772, David Zeisberger and other Moravian Brothers built villages for the Delaware Indians whom they had converted. In 1782, in order to avoid any conflict with the Europeans in Pennsylvania, the missionaries decided it was best to make them leave their Gnadenhütten (Cabins of Grace) and to withdraw to the "City of Captives," today Upper Sandusky, Ohio. But since these missionaries had ordered them to return to sow their former fields of corn the Indians were discovered by the Pennsylvania militiamen under the orders of Colonel David Williamson, who disarmed them, bound them, and exterminated them with axes and cudgels, for they wished to save their ammunition: 35 men, 37 women and 34 children were massacred in this way. They sang until their death the hymns the missionaries had taught them.

—Studebaker,

'Hello, I want Cambridge, Ohio,'—the Christian Science church,—the Portage and Sandusky Rivers that flow into Lake Erie,—the Rattlesnake River that flows into the Scioto River,—or a pearl pendant, 'skillfully cultivated, scientifically produced in a living oyster raised for at least three years in the warm waters of Japan. The romance, the charm, the flattery of cultured pearls is eternal,—they never lose their beauty.'

A slanting sunbeam on the wet leaves.

WASHINGTON, where you can order cherry ice cream in the Howard Johnson Restaurant.

—Thunderbird,

Treaty of William Penn with the Delaware Indians: '. . . I seek nothing but the honor of His name, and that we who are His workmanship, may do that which is well pleasing to Him. The man which delivers this unto you is my special friend, sober, wise and loving, you may believe him. . . .'

—Willys."

'. . . and that, having few Persons of Family among them, Strangers of Birth must be greatly respected, and of course easily obtain the best of those Offices, which will make all their Fortunes; that the Governments too, to encourage Emigrations from Europe,

not only pay the Expence of personal Transportation,
but give Land gratis to Strangers, with Negroes to
work for them, Utensils of Husbandry, and Stocks of
Cattle. These are all wild Imaginations; and those
who go to America with Expectations founded upon
them will surely find themselves disappointed . . .'
Benjamin Franklin.

Caltex,—the Monongahela River (which, after its
junction at Pittsburgh with the Allegheny River,
becomes the Ohio River) and its tributaries:
Youghiogheny River and Tenmile Creek.

A slanting sunbeam on a spattered puddle.

WASHINGTON, Warren County.

> *meadowlarks,*
> *field sparrows,*
> *oven birds,*
> *the sea,*
> *skin,*
> *thighs,*
> *elbows,*
> *toes,*
> *backs,*
> *the outskirts of New York City,*
> *fish crows,*
> *pine siskins.*
> Esso,—Rancocas, Salem and Oldmans
> Creeks, tributaries of the Delaware,—
> telephone ringing.

MILFORD, Kosciusko County, IND., a hard winter state.

Keep smiling!

'Hello, I want Cambridge, Indiana,'—the church of the Latter-Day
Saints, called the 'Mormons,'—Cedar and Dalecarlia Lakes,—or
the 'Truck Repair Manual,' new 1959 edition, page 1030 in the
catalogue. 'Over 30,000 facts about virtually all models of gasoline
trucks from 1952 to 1959. Over 2,000 illustrations, 200 practical
tables. Clear "step-by-step" instructions tell you all you need to know
to make easy repairs. Chapters on the maintenance of diesels:

—Autocar,
—Brockway,
—Chevrolet,

MILFORD, Clermont County.

—Diamond T,
—Divco,
—Dodge,

Tecumseh, chief of the Pawnee Indians, a tribe of the Algonquin group, who had succeeded in forming a coalition against the United States: 'The Great Spirit has given this great island to the Redskins; the Great Spirit has settled the White Men beyond the ocean. Today, the white Men, not content with their own lands, have come among us and have driven us from the coastal regions to the great lakes; but from here we will retreat no farther . . .' 1810. Tecumseh died in battle in 1813.

—Ford,
—GMC,
—Cummins,
more details about gasoline or diesel engines used in building work: cranes, bulldozers, etc.'

The Vermilion River that flows into Lake Erie.

The sky is clearing.

MILFORD, on the Delaware, the New Jersey border.

The shadows grow longer.

MILFORD, on the Delaware, the Pennsylvania border.

The copper sun.

CLINTON.

The glowing panes.

CLINTON, KENTUCKY, the South (for whites only).

The rising mist.

CLINTON, on the Clinch River, TENNESSEE,
(. . . whites only).

The melting sun.

CLINTON, ALABAMA, the Deep South
South (. . . only).

CLINTON, on the Wabash River that flows into the Ohio, the redbird state.

Why aren't you smiling?

Big Creek that flows into the Wabash, the Illinois border,—the synagogue,—Palestine Lake,—or the book 'Etiquette,' by Emily Post, 'answers every question about what is done; how to behave, what to wear, on every occasion, intimate or formal, 671 pages illustrated.'

CLINTON.

> *Chapel Lake Indian Ceremonials prospectus;*
> *"Michigan's Thrilling—New—Outdoor Live Indian Drama!*
> *Giant Cast of Real North American Indians!*
> *Authentic! Mysterious! Dramatic!*
> *8:30 Nightly (Except Mondays) June 25 to Labor Day.*
> *In the Huron National Forest near Tawas City and East Tawas*
> *in Iosco County, Michigan, just off US 23—Beauty Route to the*
> *Bridge!"*

> Bear Lake

The black and white warbler on a black larch branch.

> MILFORD, Oakland County.

> *'The throbbing drums of the Red Man beat again!*
> *His ceremonial fires burn bright!*
> *The voice of the Great Spirit calls!*
> *The eagle–the Thunder Bird–flies again! . . .'*

An apricot Nash, driven by an old Negro (65 miles),—Beaver and Big Portage Lakes.

A flame of clouds.

> HANOVER, Jackson County, MICHIGAN, Middle West.
>   —the border of the Canadian province of Ontario,
> —the L'Anse Indian Reservation.

> *'From the Four Points of the Compass*
> *–the place of the Four Winds,*
> *–out of the reservations, the deep forest,*
> *–as spring passes into summer,*
> *–scores of Indians, from many tribes, gather at beautiful*
> *Chapel Lake, in the Huron National Forest, in Iosco County,*
> *Michigan, to present their nightly (except Monday) spectacular,*
> *through the summer till Labor Day . . .'*

> Esso,—Big Star Lake, Carp Lake, the Chippewa Indian
> Reservation,—or a vaginal douche bag, 'to avoid being
> embarrased, buy by mail order, discreetly! The impeccable
> "hygienette" is filled directly from the faucet. Patented plastic
> stopper at the bottom of the rubber bulb.'

AUBURN, county seat of De Kalb County, IND., a hot summer state.

Why do you watch us smiling without smiling?

If you think all concentrated soups have the same taste, its time you
tried Heinz!—The Patoka and White Rivers that flow into the
Wabash.

> AUBURN, Bay County. State Flower: apple blossom.

> *'In this colorful one hour and forty-five minute authentic, live*
> *Indian Pageant and Drama, will appear proud chieftains,–the*
> *glistening bronze bodies of the warriors, in their stirring dances*
> *and contests,*
> *–the beautiful maidens,*
> *–the squaws and their stoic faces,*
> *–the joyous children,*
> *–all in gorgeous costumery and regalia, presenting their*
> *Ceremonials and age-old dances,*
> *–things heretofore unseen and unknown to the White Man!*
> *. . .'*

Coldwater and Crystal Lakes,—or a traveling douche bag,

in its case, page 217 in the general catalogue, 'flexible white rubber, curving, flexible tube . . .'

ALBION, county seat of Noble County.

Your not smiling hurts our feelings.

Busseron Creek that flows into the Wabash.

ALBION, Calhoun County.

'*At Beautiful Chapel Lake, just a short distance from US 23 and M 55, nine miles west of East Tawas and Tawas City, on a good forest road–the famous old Plank Road,–these genuine North American Indians present their Ceremonials for your pleasure! The comfortable, picturesque open-air stadium overlooks the wooded island stage. There is a rustic refreshment stand and large lighted free parking lot . . .*'

Devils Lake.

The crimson reflection on the water.

WASHINGTON.—When the sun is setting in WASHINGTON,

(Translated by Richard Howard)

JEAN RICARDOU

Born in 1932, Jean Ricardou—by profession a school-teacher—is very much the high priest of the *nouveau roman*. He is the author of at least three theoretical studies of the phenomenon, and the editor of colloquia devoted to it. He also writes novels himself that employ with single-minded rigour all the devices invented by his colleagues, which makes him very difficult to translate; not surprisingly, so far as we have been able to ascertain, this is the first specimen of his creative writing to have appeared in English. It is taken from near the middle of a novel entitled in French *La Prise de Constantinople*, but our translation cannot attempt to render all the overtones of the title, which in any case appears as *La Prose de Constantinople*, ('The *Prose* of Constantinople') on the back cover. Also punned on is the French word for cunt, *le con*; Ricardou makes clear in one of his theoretical books that *'la prise du con'* ('the seizure of the cunt') is as much what the novel is about as are the Crusaders' antics in the eastern Mediterranean in the thirteenth century.

In his critical essays, Ricardou is ever alert to puns in the novels of his colleagues: one of his pieces is entitled 'La Bataille de la phrase', 'the battle of the sentence', an elaborate play on Claude Simon's title *La Bataille de Pharsale*, or *The Battle of Pharsalus*. His own most entertaining book, *Les Lieux-Dits* ('Place-Names' or 'Named Places', 1969), is dedicated to an imaginary individual jokingly called Ed. Word.

Only time will tell whether Ricardou—self-avowedly the most cerebral of the *nouveaux romanciers*—is more than just a literary punster and constructor of puzzles aimed at exercising the ingenuity of academics. Although he takes himself very seriously as a critic, there is evidence that he uses humour and irony in his novels because he enjoys writing the sort of books he learnedly takes to pieces in his rather over-earnest essays.

This extract opens under the alchemist's symbol for water, an element which has obvious relevance to the historical subject of this novel and, more generally, equally obvious erotic connotations. It is superfluous to add that the inverted triangle also represents the *mons Veneris*, but the observation strikes the right note on which to invite the reader to read on.

(J.F.)

The Capture of Constantinople (1965)

▽

As if blurred by the semi-darkness, his silhouette is at first duplicated by a symmetrical virtual image, whose contours, in the fictive space permitted by the glass panels beyond the books, are embellished by the irregularities of reflection with notches and absurd suppositions.

Serge himself is standing silent and motionless, with his arms crossed.

Then he moves forward, draws near to the round table and the packet of Lucky Strike. Just as he was about to pick up the small red and white package, he smiles, and rapidly pulls back his hand. He contemplates it with conspicuous, exaggerated astonishment. He wipes it with his pale green handkerchief.

Then, making the same movement again, this time he is able to take a cigarette. The slowness with which he selects it seems to correspond to an attentive evaluation of the contents of the packet.

An explosion crackles, minute in the semi-darkness which it increases by contrast, and is followed by a clear halo at the end of the match.

While the tiny stick reddens, twists in various ways, stands erect—rhymes conceded to the system—with glowing fibres and then turns black, the flame lengthens and trembles on contact with the cigarette. It leaps into life again. It is extinguished at last by a brisk and bright flourish of the wrist in the air.

Stay on here, nonetheless. Take up, lucidly, an unexpected attitude, in this case the conventional and emphatic one of the combatant in action.

The left leg is bent forward; the other, on the contrary, is stretched behind. On top of the white shirt, embroidered with the intertwined initials S and L, a dark tie (on which can just be seen greenish lines of complex design) has been put on—then the suit jacket, in light metallic grey material against which the pocket in turn gives a touch of white.

The right arm is raised and the hand holds above the head the tiny cylinder with the glowing end. The left hand releases a pale green handkerchief in which the traces of the folds make up patterns which criss-cross in a jumble.

In the background, if despite the risks one's attention hazards itself a shade too much, the windows parcel out the reflection of the bookcase in accordance with the overlapping surfaces whose disjunctions proliferate. At the slightest movement of the eye, unsuspected angles and curves . . . but Serge, at the slightest movement of the eye, unsuspected angles and curves . . . but Serge abandons at the slightest movement of the eye unsuspected angles and curves, strange perspectives are revealed, but Serge drops his stereotyped posture, at the slightest movement of the eye which no doubt Alice can hardly fail to notice.

The different figures proposed do not seem, then, to illustrate a single theme, determined in advance. Instead everything appears to emerge gradually from an assemblage of parodistic scenes in accordance with a mechanism the principles of which no doubt only a privileged position in the text—sought patiently first in one direction then in another—can piece together.

Meanwhile a network of conjectures and unforeseen notches has to suffice.

So could it not be the involved trajectories of bees swirling this morning around the clumps of pansies which Serge now makes concrete by the ample ellipses of light traced by the cigarette end around the crystal vase? Serge in any case accompanies these orbits with a discreet quivering of the lips and he starts turning full circle. As these movements displace him he ends up, after several turns, by falling into the deep armchair which at one point he had carefully placed in front of Isa.

He settles himself comfortably in it and, stretching out his left arm, he now seems to be comparing, by alternate movements of the eyes, the palm of his hand with the girl's silhouette.

—You've moved again, he says.

But in too tenuous a fashion, however, for it to be necessary for him to get up, then—evading the trap of an excessively close observation of the frothy fringe or of the sinuous cleft between the head and the trunk—to approach, and to move round the armchair.

With the end of his cigarette, from which rises a thread of smoke that moves in one direction then another with every movement, Serge darkens with a fresh network of diagonal lines, on the imaginary paper, the blueish arch of the eyelids, insufficiently stressed under such lighting. On the higher cheek, the lowered lashes, joining, merge with their own shadow borne. A sinuous segment marks the fold of the lips. On each side of the face the hair falls in fragmentary parabolas, in a plethora of twists and curls which coil heavily on the shoulder, on the strapless bra held in place by the bulging of the breasts—but the pencil, inspired too by the twirling smoke or the shadows it makes, can take to tracing its innumerable metamorphoses.

Which is perhaps why Serge gives up, gets out of the armchair and walks backwards towards the bookcase. His lips are moving but the words are too indistinct to be understood in any one meaning. It is therefore not unlikely that the numbers forty and thirty-one are being pronounced, for instance, whilst behind his back his left hand has slid the glass panel across with a distant rumble, deadened and reverberated by the side of the Isle of Salts.[1] Still gropingly, a book is chosen.

Serge opens it at random, with a single movement.

Elected pope in 1198, Innocent III feels it his duty to win back the holy places. 'All princes,' he is fond of repeating, 'whatever their liege story, are Christ's vassals and must unyoke his demesne.' Into every Christian country he dispatches envoys to preach the crusade. Each preacher is to develop a common theme in accordance with whatever divine inspiration he receives.

The clergy are told to divide their property into two parts. The smaller surface is to be used to arm the crusaders. The other can be moved westward and grow or diminish in accordance with all sorts of notches and conjectures.

Various local wars, in which unexpected treacheries proliferate, stop the kings from taking up the Cross. But Foulque de Neuilly whips up the enthusiasm of more than one hundred and sixty thousand people, and on his arrival at a tournament given on the Breton heath, wins over the counts of Champagne and Blois.

An army of knights and lords thus comes to be assembled.

A fleet turns out to be necessary to get to the holy places. Eight senior dignitaries, including the Sire de Villehardouin who will later write the story of this adventure, form a deputation to request ships from the Venetian senate. The latter agrees, in return for eighty thousand silver marks and a share in the booty, to transport and feed for a year four thousand knights, eight thousand squires and sixteen thousand footsoldiers. Forty mounted galleys are added. The crusaders choose Boniface de Montferrat as their leader. At the age of

---

[1] *L'île des Sels*, a complex pun which recurs in various forms throughout the novel.

ninety the Doge Dandolo takes command of the Venetian contingent.

The crusaders hope to attack the Moslems in the region of Karnak in Upper Egypt. For complicated reasons, made clear perhaps from a certain position in the text, the Venetians deflect the expedition instead towards Constantinople.

Because they are unable to pay the full amount owing, Dandolo suggests that the Crusaders campaign in the service of Venice. They are led first to the Dalmatian shore to lay siege to Zara, Venice's competitor in the Adriatic. The pope forbids them, under pain of excommunication, to attack any Christian city. But once Zara is taken, the pope only excommunicates the Venusians, and even allows the Crusaders to continue operations with them.

Constantinople had just experienced a palace revolution. Alexis III had deposed the Emperor Isaac, put out his eyes and held him prisoner with his son Alexis, who then escaped and asked the Crusaders for help. He promises them one hundred and sixty thousand marks and eighty thousand men in return for driving out the usurper. Dandolo seizes this opportunity to draw the Crusaders at last towards Constantinople.

They disembark in 1203. Alexis has only undisciplined mercenaries at his command, their ranks depleted by many betrayals. The ablest defenders are still the Pisan merchants, Venice's enemies.

A week after the siege has started Alexis III decamps.

Isaac is removed from prison and his son, Alexis IV, is proclaimed Emperor. None of the promises is kept but the Greeks revolt and choose a new Emperor, Alexis V, who gives the crusaders a week to organize their departure.

A new siege begins.

Although short of food the crusaders dare not retreat in case they are attacked from the rear by the Greeks. One night, towards the end, the moon rises, a perfect circle, in the translucent sky above the dark ramparts.

A few risky steps sideways allow the soldiers to avoid its dangerous evocation.

Exposed in this way to the moon, a number of clear surfaces make up the battlements. The shadow cast by the citadel reaches this part of the slope in accordance with an approximate copy, and is refined in innumerable grooves by the unevenness of the ground. In the detail, indeed, some element of inversion distorts the outline: various highlit humps emerge from the area of shadow, and the illuminated zone is pockmarked with dark hollows.

If the observer indulges in a perilously close study he will no longer be able to overlook the microscopic role, on the sloping sand, of mica flakes.

In the sky, high up, dominating the ramparts and the moon, two clouds, at present of unequal size, move along, brought into existence by a single cottony mass, sacred according to certain witnesses, which one would at first have thought to be motionless. When one's gaze, distracted for a moment only, turns to contemplating again the initial phases of the break-up, it meets only an isolated cloud that gleams sufficiently to eclipse the surrounding stars and undergoes imperceptible changes in which some see a Cross, a face, the image of the Virgin, other signs still, manifested, it is said, by the localized notches and protuberances successively described.

On the other hand there is no movement on the ramparts, no sound, no call or password indistinctly uttered. If a prose attains its fiction on the battlements, turns precisely on the dot, measures the words of its to-and-fro by lining them up on the delicate lines of the paper; if it ends up in this way by getting absorbed to the point of giving its composition the unique aim of its own improvement, this happens in perfect silence.

From the side perhaps come only the sounds of water splashed up and falling again as rain, the rustling of the page, perhaps, turned carefully by Serge, or again, because a new rhyme must be granted to the system, the crunch of gravel on the drive.

This interminable investment overlooks no detail. It lasts therefore until dawn when the assault is mounted.

Like its predecessor, which inspired it, this new siege is fierce and determined. If the defences give way it is only at the absolute limit and not without having repulsed many an offensive, scared the assailants more than once, deflected them from their objectives, or set them one against the other in accordance with brief and unscheduled massacres.

In the mêlée from time to time, at a spot determined by the inflexible laws of ballistics, a soldier receives a dousing in boiling pitch. A crackling halo of fire and smoke engulfs him immediately. He can be seen twisting in various convulsions, in incandescent fragments; then he doubles up, a blackened lump which the flame, shaken and reignited by the last tremble, at last abandons.

Towards four in the afternoon the Crusaders seize the imperial banner and the miraculous image of the Virgin. Resistance slackens and gives up. Then the crusaders sack the town and, in many places.

But Serge closes the book before turning over a fresh page. On the shelf of his bookcase—easily visible now that the movement of the glass door has erased the approximate image of the room—the book's place has in part been filled by the incline of the neighbouring volume. One after the other—if one excepts minute changes increased by proximity—all the right-hand books have followed this movement so that an empty space equivalent to the one filled here is made at the end of the row. The parallelepiped left empty by the extraction of the book has thus in a way been divided into two equal gaps, two inverted prisms separated by several inches of matter.

Serge reinserts the tall volume, re-establishes the verticalities, then eclipses them again with the reflected image of the library by closing the glass panel.

And yet—or so it seems—the battle has not ended: Serge stumbles, recovers his balance, considers with care his surroundings. Brisk diagonal movements of his wrist, first in one direction then in another, repeated and redoubled with enough force to make the speed and size of the inspirations increase, enable him no doubt to slice through innumerable brambles which get thicker and thicker as he moves away from the path.

The darkness deepens.

On the ground, the carpet of moss thickens, gets more complicated.

In the distance, beyond the two windows of the bookcase, the storm suggests sporadic flickerings.

Always increasing, the thorny volume conceals itself in the undergrowth in byzantine overlaps which are simplified, here and there, by an unexpected alignment. The edge of the sword gets blunted, as does the arm's strength. It's now necessary to attack each notch twice, even three times.

The advance slows down little by little.

By now various stalks have entwined themselves round Serge's ankles and he falls on his knees at Isa's feet.

His hands which—or so it seems—were going to join together in an attitude of final supplication, remain parted however under the girl's lowered gaze, and exactly at the width of her waist. After a moment, in a deep tone, as if in threat, Serge remarks:

—You've moved.

So he has to get up, then circle the applied silhouette. Before dropping, his two vertical hands have to regulate the gap between them to match approximately the diameter of the face. His palms can thus brush the silky curls, the temples, the cheeks whose curve fills out momentarily, and then come closer together to follow the line of the neck and the start of the shoulders, in order to pull the whole body slowly backwards.

Imperceptibly, as she should, the girl closes her eyes and the greenish surface of the iris thus becomes covered by the nocturnal bluishness of the eyelids.

The red hair cascades downwards, vertically, variously, in unexpected ripples.

The two arms part symmetrically as far as they can reach.

So it is the moment to raise the silhouette—with one touch of the two hands under the nape. At the same time the arms withdraw and the fingers, scarcely parted, come to rest on the sheet of drawing paper which represents the book.

The face is lowered, surrounded already, on both sides, by the double waves of the hair.

Undergoing minute changes, the white veil has moved towards the right shoulder.

Since these different actions have parted the fastening at the back of the strapless bra by half an inch or so, Serge closes it again with a delicate gesture. But as he stooped to do this his face may have brushed up against the girl's left shoulder.

In the middle of each cheek, where the freckles present a denser constellation, a small pinkish surface has emerged, increasing rapidly towards the temples, whilst Serge, before letting Alice take his place, moves to the other door to look for the third actor (Blaise), and leads him to the blue sofa, in the semi-darkness, between the two casements.

(Translated by John Fletcher and Françoise Dupuis)

BIBLIOGRAPHY

MICHEL BUTOR

Second Thoughts, Faber & Faber, London, 1958. (Orig. publ. as *La Modification*, Editions de Minuit Paris, 1957).

Passing Time, Faber & Faber, London, 1961. John Calder, London, 1965. (Orig. publ. as *L'Emploi du temps*, Les Editions de Minuit, Paris, 1957).

Essay on a Dream of Baudelaire, Jonathan Cape, London, 1969, (Orig. publ. as *Une histoire extraordinaire, essai sur un rêve de Baudelaire*, Gallimard, Paris, 1961).

Degrees, Methuen, London, 1962. (Orig. publ. as *Degrés*, Editions Gallimard, Paris, 1960).

Les Oeuvres d'art imaginaires chez Proust Athlone Press, London, 1964.

Inventory, Jonathan Cape, London 1970. (Orig. publ. as Repertoire I, Editions de Minuit, Paris, 1968).

6 810 000 Litres of Water Per Second, H. Regnery Co., Chicago, 1969. (Orig. publ. as *6 810 000 Litres d'eau par seconde*, Editions Gallimard, Paris, 1965).

The following titles have all been published by Editions Gallimard, Paris;

Réseaú aérien	1962
Description de San Marco	1963
Illustration I	1964
Essai sur les modernes	1964
Portrait de l'artiste en jeune singe	1967
Essai sur les essais	1968
Illustration II	1969
Essais sur le roman	1970
La Rose des vents	1970
Où	1971
Dialogue avec 33 variations de Ludwig van Beethoven sur une valse de Diabelli	1971
Travaux d'approche (Poems)	1972
Illustration III	1973
Intervalle	1973
Matière de rêves I	1975
Illustration IV	1976

Matière de rêves II—Second sous-sol 1976
Troisième dessous 1977
Boomerang 1978
Envois 1980

MARGUERITE DURAS

The Square, John Calder, London 1959. (Orig. publ. as *Le square*, Editions Gallimard, Paris, 1955).

Ten-thirty on a Summer Night, John Calder, London 1962. (Orig. publ. as *Dix heures et demie du soir en été*, Editions Gallimard, Paris, 1960).

The Afternoon of Monsieur Andesmas, John Calder, London 1959. (Orig. publ. as *L'après-midi de Monsieur Andesmas,* Editions Gallimard, Paris 1962).

Hiroshima mon amour & *Une aussi longue absence* (film scripts) John Calder, London, 1966. (Orig. publ. under the same titles, Librairie Gallimard, Paris 1960 and Librairie Gallimard, Paris, 1961).

The Little Horses of Tarquinia, John Calder, London, 1960, 1985. (Orig. publ. as *Les petits chevaux de Tarquinia*, Gallimard, Paris, 1953).

Susanna Andler with *La musica* & *L'amante anglaise,* (play scripts) John Calder, London, 1975. (Orig. published under the same titles, Editions Gallimard, Paris, 1968, Editions Gallimard, Paris, 1965 & Editions Gallimard, Paris, 1965.

Three Plays—The Square, Days in the Trees, The Viaducts of Seine-et-Oise, John Calder, London, 1967. (Orig. publ. as *Le square*, Editions Gallimard, Paris, 1965, *Des journées entières dans les arbres,* Editions Gallimard, Paris, 1954, *les viaducs de Seine-et-Oise*, Editions Gallimard, Paris, 1960).

Moderato Cantabile, John Calder, London, 1966. (Orig. publ. under the same title, Les Editions de Minuit, Paris, 1958).

The Sailor from Gibraltar, John Calder, London, 1966, 1985. Orig. publ. as *Le marin de Gibraltar*, Les Editions de Minuit, Paris, 1952).

Whole Days in the Trees, John Calder, London, 1982. Orig. publ. as *Des journées entières dans les arbres*, Editions Gallimard, Paris 1953).

Les impudents, Plon, Paris, 1943.

La vie tranquille. Editions Gallimard, Paris, 1944.

Un barrage contre le Pacifique, Editions Gallimard, Paris, 1950.

Le ravissement de Lol V. Stein, Editions Gallimard, Paris, 1964.

Le vice-consul, Editions Gallimard, Paris, 1966.

La Musica (film) distr. Artistes Associés, Paris, 1966.

L'amante anglaise, Gallimard, Paris, 1965.

L'amante anglaise (play) Cahiers du Théâtre National Populaire, Paris, 1968.

Theatre II: *Suzanna Andler* (see above for Engl. tr.) *Des journées entières* (dto), *Yes, peut-être, Le shaga, Un homme est venu me voir*, Gallimard, Paris, 1968.

Détruire, dit-elle, Les Editions de Minuit, Paris, 1969.

Détruire, dit-elle (film) distr. S.M.E.P.A., Paris, 1969.

Abahn, Savana, David Gallimard, Paris, 1970.

L'amour, Gallimard, Paris, 1971.

Jaune le soleil (film) never distr., 1971

Nathalie Granger (film) distr. Films Molière.

India Song: prose, play, film, Gallimard, Paris 1973.

La femme du Gange (film) never distr., 1973.

Nathalie Granger, followed by *La femme du Gange*, Gallimard, Paris 1973.

Les Parleuses (interview with Xavière Gauthier) Les Editions de Minuit, Paris, 1974.

India Song (film) distr. Films Armorial, 1975.

Baxter, Vera Baxter (film) distr. N.E.F. Diffusion, Paris, 1976.

Son nom de Venise dans Calcutta désert (film) distr. Cinéma 9 Paris, 1976.

Des journées entières dans les arbres (film) distr. Gaumont, 1976.

Le Camion (film) Distr. Films Molière, Paris 1977.

Le Camion followed by interview with Michelle Porte, Les Editions de Minuit, Paris 1977.

L'eden Cinéma (play) Mercure de France, Paris, 1977

L'Amant, Les Editions de Minuit, Paris 1984.

Adaptations:

La Bête dans la jungle after a novella by Henry James, with James Lord. Not published.

Miracle en Alabama by William Gibson, with Gérard Jarlot, L'avant-Scène, 1963.

Les papiers d'Aspern by Michael Redgrave after a novella by Henry James, with Robert Antelme, Edition Paris-Théâtre, 1970.

Home by David Storey, Gallimard, Paris 1973.

CLAUDE MAURIAC

Dinner in Town, John Calder, London 1963. (Orig. publ. as *Le dîner en ville*, Editions Albin Michel, Paris, 1959.

The Marquise Went Out at Five, John Calder, London, 1966. (Orig. publ. as *La marquise sortit à cinq heures*, Editions Albin Michel, Paris, 1961).

Femmes Fatales, John Calder, London 1966. (Orig. publ. as *Toutes les femmes sont fatales*, Editions Albin Michel, Paris, 1961).

Introduction à une mystique de l'enfer, Editions Bernard Grasset, Paris, 1938.

Jean Cocteau ou la vérité du mensonge, Odette Lieutier, Paris 1945.

Malraux ou le mal du héros, Editions Bernard Grasset, Paris, 1947.

Proust par lui-même, Editions du Seuil, Paris, 1953

L'amour du cinéma, Albin Michel, Paris, 1954.

L'allitérature contemporaine, Albin Michel, Paris, 1958, Editions Bernard Grasset, Paris, 1969.

(The following titles are all published by Editions Bernard Grasset:

La conversation, 1964

L'oubli, 1966

Théâtre, 1968

De la littérature a l'alittérature, 1969

André Breton, 1970

Une amitié contrariée, 1970

Le temps immobile, vol. I, 1974

Les espaces imaginaires, vol. II, 1975

Et comme l'espérance est violente, vol. III, 1976

La terrasse de Malagar, vol. IV, 1977

Aimer de Gaulle, vol. V, 1978

Le rire des pères dans les yeux des enfants, vol VI, 1981

Le Bouddha s'est mis, 1979

Un coeur tout neuf, 1980

ROBERT PINGET

No Answer, John Calder, London, 1961. (Orig. publ. as *Le fiston*, Les Editions de Minuit, Paris, 1959).

Plays—Vol. 1: Clope (*Clope au dossier*, 1961) The Dead Letter (*Lettre morte*, 1959) The Old Tune (*La manivelle*, 1960)—Orig. publ. Les Editions de Minuit, Paris. Engl. tr. John Calder, London 1963.

The Inquisitory, John Calder, London 1966. (Orig. publ. as *L'inquisitoire*, Les Editions de Minuit, Paris, 1962).

Mahu, John Calder, London, 1967, 1985. Orig. publ. as *Mahu*, Les Editions de Minuit, Paris, 1952).

Baga, John Calder, London, 1967, 1985. (Orig. publ. as *Baga*, Les Editions de Minuit, Paris, 1958).

Plays—Vol. II: Architruc (*Architruc*, 1961) About Mortin (*Autour de Mortin*, 1965) The Hypothesis (*L'hypothèse*, 1961) Orig. publ.

Les Editions de Minuit, Paris. Engl. tr. John Calder, London, 1967.

The Libera Me Domine, John Calder, London, 1972. (Orig. publ. as *Le Libera*, Les Editions de Minuit, Paris, 1968).

Recurrent Melody, John Calder, London, 1975. (Orig. publ. as *Passacaille*, Les Editions de Minuit, Paris, 1969).

Fable, John Calder, London, 1980. (Orig. publ. as *Fable*, Les Editions de Minuit, Paris, 1971).

The following titles are all published by Les Editions de Minuit, Paris:

Entre Fantoine et Agapa, 1951
Le renard et la boussole, 1953
Graal flibuste, 1956
La manivelle (radio play), 1960
Quelqu'un, 1965
Identité, Abel et Bela (play) 1971
Paralchimie, nuit (play) 1973
Cette voix, 1975
L'apocryphe, 1980
Monsieur Songe, 1982
Le Harnes, 1984
Charrue, 1985

JEAN RICARDOU

L'observatoire de Cannes, Les Editions de Minuit, Paris, 1961
La prise de Constantinople, Les Editions de Minuit, Paris, 1965
Le Théâtre des métamorphoses, Les Editions du Seuil, Paris, 1982

ALAIN ROBBE-GRILLET

The Voyeur, John Calder, London, 1959. (Orig. publ. as *Le voyeur*, Les Editions de Minuit, Paris, 1955.

The Erasers, John Calder, London, 1966. (Orig. publ. as *Les gommes*, Les Editions de Minuit, Paris, 1953).

In the Labyrinth, John Calder, London, 1967. (Orig. publ. as *Dans le labyrinth*, Les Editions de Minuit, Paris, 1959).

Jealousy, John Calder, London, 1960. (Orig. publ. as *La Jalousie*, Les Editions de Minuit, Paris, 1957).

Last Year in Marienbad (cine-novel) John Calder, London, 1962. (Orig. publ. as *L'année dernière à Marienbad*, Les Editions de Minuit, Paris, 1961).

The House of Assignation, John Calder, London, 1970. (Orig. publ. as *La maison de rendez-vous*, Les Editions de Minuit, Paris, 1965).

The Immortal One, John Calder, London, 1971. (Orig. publ. as *L'immortelle*, Les Editions de Minuit, Paris, 1971).

Topology of a Phantom City, John Calder, 1978. (Orig. publ. as *Topologie d'une cité fantôme*, Les Editions de Minuit, Paris, 1976).

Snapshots, John Calder, London, 1965. (Orig. publ. as *Instantanés*, Les Editions de Minuit, Paris, 1963).

Towards a New Novel, John Calder, London, 1965. (Orig. publ. as *Pour un nouveau roman*, Les Editions de Minuit, Paris, 1963).

Project for a Revolution in New York, John Calder, London, 1973. (Orig. publ. as *Projet pour une revolution à New York*, Les Editions de Minuit, Paris, 1970).

Recollections of the Golden Triangle, John Calder, London, 1984. (Orig. publ. as *Souvenirs du triangle d'or*, Les Editions de Minuit, Paris, 1978).

Djinn, John Calder, London 1983. (Orig. publ. as *Djinn*, Les Editions de Minuit, Paris, 1981).

The following titles are all published by Les Editions de Minuit:

Glissements progressifs du plaisir (cine-novel) 1974
La Belle Captive (with René Magritte) 1976
Un regicide, 1978
Le miroir qui revient, 1984

NATHALIE SARRAUTE

Portrait of a Man Unknown, John Calder, London, 1959. (Orig. publ. as *Portrait d'un inconnu*. Editions Gallimard, Paris, 1958).

The Planetarium, John Calder, London, 1961. (Orig. publ. as *Le planétarium*, Editions Gallimard, Paris, 1959).

Trophisms and *The Age of Suspicion*, John Calder, London, 1963. (Orig. publ. as *Tropismes*, Denoel, Paris, 1939 and *L'ère du soupçon*, Librairie Gallimard, Paris, 1956).

Martereau, John Calder, London, 1964. (Orig. publ. as *Martereau* Librairie Gallimard, Paris, 1953).

The Golden Fruits, John Calder, London, 1965. (Orig. publ. as *Les fruits d'or*, Editions Gallimard, Paris, 1963).

Silence and *The Lie* (plays) John Calder, London, 1969. (Orig. publ. as *Le silence suivi de Le mensonge*, Editions Gallimard, Paris, 1967).

Between Life and Death, John Calder, London, 1970. (Orig. publ. as *Entre la vie et la mort,* Editions Gallimard, Paris, 1968).

Do You Hear Them? John Calder, London, 1975. (Orig. publ. as *Vous les entendez?* Editions Gallimard, Paris, 1972).

'*Fools Say*', John Calder, London 1977. (Orig. publ. as *Disent les imbéciles*, Editions Gallimard, Paris, 1976).

Collected Plays: It Is There (*Elle est là*) It's Beautiful (*C'est beau*) Izzum (*Isma*) The Lie (*Le mensonge*) Silence (*Le silence*) Orig. publ. as *Théâtre,* Editions Gallimard, Paris 1978. Engl. tr. John Calder, London, 1980.

The Use of Speech, John Calder, London, 1983. (Orig. publ. as *L'usage de la parole*, Editions Gallimard, Paris, 1980).

Childhood, John Calder, London, 1984. (Orig. publ. as *Enfance*, Editions Gallimard, Paris, 1983).

CLAUDE SIMON

Conducting Bodies, John Calder, London, 1975. (Orig. publ. as *Les corps conducteurs*, Les Editions de Minuit, Paris, 1971).

Triptych, John Calder, London, 1977. (Orig. publ. as *Triptyque*, Les Editions de Minuit, Paris, 1973).

The Flanders Road, John Calder, London, 1985. (Orig. publ. as *La route de Flandres*, Les Editions de Minuit, Paris, 1960).

The World About Us, Ontario Review Press, Toronto, 1983. (Orig. publ. as *Leçon de choses*, Les Editions de Minuit, Paris, 1975).

Le tricheur, Les Editions de Minuit, Paris, 1945

La corde raide, Les Editions de Minuit, Paris, 1947

Gulliver, Calmann-Lévy, Paris, 1952

Le sacre du printemps, Calmann-Lévy, Paris, 1954

Le vent, Les Editions de Minuit, Paris, 1957

L'herbe, Les Editions de Minuit, Paris, 1958

Le palace, Les Editions de Minuit, Paris, 1962

Femmes, (on 23 paintings by Joán Miro) Maeght, 1966

Histoire, Les Editions de Minuit, Paris, 1967

La bataille de Pharsale, Les Editions de Minuit, 1969

Orion aveugle, Skira, 1970

Les Georgiques, Les Editions de Minuit, 1981

GENERAL CRITICISM

BARTHES, Roland: *Writing Degree Zero—Critical Essays*, Jonathan Cape, London, 1967, Evanston, Illinois, 1972.

CULLER, Jonathan: *Structuralist Poetics*, Routledge & Kegan Paul, London, 1975.

FLETCHER, John: *Claude Simon and Fiction Now*, Calder & Boyars, London, 1975.

——*New Directions in Literature*, Calder & Boyars, London, 1968.

HEATH, Stephen: *The Nouveau Roman—A Study in the Practice of Writing*, Paul Elek, London, 1972.

JOSEPOVICI, Gabriel: *The World and the Book*, Macmillan, London, 1971.

MATHEWS, J.M. (ed): *Un Nouveau Roman—recherches et tradition*, Minard, Paris, 1964.

MERCIER, Vivian: *The New Novel from Queneau to Pinget*, Ferrer, Straus & Giroux, New York, 1971.

PUGH, Anthony Cheal: *Claude Simon—The Narrator and His Double*, Twentieth Century Studies, Dec. 1971—30-40.

RICARDOU, Jean: *Nouveau Roman: hier, aujourd'hui*, du Seuil, Paris, 1972.

——*Pour une théorie du nouveau roman*, du Seuil, Paris, 1971.

ROBBE-GRILLET, Alain: *Pour un nouveau roman*, Minuit, Paris, 1963.

ROUDIEZ, Leon S: *French Fiction Today—A New Direction*, Rutgers University Press, New Brunswick, 1972.

SOLLERS, Philippe: *Logiques*, du Seuil, Paris 1968.

SPENCER, Sheron: *Space, Time and Structure in the Modern Novel*, University Press, New York, 1971.

STURROCK, John: *The French New Novel*, Oxford University Press, Oxford, 1969.

WEIGHTMAN, John: *The Concept of the Avant-Garde—Explorations in Modernism*, Alcove Press, London, 1973.

ACKNOWLEDGEMENTS

Copyright information and acknowledgements are as follows:

Introduction Part 1, introductory material to Claude Simon, Claude Mauriac, Michel Butor and Jean Ricardou © John Fletcher, 1986. Introduction Parts 2 & 3, introductory material to Nathalie Sarraute, Marguerite Duras, Robert Pinget, Alain Robbe-Grillet © John Calder, 1986.

Tropisms originally published by Editions Denoël, 1939 and republished by Les Editions de Minuit, 1957. English translation © Maria Jolas and John Calder (Publishers) Ltd, 1963. *The Planetarium* and *Between Life and Death* originally published by Editions Gallimard, 1959, 1968. English translation © Maria Jolas and John Calder (Publishers) Ltd, 1961 and 1970 respectively. *It's Beautiful* originally published by Editions Gallimard, 1978. English translation © Barbara Wright and John Calder (Publishers) Ltd, 1980.

The Flanders Road originally published by Les Editions de Minuit, 1960 and in English by George Braziller Inc, New York, and Jonathan Cape, London, 1961 and 1962 respectively. Re-issued by John Calder (Publishers) Ltd, 1985. English translation by Richard Howard © George Braziller Inc, 1961, 1985. *Histoire* originally published by Les Editions de Minuit, 1967. English translation © George Braziller Inc, 1969. *Triptych* originally published by Les Editions de Minuit, 1973. English translation © Helen Lane and John Calder (Publishers) Ltd, 1977.

The Square originally published by Editions Gallimard, 1955. English translation © Sonia Pitt-Rivers and Tina Morduch, 1959. *Moderato Cantabile* originally published by Les Editions de Minuit, 1958. English translation © Richard Seaver and John Calder (Publishers) Ltd, 1966.

The Marquise Went Out at Five originally published by Editions Albin Michel, 1961. English translation © Richard Howard and John Calder (Publishers) Ltd, 1966.

Baga, *The Inquisitory* and *Fable* all originally published by Les Editions de Minuit, 1958, 1962, 1971. English translations © John Calder (Publishers) Ltd, 1967, 1966, 1980 and by John Stevenson, Donald Watson and Barbara Wright respectively.

Jealousy, *Project for a Revolution in New York*, *Last Year in Marienbad* originally published by Les Editions de Minuit, 1957, 1970, 1961. English translations © Richard Howard and John Calder (Publishers) Ltd, 1960, 1973, 1962. *Snapshots* originally published by Les Editions de Minuit, 1963. English translation © Barbara Wright and John Calder (Publishers) Ltd, 1965.

Second Thoughts originally published by Les Editions de Minuit, 1957. English translation © Faber & Faber and Jean Stewart, 1958. *Mobile* originally published by Editions Gallimard, 1962. English translation © George Braziller Inc and Richard Howard 1964.

The Capture of Constantinople originally published by Les Editions de Minuit, 1965. This translation © John Fletcher and Françoise Dupuy.